Communications
in Computer and Information Science   165

Estevam Rafael Hruschka Jr.   Junzo Watada
Maria do Carmo Nicoletti (Eds.)

Integrated Computing Technology

First International Conference, INTECH 2011
Sao Carlos, Brazil, May 31 – June 2, 2011
Proceedings

 Springer

Volume Editors

Estevam Rafael Hruschka Jr.
Federal University of Sao Carlos, Brazil
E-mail: estevam.hruschka@gmail.com

Junzo Watada
Waseda University
Wakamatsu, Kita-Kyushu, Japan
E-mail: junzow@osb.att.ne.jp

Maria do Carmo Nicoletti
Federal University of Sao Carlos, Brazil
E-mail: carmo@dc.ufscar.br

ISSN 1865-0929   e-ISSN 1865-0937
ISBN 978-3-642-22246-7   e-ISBN 978-3-642-22247-4
DOI 10.1007/978-3-642-22247-4
Springer Heidelberg Dordrecht London New York

Library of Congress Control Number: Applied for

CR Subject Classification (1998): H.3, F.1, H.4, J.3, H.2.8, I.4

Typesetting: Camera-ready by author, data conversion by Scientific Publishing Services, Chennai, India

Printed on acid-free paper

Springer is part of Springer Science+Business Media (www.springer.com)

Message from the Chairs

We are pleased to present the proceedings of the First International Conference on Integrated Computing Technology (INTECH 2011). This scholarly conference was co-sponsored by Springer and organized and hosted by the University of Sao Carlos in Brazil, during May 31- June 02, 2011 in association with the Digital Information Research Foundation, India.

The INTECH conference brings forth discussions on integrating models, frameworks, designs, content, networks and knowledge through more robust and high-quality research. All accepted papers are blind reviewed before they are included in the refereed conference proceedings.

This scientific conference included guest lectures and the presentation of 16 research papers in the technical session. This meeting was a great opportunity to exchange knowledge and experience for all the participants who joined us from all over the world and to discuss new ideas in the area of computing technology. We are grateful to the University of Sao Carlos in Brazil for hosting this conference. We use this occasion to express our thanks to the Technical Committee and to all the external reviewers. We are grateful to Springer for co-sponsoring the event. Finally, we would like to thank all the participants and sponsors.

April 2011

Estevam Rafael Hruschka Junior
Junzo Watada
Maria do Carmo Nicoletti

Preface

On behalf of the INTECH 2011 Program Committee and the University of Sao Carlos in Brazil, we welcome you to the proceedings of the First International Conference on Integrated Computing Technology (INTECH 2011). The INTECH 2011 conference explored new advances in computing technology and its applications. It brought together researchers from various areas of computer and information sciences who addressed both theoretical and applied aspects of computing technology applications. We hope that the discussions and exchange of ideas that took place will contribute to advancements in the technology in the near future.

The conference received 103 papers, out of which 24 were accepted, resulting in an acceptance rate of 25%. These accepted papers are authored by researchers from many countries covering many significant areas of computing technology. Each paper was evaluated by a minimum of two reviewers. Finally, we believe that the proceedings document the best research in the studied areas. We express our thanks to the University of Sao Carlos in Brazil, Springer, the authors, and the organizers of the conference.

Estevam Rafael Hruschka Junior
Junzo Watada
Maria do Carmo Nicoletti

Table of Contents

Reputation Based Trust Model for Grid with Enhanced Reliabilty

P. Vivekananth

Lecturer, BOTHO COLLEGE
Gaborone
Botswana
vivek.jubilant@gmail.com

Abstract. Grid computing is a next evolutionary level of distributed computing. It integrates the users and resources which are scattered in various domains. The Grid and its related technologies will be used only if the users and the providers mutually trust each other. The system must be as reliable and robust as of their own. The reliability can be defined as the probability of any process to complete it's task successfully as the way it was expected. In grid the reliability of any transaction can be improved by considering trust and reputation. Trust depends on one's own individual experiences and referrals from other entities. This paper proposes a model which improves reliability in grid by considering reputation and trust.

Keywords: Trust, Reputation, Reliabilty.

1   Introduction

A Grid integrates and coordinates resources and users within different domains. Grid computing is interconnected computer systems where the machines share the resources which are highly heterogeneous. To achieve reliable transactions mutual trust must be established between the initiator and the provider. Trust is measured by using reputation and reputation is the collective opinion of others.

Trust can be defined as strong belief in an entity to act dependably, securely and reliably in a specific context. When we say that we trust someone or someone is trust worthy [1], we assume that the probability that he/she will perform an action that is beneficial to us is high. On the other hand when we say some one is un trust worthy we imply that the beneficial probability is very low and detrimental probability is high.

According to Abdul-Rahman and Hailes [2], a reputation is the expectation about an entity's behavior based on information about or observations of its past behavior. Reputation is what is generally said or believed about a person or thing's character [3]. Therefore, reputation is a measure of trustworthiness, in the sense of reliability. Reputation can be the source of building trust. Reputation can be considered as a collective measure of trustworthiness (in the sense of reliability) based on the referrals or feed backs from members in the same community. An individual's subjective trust can be derived from a combination of received referrals and personal experience.

E.R. Hruschka Junior et al. (Eds.): INTECH 2011, CCIS 165, pp. 1–11, 2011.
© Springer-Verlag Berlin Heidelberg 2011

The main purpose of security mechanisms in any distributed environment such as grid is to provide protection against malicious parties. There is a whole range of security challenges that are yet to be met by traditional approaches. Traditional security mechanisms such as authentication and authorization will typically protect resources from malicious users, by restricting access to only authorized users. However, in many situations one has to protect themselves from those who offer resources so that the problem in fact is reversed. Information providers can deliberately mislead by providing false information, and traditional security mechanisms are unable to protect against this type of security threat.

Trust and reputation systems on the other hand can very well provide protection against such threats. Reputation models can be modeled in such a way that could provide reliability for both users and providers. Reputation systems provide a way for building trust through social control by utilizing community based feedback about past experiences of peers to help making recommendation and judgment on quality and reliability of the transactions..Reputation and Trust systems are soft security mechanisms which can assure behavior conformity. The reliability of any transaction obviously increases when feed backs of past experience of same type of jobs are considered and given with more weightage. The rest of the sections are organized as follows. Section 2 analyzes the similar previous work. Section 3 discusses about the proposed model. Section 4 gives details of experiments and analysis of results and section 5 concludes.

2   Related Work

The simplest form of computing reputation scores is proposed by Resnick and Zeckhauser [4] who simply measure the reputation by finding the *sum of* the number of positive ratings and negative ratings separately, and keep the total score as the positive score minus the negative score . The advantage is that it is very simple model where anyone can understand the principle behind the reputation score, while the disadvantage is that it is primitive and therefore gives a poor picture on participants' reputation score.

Advanced models in this category compute a weighted average of all the ratings, where the rating weight can be determined by factors such as the rater trustworthiness/reputation, the age of the rating, the distance between rating and current score, etc. Xiong and Liu in their paper [5] use an adjusted weighted average of amount of satisfaction that a user gets for each transaction. The parameters of the model include the feedback from transactions, the number of transactions, the credibility of feedbacks, the criticality of the transaction.

Zacharia and Maes [6] review some systems in 2000 that address reputation management in e-commerce sites. Regarding on-line trading environments, Dellarocas [7] analyzes reputation mechanisms from a game-theoretical point of view. He allows opportunistic players to take part of the game and his analysis is fully based on mathematics developments.

Probabilistic / Bayesian models directly model the statistical interaction between the consumers and the providers. Wang and Vassileva [8] use a naive Bayesian network which is generally used for representing and analyzing models involving uncertainty, to represent the trust of a user with a provider, the concept of trust being defined in terms of both the capability of the provider in providing services and the reliability of the user in providing recommendations about other users.

Baolin Ma, Jizhou Sun [9] talk about trust model based on reputation. In this model both direct and indirect trust are calculated by using reputation. Direct trust is calculated and the value of direct trust is used to find the value of indirect trust. Gregor von laszewki [10] provide a way for efficient resource selection by considering Eigen trust algorithm. Their approach is similar to Azzedin approach [11] except for a new parameter context. Ayman Tajeddine et al. [12] propose an impressive reputation based trust model. In this approach the initiator host calculates reputation value of target host based on its previous experiences and gathered feedbacks from other hosts. The recommenders can be from the same administrative control (neighbor) or from different trusted domain (friends) or from a completely strange domain (stranger).

Srivaramangai [13] talk about the trust system is made more robust by eliminating the unreliable feedbacks by using rank correlation method. The model is further improved in Srivaramangai [14] by adding two way test criteria.

3   Proposed Model

The proposed model is further enhancement. In the last two models proposed, two types of trust have been taken, namely direct trust and indirect trust . Indirect trust is measured from the reputation score of other entities. In the first model the initiator eliminates the feed backs of entities whose evolution procedure are not correlated to that of its' own. The second model is further enhanced by adding two way test criteria. In that model the transaction is allowed only when the user trust score as evaluated by the provider is greater than the pre defined threshold value and the provider trust score is greater than the threshold of the user. These two models and other existing models take the direct trust score from the table. There is no categorization of type of jobs. This model measures direct trust based upon different parameters such as context, size and complexity. It categorizes the jobs. The model assumes that the feedback value given by the user for one kind of job provided by one entity is different from another kind of job by the same entity. So the model uses three types of trust namely DT1, DT2 and indirect trust. DT1 represents trust of user on the provider as a result of same kind of transactions and DT2 for different type of transactions. Indirect trust is calculated by same expression as that of previous models. This model adheres to the fact that the reputation values are not always constant. When there is no transaction between two entities for a longer period of time than the value of reputation should be brought down. So this model adopts a function called decay function which will decrease the value of reputation when there is no transaction for a given interval.   After each transaction is over the updation is done.

3.1   Computation of Trust

In this model three types of jobs are considered. The jobs can be the transfer of files, printing or computing. Further, the size of the jobs can fall under three categories- small, medium and large. The system assigns the complexity factor based upon context and size (Table 1). Nine different combinations of contexts and sizes of jobs are considered and a complexity factor is assigned for each of the combinations. Thus there are nine types of transactions; from Table 1, it follows that the complexity factor is highest (=1) for large computational jobs, and the smallest (=0.25) for simple file transfer jobs.

Let us consider a scenario where A is the user and wants to use the resource, say the printer of the provider P. Let the job size be medium. Thus, from (Table 1) , the transaction type is 5. Before submitting the job to P, the user A has to be satisfied about the trust worthiness of P. The system refers to all the previous transactions between the user A and the provider P. (Table 2). If there are any transactions of the same type-s, context and size being the same as per the current requirement, then the average of the reputation values of all these transactions is taken as DT1.Thus DT1 $_{x,y,s}$ the direct trust of the user x on y based on the same type of transactions as the present requirement, is given by expression 1.

$$DT1_{x,y,s} = \frac{\forall i \in type\ s\ \sum_{i=1} r_i}{f_s} \tag{1}$$

where f_s refers to the frequency of the same type of transactions and r_i corresponds to the reputation value based on the i_{th} transaction.

Perusing Table 2, we find that there are two transactions of the type 5 (\$No:2 ,9) corresponding to C2,M combination. Thus DT1 is evaluated as $DT1_{x,y,s} =$ $\frac{3.98+2.85}{2} = 3.41$

Table 1. Complexity Table

job type	Context	Size	Complexity Factor
1	C1	S	0.25
2	C1	M	0.4
3	C1	L	0.5
4	C2	S	0.4
5	C2	M	0.5
6	C2	L	0.6
7	C3	S	0.6
8	C3	M	0.8
9	C3	L	1

C1: File transfer, C2: Printing,
C3: Computing.

Table 2. Transactions between A and P

S.NO	Context	Size	Reputation	Job type
1	C2	L	2.9	6
2	C2	M	3.98	5
3	C1	S	2.36	1
4	C1	M	2.85	2
5	C1	L	2.91	3
6	C2	L	2.25	6
7	C2	S	3.53	4
8	C3	S	2.01	7
9	C2	M	2.85	5
10	C1	M	3.05	2
11	C3	M	1.81	8
12	C1	S	3.05	1

The trust of an object l about an object I at context c is given by

$$trust_{x,y,c} = \frac{\alpha[DT_{x,y,c}] + \beta[IT_{x,y}]}{\alpha + \beta} \tag{2}$$

where $\alpha > \beta$ and $\alpha + \beta = 1$.

$DT_{x,y,c}$ represents direct trust, $IT_{x,y}$ represents indirect trust.

$$IT_{x,y} = IT1_{x,y} + IT2_{x,y} \tag{3}$$

$$IT1_{x,y} = \frac{\sum_{i=1}^{n} \delta_{1i} \, rep \frac{y}{z_i}}{\sum_{i=1}^{n} \delta_{1i}} \tag{4}$$

$$IT2_{x,y} = \frac{\sum_{i=1}^{n} \delta_{2i} \, rep \frac{y}{t_i}}{\sum_{i=1}^{n} \delta_{2i}} \tag{4}$$

$\delta 1, \delta 2$ are credibility factors.

z_i represents i^{th} entity in the neighbor domain and t_i represents i^{th} entity in the friend domain.

Indirect trust is calculated by considering the recommendations from reliable entities. The factors such as credibility, compatibility, activity and specificity are considered for measuring indirect trust. The elimination of feed backs is done by using the compatibility factor.

$$crediblity = a * Compatablity + b * activity + c * specificity$$
Where a+b+c = 1 and a> b>c. $\tag{5}$

$$Compatablity = 1 - \frac{6\sum_{i=1}^{n} \sum dr_i^2}{n(n^2-1)} \tag{6}$$

$$activity = \frac{Number\ of\ interactions\ by\ an\ entity\ as\ a\ user}{Total\ number\ of\ interactions\ by\ all\ entities} \tag{7}$$

$$specificity = \frac{Number\ of\ interactions\ by\ an\ entity\ as\ a\ provider}{Total\ number\ of\ interactions\ by\ all\ entities} \qquad (8)$$

$$\sum_{i=1}^{n} \delta_{1i}\ rep\ \frac{y}{z_i}$$ represents weighted sum of repuations of y

as represented by neighbours.

$$\sum_{i=1}^{n} \delta_{2i}\ rep\ \frac{y}{t_i}$$ represents weighted sum of repuations of y

as represented by friends.

$$DT_{x,y,c} = \gamma[DT1_{x,y,c}] + \theta[DT2_{x,y,c}] \qquad (9)$$

Where γ and θ are suitable weighing factors and $> \theta$ and $\gamma + \theta = 1$.

$DT1_{x,y,c}$ Direct trust of x on y which is obtained from the transactions of same type.

$DT2_{x,y,c}$ Direct trust of x on y which is obtained from the transactions of different type.

$$DT1_{x,y,c} = \frac{\sum_{i=1}^{n} r_i}{n} \qquad (10)$$

r_i represents Reputation value of entity y by x on i^{th} transaction and n represents the Total number of transactions .

$$DT2_{x,y,c} = \frac{\sum_{i=1}^{n} c_i r_i}{\sum_{i=1}^{n} f_i} \qquad (11)$$

c_i represents suitable credibility and r_i the reputation value of entity y by x on i^{th} transaction and f_i represents the frequency .

4   Experiments and Results

Simulation study has been conducted for the existing model and the proposed model.

Model 1 : Existing model as proposed by [12].

Model 2 : Present model eliminates biased feed backs by using compatibility factor and applies two way test criteria to decide the transaction . This model also includes parameters for measuring direct trust . In this model 20 users and 20 providers are taken. Out of 150 cases, there is perfect agreement for 134 cases, disagreement for 16 cases. Table 3 gives cumulative result and Table 4 describes the disagreement cases. The model assumes user 1-5 and provider 1-5 are malicious.

Table 3. Cumulative Result 1

Simulation	YY	NN	YN	NY	TOTAL
1.	56	78	12	4	150
Percentage	37	52	8	3	100

Table 4. Disagreement Cases 1

S.NO	User	Provider	Model1	Model2
1	15	3	YES	NO
2	19	1	YES	NO
3	11	2	YES	NO
4	15	2	YES	NO
5	10	5	YES	NO
6	8	3	YES	NO
7	16	4	YES	NO
8	16	5	YES	NO
9	10	3	YES	NO
10	5	11	YES	NO
11	18	4	YES	NO
12	10	3	YES	NO
13	14	15	NO	YES
14	14	14	NO	YES
15	20	17	NO	YES
16	18	20	NO	YES

As depicted by Table 4 there are 16 disagreement cases. In the first 12 cases either the provider or the user is assumed malicious nodes. So the proposed model rightly denies the transaction. Since the model applies two way test criteria that is it checks for both malicious user and provider it denies the transactions. The last four cases both the users and providers are reputed so the transactions is granted by our model. The through put is also fair enough that is 52 % and the reliability is further increased than our previous model by including the job type. Figure 1 shows the allocation by the two models.

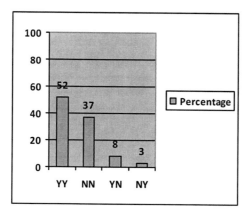

Fig. 1. Allocation by two models

Table 5. Cumulative Results 2

Simulation	YY	NN	YN	NY	TOTAL
1.	31	60	4	5	100
2	20	68	4	8	100
3	21	72	3	4	100
Cumulative Percentage	25	66	3.6	5.4	100

Table 6. Disagreement Cases 2

S.NO	User	Provider	Model1	Model2
1	13	3	yes	no
2	11	1		
3	6	4		
4	11	2		
5	17	5		
6	6	3		
7	17	5		
8	12	5		
9	16	4		
10	8	1		
11	9	5		
12	5	2	no	yes
13	6	20		
14	19	14		
15	6	8		
16	3	1		
17	18	15		
18	3	1		
19	3	2		
20	7	20		
21	17	7		
22	13	20		
23	9	6		
24	7	18		
25	15	12		
26	10	20		
27	9	18		
28	3	12		

On the whole it was found that 91% agreement was there out of three simulations between two models. The remaining 9% disagreement due to the addition of new factors such as context and complexity. Here also the user 1 to user 5 and provider 1 to provider 5 are assumed malicious nodes. The proposed model further improves reliability by preventing malicious nodes to participate in the transactions.

Second simulation study was conducted by taking the previous model proposed by us [14] and the proposed model was found to be more accurate because of the additional parameters. This time simulation was run three times each with 100 runs. The results were given in table 4 and 5.

Table 4 depicts all the disagreement cases. Transactions 1 to 11 are granted by our previous model where as rejected in the proposed model. In all these transactions the providers are assumed to be malicious. So our proposed model rightly corrects the error occurred in the previous model. Transactions 12 to 28 are granted by new model where as rejected by the previous model. In all these transactions either both the providers and users are malicious or good. That is the reason the transactions are approved by the new system. Thus the new system eliminates the small percentage of erroneous decision from the previous model. The system is made more reliable. Figure 2 shows the allocation by the two models.

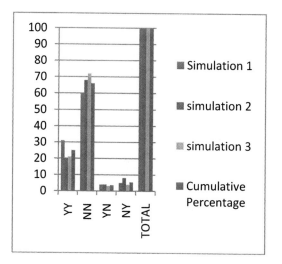

Fig. 2. Cumulative result

5   Conclusions

This paper present has presented a new comprehensive trust model in the sense it takes cognizance of both provider and user sensibilities. The model includes new expression for measuring direct trust by categorizing the type of jobs. Further by eliminating biased feedbacks from both user and provider groups the resultant transactions become more reliable and secure. Simulation study describes the superiority of the proposed comprehensive trust model over the existing models.

References

1. Silaghi, G.C., Arenas, A.E., Silva, L.M.: Reputation-based trust management systems and their applicability to grids ',CoreGRID Technical Report Number TR-0064 (2007), http://www.coregrid.net
2. Abdul-Rahman, A., Hailes, S.: Supporting trust in virtual communities. In: HICSS 2000: Proceedings of the33rd Hawaii International Conference on System Sciences, vol. 6, pp. 6007–6016. IEEE Computer Society, Washington, DC, USA (2000)
3. Bearly, T., Kumar, V.: Expanding trust beyond reputation in peer-to-peer systems. In: Galindo, F., Takizawa, M., Traunmüller, R. (eds.) DEXA 2004. LNCS, vol. 3180, pp. 966–970. Springer, Heidelberg (2004)
4. Resnick, P., Zeckhauser, R.: 'Trust among strangers in internet transactions. Empirical analysis of eBay's reputation system 11, 127–157 (2002)
5. Xiong, L., Liu, L.: 'PeerTrust: Supporting Reputation-Based Trust for Peer-to-Peer Electronic Communities. IEEE Transactions on Knowledge and Data Engineering 16(7), 843–857 (2004)
6. Zachari, G., Maes, P.: 'Trust management through reputation mechanisms. Applied Artificial Intelligence 14(9), 881–907 (2000)
7. Dellarocas, C.: 'Reputation mechanism design in online trading environments with pure moral hazard. Info. Sys. Research 16(2), 209–230 (2005)
8. Wang, Y., Vassileva, J.: Trust and reputation model in peer-to-peer networks. In: Proceedings of the Third International Conference on Peer-to-Peer Computing, Linköping, Sweden, pp. 150–157 (2003)
9. Ma, B., Sun, J.: Reputation-based Trust Model in Grid Security System. Journal of Communication and Computer 3(8), 41–46 (2006)
10. Kurian, B., von laszewki, G.: Reputation based grid resource selection. In: The Proceedings of the Workshop on Adoptive Resource Selection, pp. 28–36 (2003)
11. Azzedin, F., Maheswaran, M.: Evolving and Managing Trust in Grid Computing Systems. In: Proceedings of the Canadian Conference on Electrical & Computer Engineering, vol. 3, pp. 1424–1429 (2002)
12. Tajeddine, A., Kayssi, A., Cheab, A., Artail, H.: A comprehensive reputation-based trust model for distributed systems. In: The IEEE Workshop on the Value of Security through Collaboration (SECOVAL), Athens, Greece, September 5–9, vol. 1(3-4), pp. 416–447 (2005)
13. Srivaramangai, P., Srinivasan, R.: Reputation Based Trust Model With Elimination Of Unreliable Feed backs. International Journal of Information technology and Knowledge Management 2(2), 455–459 (2009)

14. Srivaramangai, P., Srinivasan, R.: Reputation based Two Way Trust Model for Reliable Transactions In Grid Computing. International Journal of Computer Science 7(5), 33–39 (2010)
15. Vivekananth, P.: An Overview of Trust models and proposal of new model based on Resource Selection in Grid Computing. International Journal of Engineering and Technology 2(4), 387–389 (2010)
16. Vivekananth, P.: Trusted Resource allocation in Grid Computing by using Reputation. International Journal of Computer Science & Communication 1(2), 23–25 (2010)

Biomedical Resource Discovery Considering Semantic Heterogeneity in Data Grid Environments*

Imen Ketata, Riad Mokadem, and Franck Morvan

Institut de Recherche en Informatique de Toulouse IRIT, Paul Sabatier University,
118 Route de Narbonne F-31062, Toulouse Cedex 9, France
{ketata,mokadem,morvan}@irit.fr

Abstract. Informatics application in biomedicine accumulates large amount of data constituting a big data source network. These sources are highly heterogeneous, dynamic and distributed in large scale environments. Resource discovery in such environments presents an important step for the SQL-query processing. Many research studies have focused on this issue. However, structural heterogeneity problems have been more widely studied than semantic ones. In this paper, we deal with the resource discovery in large-scale environments (as data grid systems) considering data semantic heterogeneity of biomedical sources. The main advantages of the proposed resource discovery method are: (i) allowing a permanent access, through an addressing system, from any domain ontology DO_i to another DO_j (inter-domain discovery) despite peers' dynamicity, (ii) reducing the maintenance cost and (iii) taking into account the semantic heterogeneity.

Keywords: Data Grid, Biomedical Data Sources, Resource Discovery.

1 Introduction

Computer applications in the biomedical domain accumulate a large number of data sources. These sources are voluminous, daily published (dynamicity of the environment) and with high heterogeneity. Thanks to its large storage capacity and scalability, the data grid is the most appropriate infrastructure adopted in this domain. Resource discovery presents an important step in the SQL-query processing in such environment. Several resource discovery solutions have been proposed. However, the structural heterogeneity problems [7] have been more widely studied than semantic ones. In this paper, we deal with the resource discovery in a large-scale environment as data grid systems, with considering semantic heterogeneity (e.g., polysemy, synonymy, abbreviation, etc).

* This work was supported in part by the French National Research Agency ANR, PAIRSE Project, Grant number -09-SEGI-008.

E.R. Hruschka Junior et al. (Eds.): INTECH 2011, CCIS 165, pp. 12–24, 2011.

There are first the traditional approaches based on centralized [27], [16] and [18] and hierarchical systems [24] and [8]. Whereas, they do not achieve scalability in such environments [13] when the peer-to-peer systems have proved their efficiency with respect to this scalability (e.g., the biomedical application: "Drug Target Validation [7]). However, most of the resource discovery works, dealing with peer-to-peer techniques do not effectively respond to the semantic heterogeneity problems because of the use of keyword method. For example, matching relations are established between keywords in PeerDB [21]. Whereas, this approach may return wrong results because of the strong semantic heterogeneity in biomedical domain, e.g., Doctor in biomedical domain corresponds to a Practitioner and Doctor in a biological domain corresponds to a Biologist having a Ph.D. degree in biology. Piazza [12] also establishes correspondence relations (*mapping*) between peers (in pairs or by groups) generating a large number of mappings. Keeping these mappings up to date becomes a complicated task. To discover resources more semantically, Hyperion [4] uses expressions and tables of mapping [17] to illustrate these correspondence relations. This technique helps to describe any semantic relationship between existing peer's schemas, whereas, such mapping is manual. Hence, having a completed and updated resource discovery result with this kind of mapping is not always obvious and easy. Otherwise, besides keyword approach, there is also global ontology solution [11] and [7]. However, using such ontology shared by all peers in the network is still a very complex task regarding the large number of domains in biomedical environment. The emergence of domain ontology solution, i.e., an ontology is associated to each domain [20], deals more efficiently with problems of semantic heterogeneity. For example, [3] applies a peer-to-peer technique as Chord [26] for an efficient resource discovery by handling the problem of semantic heterogeneity using domain ontologies. Hence, a domain ontology is duplicated in each peer. Nevertheless, semantic mappings between domain ontologies, specifying how those latter are linked together have not been processed.

In this paper, we introduce a method for data resource discovery in a biomedical data grid environment considering data semantic heterogeneity. The resource discovery concerns metadata describing the data sources. For this goal, peers are grouped by domains and an ontology [15] is associated to each domain in which all peers use the same vocabulary. Thus, a community called Virtual Organization (VO) is associated to each domain. For efficiency purposes, we are based on structured peer-to-peer technique, e.g., a Distributed Hash Table (DHT) [26]. Hence, the broadcast of resource discovery queries in one VO is realised by a classic DHT lookup. Otherwise, when a resource discovery query is transmitted from one domain ontology to another, this technique is no applied. In this case, the search is mainly based on mapping's relationships taking into account the dynamic nature of peers. Our method allows permanent access from any domain ontology DO_i to another one DO_j ($i \neq j$) despite peers' dynamicity. Thus, we have developed an addressing system allowing a low cost maintenance system. The main advantages of our method are: (i) applying the principle of data locality during the metadata discovery phase, (ii) allowing a robust inter-domain discovery with respect to the connection / disconnection of a large node number requiring low maintenance cost and (iii) taking into account the semantic heterogeneity.

The rest of this paper is organized as follows. In the second section, we propose a resource discovery method dealing with semantic heterogeneity. We illustrate our method by resource discovery process examples. We also discuss the maintenance process. We present some related work in the third section. Finally, we conclude our work by considering some prospects.

2   Resource Discovery Taking into Account Semantic Heterogeneity

The resource discovery process is an important step in the query processing in a large-scale environment. In such environment, every node manages several data sources. Moreover, the instability of such environment presents a major problem. Thus, we can not have a centralized and global schema to locate all resources. The duplication of this type of schema will also cause update problems. Consequently, the most appropriate solution is the distribution of such schema [19]. In this section, we focus on the distributed resource discovery on large-scale environments taking into account the semantic aspect. Specifically, we are interested in the metadata which describes data sources in a biomedical database context with minimizing maintenance costs. We cite the example of metadata discovery of a relation R which we associate to a concept in an ontology. These metadata contain: (i) attributes of R, (ii) placement of R (IP address of each fragment, fragmentation, information duplication and construction rules of R) and (iii) the different statistics of R, e.g., the size.

2.1   Architecture

Developing a global ontology is a difficult task to achieve, given the diversity of domains in a biomedical environment. Indeed, each biomedical domain accumulates large masses of heterogeneous data sources. One solution is to decompose the environment into domains as shown in Fig. 1. Hence, each domain can be handled independently. Thus, a community called Virtual Organization (VO) is associated to each domain of biomedicine (see Fig. 1). By this way we allow to take into account the locality and autonomy principles of each VO. On the other hand, solving problems such as synonymy and polysemy in resource discovery process is a difficult task to accomplish using only the schema principle. Then, a domain ontology [20] is associated to every VO (biomedical domain) as shown in Fig. 1. Hence, all peers in one VO use the same language (vocabulary).

   For resource discovery efficiency reasons, a structured peer-to-peer system is associated with each VO. Thus, a DHT (Distributed Hash Table) [26] is associated to peers belonging to the same domain ontology. The resource discovery within a single domain ontology is then a classic discovery by a DHT. Now, the way in which domain ontologies communicate between each other should be defined. Indeed, ontologies must be connected. Hence, we use relations (rules) of mapping between peers belonging to different domain ontologies. After that, we define a protocol to link VOs between each other.

Let $N(VO_i)$ be the set of virtual organizations connected to VO_i through mapping relationships (VOs neighbors of VO_i). VOs as well as mapping relationships form a graph noted: $G(N, E)$, with N the set of vertices presenting the set of VOs and E the edges presenting mappings. We note that the edge $e_{ij} \in E$ only if there exists a mapping between VO_i and VO_j. Let $|N(VO_i)|$ be the number of VOs neighboring VO_i.

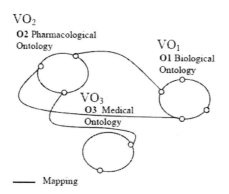

Fig. 1. Example of Virtual Organisation Distribution

To ensure the completeness of resource discovery results, the graph must be connected. Thus, we assume in the rest of this paper, that the graph is connected. So, for two vertices $VO_i \in N$ and $VO_j \in N$, there is a path $P_{ij} \in E$ from VO_i to VO_j. Also, since grid is an unstable environment, a peer P_k belonging to a VO_i should be able to initiate, at any time, a discovery process on a peer $P_{k'}$ belonging to VO_j / $VO_j \in N(VO_i)$ and $i \neq j$. Then, for each node in a VO_i we associate $|N(VO_i)|$ access points (AP_k) in the DHT. Access points are peers connected to different nodes of VOs (biomedical domains) available via the network. We note that two nodes belonging to a first VO_i do not necessarily have the same access point to a second VO_j. By this way we can avoid having a central access point to one VO (bottleneck). This can also help to avoid the single point of failure in case of disconnection of the access point, especially in an unstable environment as grid. After describing how VOs are connected, we will focus on the resource discovery process.

2.2   Resource Discovery

In our system, we classify resource discovery queries into two types: query within a single domain ontology (intra-domain ontology) and queries between domain ontologies (inter-domain ontologies). For inter-domain ontology query (between domains), we define a protocol to connect the VOs between each other.

2.2.1   Intra-domain Ontology Resource Discovery
As noted earlier, the intra-domain ontology queries are evaluated according to the routing system of a classic Distributed Hash Table DHT [26]. Indeed, structured

peer-to-peer systems have proved their efficiency with respect to the scalability and research process. Thus, a hash function is applied whose key is the name of the relation (the concept to discover). If the node, which is defined as responsible of the resource to be discovered, belongs to the same ontology in which the query was occurred, the query is an intra- domain ontology query (Fig. 2). In this case, the complexity to find this node is O(log(N)) where N presents the number of nodes [26]. The result of this discovery is the metadata describing the relation (concept).

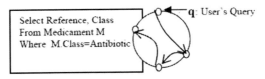

Fig. 2. Example of Intra-Domain Ontology Resource Discovery Query

2.2.2 Inter-domain Ontology Resource Discovery

To have a final resource discovery result with the most complete responses, the research should also be made in other peers from other biomedical domains (VOs).

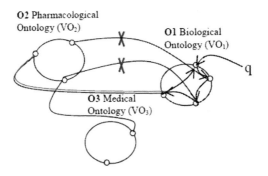

Fig. 3. Example of Inter-Domain Ontology Resource Discovery Query Process

Let P_i be the node receiving the user query. For an inter-domain ontology resource discovery, P_i contacts all its access points. The discovery process is realized by translating the original concept of the initial VO_i (where the user's query has been occurred) to a VO_k through a mapping. To avoid the endless waiting of an access point response, we define an interval of time, e.g., a RTT (Round-Trip-Time). Thus, if an access point does not respond after one RTT, it is considered to be disconnected. In this case, the peer P_i looks for another access point by contacting the nearest neighbor in the DHT. This research is done on the P_i's neighbor and then its neighbor and so on, until retrieving a peer presenting an access point to the researched distant VO_k. If all neighbors have been contacted without any response, the concerned VO_j is considered to be disconnected and only the administrator can reconnect it. We discuss this case in the further disconnection section. We demand to this access point one of its neighbors. This is done to avoid that all nodes of the graph converge towards a single access point. The response of resource discovery found is sent to the first query sender node P_i and noted *RSender* in the Inter-Domain Ontology Resource Discovery Algorithm (Fig. 4). At this moment, we take the opportunity to update VO_j's access points. We keep, of course, the path that the query followed along the discovery process for its translation from one VO to another. Indeed, this path will be used to translate the user's query (concepts) when it is sent from one domain ontology to another. Fig. 4 shows the algorithm of inter-domain ontology discovery. To simplify this algorithm we have not described the update of the access points in case of disconnection.

```
//R: Relation to be discovered (presenting researched
//concept name).
//RSender: Initiator resource discovery node (which
//have received the user query).
//VO: Current virtual organisation
//APk: Access point from one VO towards another.
//APS: Set of access points.
//Path: Resource discovery process path.
//Lookup(R, VOAPk, RSender, Path): Discover the relation
//R in the VO via the APk node.
//TTL: Time-To-Live (limit of the propagation range of
//a message).

Metadata ← Lookup(R, VOAPk, RSender, Path);
//Intra-domain-ontology research
TTL ← TTL - 1;

If(TTL != 0) then
For each APk є APS
Metadata ← Metadata U Lookup(Translate(R, VO, VOAPk),
VOAPk, RSender, Path U VO); //Inter-domain-ontology
//research

If (not Empty(Metadata)) then
Return(Metadata, RSender, Path U VO);
```

Fig. 4. Inter-Domain Ontology Resource Discovery Algorithm

Example 1

Let's have two virtual organisations:
VO_1: Biological domain and
VO_2: Pharmacological domain.

Suppose that a node N_{11} in a VO_1 (biological VO), receives a user's query. In addition to the intra-domain ontology query, this node have to connect to another VO_2 (pharmacological VO) in order to have a more complete response for a relation (concept) in the user's query.

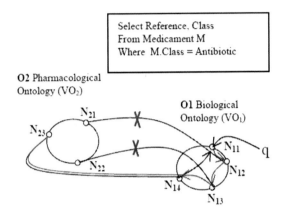

Fig. 5. Example of Inter-Domain Ontology Resource Discovery Process

First, N_{11} looks for, in its neighbors, the nearest access point towards VO_2 which is N_{12} (connected to N_{21} in VO_2). Supposed that N_{21} is disconnected. Then, N_{11} will look for the nearest neighbor of N_{12} with an access point to VO_2 and then the neighbor of this neighbor and so on (recursively) until finding an access point connected to VO_2. It corresponds to N_{14} in our example. Once this VO_2 is reached, the result (the metadata of the researched resource) is sent to the node initiating this discovery process (RSender) which is N_{11} in our example. Then, this node update its new access point (N_{14}) towards VO_2 (Fig. 5).

2.3 Maintenance

Since the dynamicity properties of grid environment, each node can join or leave the system at any time. In consequence, the system update will be required. In structured peer-to-peer systems such as Chord [26], the update of the DHT generates $Log^2(N)$ messages for each connection / disconnection of a node. In this section, we show that our method can significantly reduce the cost of the system maintenance. In this context, we discuss two types of maintenance: (a) maintenance of the DHT and (ii) maintenance of the nodes with access points to other VO_j belonging to $N(VO_i)$.

We will not deal with the first case because maintaining the system is done by a classic maintenance of a DHT [26]. This occurs at the connection / disconnection of a node. Otherwise, the connection / disconnection of nodes presenting access points raises more complicated update problems. Maintaining such system is updating the access point nodes in their connection (disconnection). In what follows, we will consider two cases: (i) the connection of a node and (ii) the disconnection of a node.

2.3.1 Node Connection

Supposed that a new node, called NewN, is connected to a VO_i. It looks for the access points to all other VOs. For this reason, it contacts the nearest neighbor in VO_i to get its access points to these VOs. If an access point towards a VO_k ($k != i$) does not respond during a certain period of time (RTT), it is considered to be disconnected. Then, NewN contacts the neighbor of its neighbor. This corresponds to (Neighbor (Following)) in the maintenance algorithm shown in Fig. 6. It repeats this recursively until getting connected access point to the appropriate VO_k. The test is done via the check( ) function. If all the neighbors are contacted without response (a failure case), the appropriate VO_k is considered to be disconnected. If the access point is found, NewN sends it a message to get its neighbor in the distant appropriate VO_k. This explain the instruction ($AP_K \rightarrow$ Following()) in Fig. 6. Then, NewN has a new access point to this VO_k.

```
//AP: Set of access points.
//Check(k): Check the connexion of a node Pi with
//respect to a VOk.
//P(k): Access point retrieved in VOk after a check
//test.

For k e N(VO)
{
Found  False;
Following = This.Neighbor;
  While(Following != This) and (not Found)
  {
  Found  Check(APk  Following());
  If (Found) then
  APK  Following();
  Else Following = Neighbor(Following);
  }
}
```

Fig. 6. Maintenance Algorithm of Routing System (Node Connection Case)

Example 2

Let's have the same two VOs as example 1:
VO_1: Biological domain and
VO_2: Pharmacological domain.
And let's take also a third VO_3: Medical domain.

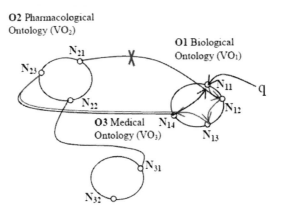

Fig. 7. Example of a System Maintenance after a Node Connection

Suppose that a new node N_{11} is connected to a VO_1. This node wants to get access point to the other VO_2 and VO_3. For this, it contacts the nearest neighbor N_{12} to get its access points to these two VOs. In fact, N_{11} contacts N_{21} (the access point from VO_1 to VO_2). N_{21} does not respond during the RTT, it is considered to be disconnected and N_{11} contacts the neighbors of N_{12} recursively, to establish other access point to the appropriate VO_2. Therefore, N_{11} contacts the next neighbor N_{14}, an access point to VO_2. The corresponding node in VO_2 is N_{23}. Thus, N_{11} gets N_{23} as access point towards VO_2 and thereafter sends it a message to get its neighbors in VO_2. N_{11} process by the same way to get an access point to VO_3. But in our example there is no access point from VO_1 to VO_3. That is way VO_3 is considered to be disconnected.

2.3.2 Node Disconnection

Supposed that one node, called NDisc disconnects from the system. A classic update of a DHT [26] is employed. When NDisc is an access point to a $VO_j \in N(VO_i)$, all the associated nodes in $N(VO_i)$ must be updated. Two solutions emerge. One solution is that NDisc propagates the information to every VO_i towards which it is connected. We do not adopt this strategy since it proceeds by the flooding. Another solution, adopted in our system, is to apply a lazy maintenance. Each node that has just disconnected does not have to send anything to the appropriate nodes. None of the concerned $VO_j \in N(VO_i)$ is informed by this disconnection. The access points towards this VO_j will be updated during the process of inter-domain ontology resource discovery. This reduces the number of node messages. The process of resource discovery is frequently performed so that the system can be updated. Consequently, the maintenance cost is significantly reduced.

Example 3

Let's have the same two VOs as examples 1 and 2:
VO_1: Biological domain and
VO_2: Pharmacological domain.

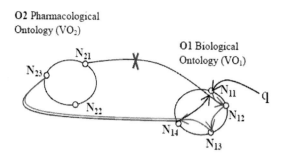

Fig. 8. Example of a System Maintenance after a Node Disconnection

The disconnection of a node N_{12} from the network implies a classic update of a DHT associated to the VO to which it belongs [26]. More, when N_{12} is an access point to other VOs, all the access points associated with N_{12} must be updated. As we adopt lazy maintenance in our system, the disconnected node N_{12}, does not inform any associated nodes (N_{21} which belongs to VO_2 in our example). Thus, VO_2 is not informed by the disconnection of N_{12}. The access points towards this VO will be updated during the process of inter-domain ontology resource discovery. Consequently, the maintenance cost is significantly reduced.

3   Related Work

Many research works have used the peer-to-peer techniques for resource discovery in large-scale environment [21], [17], [4], [5], [25], [10], [11], [28], [7], [9], [2] and [3]. But, only few studies have focused on the semantic aspect during this discovery [22], [23] and [6]. [5] Introduces the semantic in web service discovery. It uses the unstructured peer-to-peer architecture based on the Gnutella protocol [1] and keywords' mappings. It handles the semantic by using the QDN (Querical Data Network) where the identity of a peer is identified by its data. However, discovery query service employs a broadcast mechanism by flooding, which can saturate the network. Resource discovery in PeerDB [21] and XPeer [25] were also based on keyword search, which is unreliable. Firstly, the connections made between these keywords require user's intervention to select significant query. Secondly, it generates a bottleneck and requires the resolving of fault tolerance problems. In this context, [4] and [10] are based on semantic relationship between elements of peer's schemas (mapping's tables [17]). However, the domain experts' intervention is not always obvious. The resource discovery service in [14] deals with semantics in a grid environment. Each pair has its own ontology presented by a DAG (Directed Acyclic Graph). To discover resources, structured peer-to-peer systems (DHT) are used. They allow the distribution of local graphs (DAGs) through the peer-to-peer network nodes. Thus, a distributed virtual view of all peers' graphs is conceived. [28] Also uses the DHT for the message broadcast between communities. Discovery service is based on the GSBSL method (Location Based Greedy Search). But, the problem of semantic heterogeneity between graphs is also present. SenPeer [9], a peer-to-peer distributed data management system, also uses the principle of keywords but introduces semantics by organizing peers by semantic domains. Each peer can get its data semantically as a graph structured formalism with keywords. Other studies are based on a global ontology or schema shared by all peers [11], [7], [2] and [3]. The Bibster system [11], for example, uses a routing system based on semantic similarity between the discovery query and each pair expertise description in order to select relevant peers. [7] Introduces the semantic mapping describing all semantic relationship between the elements of peer's schemas. APPA [2] is based on a common schema called CSD (Common Schema Description) to distribute and share data between peers considering semantics. However, the use of a global ontology or schema is still a difficult task to achieve, due to the strong diversity of domains in the biomedical environment.

4   Conclusion and Future Works

We have proposed a resource discovery method in a large-scale environment taking into account the semantic aspect. Our solution allows the discovery of metadata describing biomedical data sources despite their semantic heterogeneity.

In the proposed solution, a domain ontology is associated to each biomedical domain whose peers constitute a virtual organization. Resource discovery queries within a domain (intra-domain ontology) follow the routing system of a classic DHT. For inter-domain ontology queries, we rely on the mapping relationships between peers belonging to different domain ontologies. We define a protocol to link virtual organizations between each other. Our method provides a permanent access from any domain ontology to any other one. It reduces resource discovery costs especially for intra-domain ontology query. It also provides low system maintenance costs despite the connection / disconnection of a large number of nodes.

Our method is particularly applicable to data grids which are particularly characterized by the high dynamicity of nodes and heterogeneity of data sources. For our future work, we are planning to carry out a performance evaluation of our method based on real experiences involving several heterogeneous data sources in biomedical environment.

References

1. Gnutella Development Home Page, http://gnutella.wego.com/
2. Akbarinia, R., Martins, V.: Data Management in the APPA System. Journal of Grid Computing (2007)
3. Alking, R., Hameurlain, A., Morvan, F.: Ontology-Based Data Source Localization in a Structured Peer-to-Peer Environment. In: IDEAS, Coimbra, Portugal (2008)

4. Arenas, M., Kantere, V., Kementsietsidis, A., Kiringa, I., Miller, R.J., Mylopoulos, J.: The Hyperion Project: From Data Integration to Data Coordination. SIGMOD Record Journal (2003)
5. Banaei-Kashani, F., Chen, C.-C., Shahabi, C.: WSPDS: Web Services Peer-to-peer Discovery Service. In: The International Conference on Internet Computing, Las Vegas, Nevada, USA (2004)
6. Comito, C., Mastroianni, C., Talia, D.: A Semantic-aware Information System for Multi-Domain Applications over Service Grids. In: IPDPS, Rome, Italy (2009)
7. Cruz, I.F., Xiao, H., Hsu, F.: Peer-to-Peer Semantic Integration of XML and RDF Data Sources. In: International Workshop on Agents and Peer-to-Peer Computing AP2PC, New York, NY, USA (2004)
8. Elmroth, E., Tordsson, J.: An interoperable, Standards based Grid Resource Broker and Job Submission Service. In: The International Conference on e-Science and Grid Computing, Melbourne, Australia (2005)
9. Faye, D., Nachouki, G., Valduriez, P.: SenPeer: Un système Pair-à-Pair de médiation de données. ARIMA Journal (2006)
10. Rodríguez-Gianolli, P., Garzetti, M., Jiang, L., Kementsietsidis, A., Kiringa, I., Masud, M., Miller, R.J., Mylopoulos, J.: Data Sharing in the Hyperion Peer Database System. In: VLDB Conference, Trondheim, Norway (2005)
11. Haase, P., Broekstra, J., Ehrig, M., Menken, M.R., Mika, P., Olko, M., Plechawski, M., Pyszlak, P., Schnizler, B., Siebes, R., Staab, S., Tempich, C.: Bibster – A semantics-based bibliographic peer-to-peer system. In: McIlraith, S.A., Plexousakis, D., van Harmelen, F. (eds.) ISWC 2004. LNCS, vol. 3298, pp. 122–136. Springer, Heidelberg (2004)
12. Halevy, A.Y., Ives, Z.G., Mork, P., Tatarinov, I.: Piazza: Data Management Infrastructure for Semantic Web Applications. In: WWW, Budapest, Hungary (2003)
13. Çokuslu, D., Hameurlain, A., Erciyes, K.: Grid Resource Discovery Based on Web Services. In: ICITST, London, UK (2009)
14. Heine, F., Hovestadt, M., Kao, O.: Towards Ontology-Driven P2P Grid Resource Discovery. In: IEEE/ACM International Workshop on Grid Computing (GRID), Pittsburgh, Pennsylvania (2004)
15. Jonquet, C., Musen, M.A., Shah, N.: A system for ontology-based annotation of biomedical data. In: Bairoch, A., Cohen-Boulakia, S., Froidevaux, C. (eds.) DILS 2008. LNCS (LNBI), vol. 5109, pp. 144–152. Springer, Heidelberg (2008)
16. Kaur, D., Sengupta, J.: Resource discovery in web services based grids. World Academy of Science, Engineering and Technology (2007)
17. Kementsietsidis, A., Arenas, M., Miller, R.: Managing Data in Peer-to-Peer Systems: Semantics and Algorithmic Issues. In: SIGMOD, San Diego, California (2003)
18. Moltó, G., Hernández, V., Alonso, J.M.: A service oriented WSRF-based architecture for metascheduling on computational grids. The International Journal of Grid Computing and eScience: Future Generation Computing Systems (2008)
19. Mokadem, R., Hameurlain, A., Tjoa, A.M.: Resource Discovery Service while Minimizing Maintenance Overhead in Hierarchical DHT Systems. In: International Conference on Information Integration and Web-based Applications & Services (iiWAS), Paris, France (2010)
20. Navas, I., Sanz, I., Aldana, J.F., Berlanga, R.: Automatic generation of semantic fields for resource discovery in the semantic web. In: Andersen, K.V., Debenham, J., Wagner, R. (eds.) DEXA 2005. LNCS, vol. 3588, pp. 706–715. Springer, Heidelberg (2005)
21. Ng, W.S., Ooi, B.C., Tan, K.-L., Zhou, A.: PeerDB: A P2P-based System for Distributed Data Sharing. In: International Conference of Data Engineering, Bangalore, India (2005)

22. Pirrò, G., Ruffolo, M., Talia, D.: An algorithm for discovering ontology mappings in P2P systems. In: Lovrek, I., Howlett, R.J., Jain, L.C. (eds.) KES 2008, Part II. LNCS (LNAI), vol. 5178, pp. 631–641. Springer, Heidelberg (2008)
23. Pirró, G., Talia, D., Trunfio, P.: ERGOT: Combining DHTs and SONs for Semantic-Based Service Discovery on the Grid. Technical Report, CoreGRID
24. Ramos, T.G., Magalhaes, A.C.: An extensible resource discovery mechanism for grid computing environments. In: CCGRID: IEEE International Symposium on Cluster Computing and the Grid. IEEE Computer Society, Singapore (2006)
25. Sartiani, C., Manghi, P., Ghelli, G., Conforti, G.: XPeer: A Self-organizing XML P2P Database System. In: EDBT Workshop on P2P and Databases, Heraklion, Crete, Greece (2004)
26. Stoica, I., Morris, R., Karger, D., Kaashoek, M.F., Balakrishnany, H.: Chord: A Scalable Peer-to-peer Lookup Service for Internet Applications. In: SIGCOMM, San Diego, California, USA (2001)
27. Yu, J., Venugopal, S., Buyya, R.: Grid market directory: A web services based grid service publication directory. Technical report, Grid Computing and Distributed Systems, GRIDS (2003)
28. Zhu, C., Liu, Z., Zhang, W., Xiao, W., Huang, J.: An Efficient Decentralized Grid Service Discovery Approach based on Service Ontology. In: The IEEE/WIC/ACM International Conference on Web Intelligence (WI), Beijing, China (2004)

On Combining Higher-Order MAP-MRF Based Classifiers for Image Labeling

Alexandre L.M. Levada[1], Nelson D.A. Mascarenhas[1], and Alberto Tannús[2]

[1] Departamento de Computação, Universidade Federal de São Carlos
alexandre@dc.ufscar.br, nelson@dc.ufscar.br
http://www.dc.ufscar.br/~alexandre
[2] Instituto de Física de São Carlos, Universidade de São Paulo
goiano@ifsc.usp.br

Abstract. In this paper we present a framework for combining MAP-MRF based classifiers for solving image labeling problems, by deriving a classification rule that uses a Gaussian Markov Random Field to model the observed data and a higher-order Potts MRF model as prior knowledge. In this scenario, the Potts model parameter acts like a regularizarion parameter, controlling the tradeoff between data fidelity and smoothing. Maximum Pseudo-Likelihood equations are applied to automatically set this parameter value. The proposed methodology consists in using several initial conditions for the iterative combinatorial optimization algorithms in order to escape local maxima solutions. Experiments with NMR image data show, in quantitative terms, that the joint use of multiple initializations and higher-order neighborhood systems significantly improves the classification performance.

Keywords: Markov Random Fields, Combinatorial Optimization, Image Labelling, Bayesian Inference, Maximum Pseudo-Likelihood, Information Fusion.

1 Introduction

Image labeling is one of the most challenging tasks in computer vision and image processing applications, since it is an extremelly complex procedure. Part of this complexity is due to the huge variety of existing data, among which we can cite natural scenes, computerized tomography (CT), magnetic ressonance (MRI), ultrasound and synthetic aperture radar (SAR) images. This fact makes the development of sufficiently robust classification techniques almost an impossible mission. Tipically, each type of image has its own characteristics, following a specific statistical model. Moreover, a serious problem often faced in image labeling is the presence of noise in the observed data. Usually, low exposure times during the image acquisition stage is the main reason for the appeerence of noise in image data. Additionally, most digital images are corrupted by additive Gaussian noise, introduced by many eletronic devices. Hence, traditional pointwise classification methods are not suitable for image labeling since they do not take into account the local dependence between pixels.

E.R. Hruschka Junior et al. (Eds.): INTECH 2011, CCIS 165, pp. 25–39, 2011.

In this paper, we are concerned with the multispectral image contextual classification problem using a MAP-MRF Bayesian framework (*Maximum a posteriori estimation with a Markovian prior*) that combines two MRF models: a Gaussian Markov Random Field (GMRF) for the observations (likelihood) and a Potts model as a smoothing prior, acting as a regularization term in the presence of noisy data, by reducing the solution space through the addition of constraints in the final solution.

Usually, to avoid both computational cost and slow convergence speed of the optimal algorithm, known as *Simulated Annealing* (SA), several sub-optimal combinatorial optimization algorithms are widely used in practice. It has been reported that, in some cases, SA can even become unfeasible in the solution of real world image processing applications. However, despite their apparent advantages, these sub-optimal algorithms also have some drawbacks: strong dependence on the initial conditions and convergence to local maxima/minima.

Thus, to attenuate these intrinsic sub-optimal algorithms limitations, looking for an improvement in classification performance, but at the same time keeping a reasonable computational cost, in this work we propose an approach for combining contextual classifiers. The basic idea consists in using higher-order MRF's, multiple simultaneous initializations and information fusion strategies [9] as a way to incorporate more information in the pixelwise decision rule, aiming to make the final solution less sensitive to the initial conditions.

The main contributions of the proposed MAP-MRF framework can be summarized in two main points. First, with the proposed method it is possible to incorporate more information in the pixelwise classification: either by using higher-order neighborhood systems, which improves contextual modeling, or by fusion of multiple contextual information. Finally, the proposed MAP-MRF approach is far less expensive and faster than *Simulated Annealing*.

The remaining of the paper is organized as follows: Section 2 describes the state of the art in image classification problems. Section 3 presents the proposed MAP-MRF contextual classification model. Section 4 describes the maximum pseudo-likelihood MRF parameter estimation, briefly discussing the accuracy of this method. Section 5 shows some rules for information fusion in contextual image labeling and metrics for quantitative performance evaluation. Section 6 shows the experimental setup, describing the obtained results. Finally, Section 7 presents the conclusions and final remarks.

2   State-of-the-Art in MAP-MRF Image Labeling

Definitely, the incorporation of contextual information in decision making brings benefits to the classification of spatial data. Markov Random Field models have been used successfully in contextual classification tasks, since these models are able to capture the dependency between neighboring elements in an elegant and sistematic way. In MAP-MRF image labeling, state-of-the-art methods comprise variational Bayesian aprroaches, graph-based techniques and Mixture Models. However, each one of them has positive and negative aspects that we will briefly discuss in the following.

The main point in favor of the variational approach is that we can perform joint estimation of the parameter models and the label field in an integrated framework [16, 19, 22]. However, in this approach, mathematical tractability is complex and hard, especially in non-gaussian models, which makes its usage a painful task.

Among the state-of-the-art methods for image lablelling, we can also highlight multiresolution hierarquical approaches using semi-supervised learning and gaussian mixture models [5, 12, 12, 14, 21, 24]. During the last years, these methods have become popular among the pattern recognition and machine learning comunity, since they define an extremely general framework for solving classification problems. However, one drawback related to this approach is the computational time and cost, because of the EM (Expectation-Maximization) algorithm, whose convergence rate is quite slow.

Another possibility that have been investigated in MAP-MRF image labeling are the widely known graph-based algorithms [13, 23], which have shown to be a fast and efficient method. The motivation for these algorithms is that it has been shown an equivalence between MAP estimation and the max-flow/min-cut problem defined on the corresponding graph (since an image is a rectangular lattice). However, the major drawback of graph-based algorithms for MAP-MRF estimation is that only some cost functions satisfying a set of constraints can be maximized [8]. In other words, it cannot be considered as a general method.

Therefore, the main advantage of the proposed method against the existing state-of-the-art approaches is that we can easily incorporate more contextual information, by means of higher order neighborhood systems, and also by using several initial conditions simultaneously, which avoids convergence to poor local maxima solutions. Besides, the proposed MAP-MRF approach is extremelly general, since we can consider a huge variety of statistical models and also it uses fast suboptimal combinatorial optimization algorithms that converge in few iterations. Last, but not least, the proposed combined scheme is easily parallelizable, reducing the computational time even more.

3   MAP-MRF Approach for Image Labeling

Basically, the proposed methodology for combining contextual classifiers follows the block diagram illustrated in Figure 1. Given a multispectral image as input, the first step consists in defining both spectral (likelihood) and spatial (MRF prior) statistical models. After that, the definition of training and test sets is necessary since we are dealing with supervised classification. From the training set, the class conditional densities parameter estimation is performed.

Eventually, some feature extraction method may be required to reduce the dimensionality of the classification problem. At this point, we have the initialization stage, where several pattern classifiers are used to generate different initial conditions for the sub-optimal iterative combinatorial optimization algorithms (ICM, GSA and MPM). Many classification methods can be applied for the generation of the initializations, from neural network based classifiers to Support

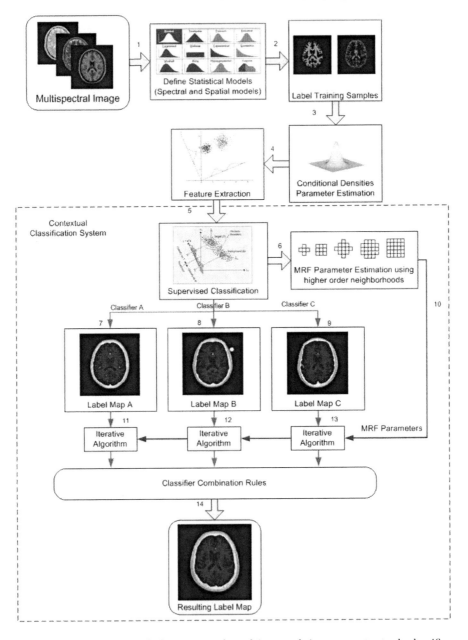

Fig. 1. Block diagram of the proposed multispectral image contextual classification system using combination of sub-optimal iterative combinatorial optimization algorithms

Vector Machines (SVM). In this work we selected seven statistical pattern classifiers: Linear (LDC) and Quadratic (QDC) Bayesian classifiers (under Gaussian hypothesis), Parzen-Windows classifier (PARZENC), K-Nearest-Neighbor classifier (KNNC), Logistic classifier (LOGLC), Nearest Mean classifier (NMC) and a Decision-Tree classifier (TREEC). An extensive literature on pattern classifiers can be found in [3, 4, 15, 17]. The iterative combinatorial optimization algorithms improve the initial solutions by making use of the MRF parameters estimated by the proposed MPL approach. Finally, the classifier combination stage is responsible for the data fusion by incorporating information from different contextual observations in the decision making process using six rule-based combiners: *Sum, Product, Maximum, Minimum, Median* and *Majority Vote* [7, 9].

3.1 Double Higher-Order MRF Model for Multivariate Data Classification

Given the initial conditions, the iterative contextual classification is achieved by updating each image pixel by a new label that maximizes the posterior distribution. Let $x_W^{(p)}$ be the label field at the p-th iteration, y the observed multispectral image, $\theta = [\theta_1, \theta_2, \theta_3, \theta_4]$ the 4-D vector of GMRF hyperparameters (directional spatial dependency parameters), ϕ the vector of GMRF spectral parameters for each class (μ_m, Σ_m) and β the Potts model hyperparameter (regularization parameter). Considering a multispectral GMRF model for the observations and a Potts model for the *a priori* knowledge, according to the Bayes' rule, the current label of pixel (i, j) can be updated by choosing the label that maximizes the functional given by equation (1) [20], where $\hat{\theta}^{ct}$ is a diagonal matrix whose elements are the horizontal, vertical and diagonals hyperparameters (4×4), $ct = 1, \ldots, K$, where K is the number of bands, $\hat{\Theta}^T$ is a matrix built by stacking the $\hat{\Theta}^{ct}$ diagonal matrices from each image band $(4 \times 4K)$, that is, $\hat{\Theta}^T = \left[\hat{\theta}^{ct1}, \hat{\theta}^{ct2}, \ldots, \hat{\theta}^{ctK}\right]$ and $y_{\eta_{ij}}$ is a vector whose elements are defined as the sum of the two neighboring elements on each direction (horizontal, vertical, and diagonals) for all the image bands $(4K \times 1)$.

$$Q\left(x_{ij} = m \left| x_W^{(p)}, y, \theta, \phi, \beta \right.\right) = \tag{1}$$

$$-\frac{1}{2}ln\left|\hat{\Sigma}_m\right| - \frac{1}{2}\left\{y_{ij} - \hat{\mu}_m\left[\hat{\Theta}^T y_{\eta_{ij}} - 2\left(\sum_{ct}\hat{\theta}^{ct}\right)\hat{\mu}_m\right]\right\}^T \times \hat{\Sigma}_m^{-1}$$

$$\times \left\{y_{ij} - \hat{\mu}_m\left[\hat{\Theta}^T y_{\eta_{ij}} - 2\left(\sum_{ct}\hat{\theta}^{ct}\right)\hat{\mu}_m\right]\right\} + \hat{\beta}U_{ij}\left(m\right)$$

Basically, this decision rule works as follows: in case of extremely noisy situations, no confidence is placed in the contextual information, since β is small and the decision is made mostly based on the likelihood term. On the other side, when contextual information is informative, that is, β is significant, spatial information is considered in the decision rule. It is worthwhile to note that, in this context, the Potts model β parameter controls the tradeoff between data fidelity and prior knowledge, so its correct setting is really meaningful for contextual classification. This double-MRF model was originally proposed by [20], however it was restricted to first-order beighborhood systems. Here, besides extending this compound model to second-order systems, we use a novel pseudo-likelihood equation for Potts model parameter estimation and combination of multiple contextual classifiers.

4   Maximum Pseudo-Likelihood Estimation

As we have seen on the previous section, the choice of the regularization parameter (β) plays an important role on the proposed classification method. Many studies report that the choice of this parameter value is still made manually, by simple trial-and-error, in a variety of applications. The main reason for this is the computational intractability of maximum likelihood, a reference method for parameter estimation, due to the presence of the partition function on the joint Gibbs distribution. An alternative proposed by Besag to surmount this problem is to use the local conditional density functions, or the set of local characteristics, to perform maximum pseudo-likelihood (MPL) estimation [1]. Besides being a computationally feasible method, from a statistical perspective, MPL estimators possess a series of interesting properties, such as asymptotic unbiasedness and normality [6]. In this section, a pseudo-likelihood equation for estimation of the Potts MRF model parameter on third-order neighborhood systems, that is, considering interactions of a given pixel with its 12 nearest neighbors, is shown. Additionally, the accuracy of the estimation method is assessed by an approximation for the asymptotic variance of MPL estimators.

4.1   Potts Model MPL Estimation

In order to perform contextual classification in higher-order systems, novel methods for Potts model parameter estimation are required. In this work, we use a novel pseudo-likelihood equation for this estimation on third order neighborhood, based on the expansion of the pseudo-likelihood function in the entire dictionary of possible cliques within the neighborhood system [10]. The MPL estimator of the regularization parameter $\hat{\beta}$ is given by the solution of (2), where Ω denotes the entire image lattice. It has been verified that in third order systems, there are 77 contextual patterns that offer different contributions to the pseudo-likelihood equation [10].

$$\sum_{(i,j)\in\Omega} U_{ij}\left(m_{ij}\right) - \frac{12e^{12\hat{\beta}}}{e^{12\hat{\beta}}+M-1}K_1 - \frac{11e^{11\hat{\beta}}+e^{\hat{\beta}}}{e^{11\hat{\beta}}+e^{\hat{\beta}}+M-2}K_2 - \frac{10e^{10\hat{\beta}}+2e^{2\hat{\beta}}}{e^{10\hat{\beta}}+e^{2\hat{\beta}}+M-2}K_3$$

$$-\frac{9e^{9\hat{\beta}}+3e^{3\hat{\beta}}}{e^{9\hat{\beta}}+e^{3\hat{\beta}}+M-2}K_4 - \frac{8e^{8\hat{\beta}}+4e^{4\hat{\beta}}}{e^{8\hat{\beta}}+e^{4\hat{\beta}}+M-2}K_5 - \frac{7e^{7\hat{\beta}}+5e^{5\hat{\beta}}}{e^{7\hat{\beta}}+e^{5\hat{\beta}}+M-2}K_6 - \frac{12e^{6\hat{\beta}}}{2e^{6\hat{\beta}}+M-2}K_7$$

$$-\frac{12e^{4\hat{\beta}}}{3e^{4\hat{\beta}}+M-3}K_8 - \frac{5e^{5\hat{\beta}}+4e^{4\hat{\beta}}+3e^{3\hat{\beta}}}{e^{5\hat{\beta}}+e^{4\hat{\beta}}+e^{3\hat{\beta}}+M-3}K_9 - \frac{10e^{5\hat{\beta}}+2e^{2\hat{\beta}}}{2e^{5\hat{\beta}}+e^{2\hat{\beta}}+M-3}K_{10} - \frac{6e^{6\hat{\beta}}+6e^{3\hat{\beta}}}{e^{6\hat{\beta}}+2e^{3\hat{\beta}}+M-3}K_{11}$$

$$-\frac{6e^{6\hat{\beta}}+4e^{4\hat{\beta}}+2e^{2\hat{\beta}}}{e^{6\hat{\beta}}+e^{4\hat{\beta}}+e^{2\hat{\beta}}+M-3}K_{12} - \frac{6e^{6\hat{\beta}}+5e^{5\hat{\beta}}+e^{\hat{\beta}}}{e^{6\hat{\beta}}+e^{5\hat{\beta}}+e^{\hat{\beta}}+M-3}K_{13} - \frac{7e^{7\hat{\beta}}+3e^{3\hat{\beta}}+2e^{2\hat{\beta}}}{e^{7\hat{\beta}}+e^{3\hat{\beta}}+e^{2\hat{\beta}}+M-3}K_{14}$$

$$-\frac{7e^{7\hat{\beta}}+4e^{4\hat{\beta}}+e^{\hat{\beta}}}{e^{7\hat{\beta}}+e^{4\hat{\beta}}+e^{\hat{\beta}}+M-3}K_{15} - \frac{8e^{8\hat{\beta}}+4e^{2\hat{\beta}}}{e^{8\hat{\beta}}+2e^{2\hat{\beta}}+M-3}K_{16} - \frac{8e^{8\hat{\beta}}+3e^{3\hat{\beta}}+e^{\hat{\beta}}}{e^{8\hat{\beta}}+e^{3\hat{\beta}}+e^{\hat{\beta}}+M-3}K_{17}$$

$$-\frac{9e^{9\hat{\beta}}+2e^{2\hat{\beta}}+e^{\hat{\beta}}}{e^{9\hat{\beta}}+e^{2\hat{\beta}}+e^{\hat{\beta}}+M-3}K_{18} - \frac{10e^{10\hat{\beta}}+2e^{\hat{\beta}}}{e^{10\hat{\beta}}+2e^{\hat{\beta}}+M-3}K_{19} - \frac{12e^{3\hat{\beta}}}{4e^{3\hat{\beta}}+M-4}K_{20}$$

$$-\frac{4e^{4\hat{\beta}}+6e^{3\hat{\beta}}+2e^{2\hat{\beta}}}{e^{4\hat{\beta}}+2e^{3\hat{\beta}}+e^{2\hat{\beta}}+M-4}K_{21} - \frac{8e^{4\hat{\beta}}+4e^{2\hat{\beta}}}{2e^{4\hat{\beta}}+2e^{2\hat{\beta}}+M-3}K_{22} - \frac{8e^{4\hat{\beta}}+3e^{3\hat{\beta}}+e^{\hat{\beta}}}{2e^{4\hat{\beta}}+e^{3\hat{\beta}}+e^{\hat{\beta}}+M-4}K_{23}$$

$$-\frac{5e^{5\hat{\beta}}+3e^{3\hat{\beta}}+4e^{2\hat{\beta}}}{e^{5\hat{\beta}}+e^{3\hat{\beta}}+2e^{2\hat{\beta}}+M-4}K_{24} - \frac{5e^{5\hat{\beta}}+6e^{3\hat{\beta}}+e^{\hat{\beta}}}{e^{5\hat{\beta}}+2e^{3\hat{\beta}}+e^{\hat{\beta}}+M-4}K_{25} - \frac{5e^{5\hat{\beta}}+4e^{4\hat{\beta}}+2e^{2\hat{\beta}}+e^{\hat{\beta}}}{e^{5\hat{\beta}}+e^{4\hat{\beta}}+e^{2\hat{\beta}}+e^{\hat{\beta}}+M-4}K_{26}$$

$$-\frac{10e^{5\hat{\beta}}+2e^{\hat{\beta}}}{2e^{5\hat{\beta}}+2e^{\hat{\beta}}+M-4}K_{27} - \frac{6e^{6\hat{\beta}}+6e^{2\hat{\beta}}}{e^{6\hat{\beta}}+3e^{2\hat{\beta}}+M-4}K_{28} - \frac{6e^{6\hat{\beta}}+3e^{3\hat{\beta}}+2e^{2\hat{\beta}}+e^{\hat{\beta}}}{e^{6\hat{\beta}}+e^{3\hat{\beta}}+e^{2\hat{\beta}}+e^{\hat{\beta}}+M-4}K_{29}$$

$$-\frac{6e^{6\hat{\beta}}+4e^{4\hat{\beta}}+2e^{\hat{\beta}}}{e^{6\hat{\beta}}+e^{4\hat{\beta}}+2e^{\hat{\beta}}+M-4}K_{30} - \frac{7e^{7\hat{\beta}}+4e^{2\hat{\beta}}+e^{\hat{\beta}}}{e^{7\hat{\beta}}+2e^{2\hat{\beta}}+e^{\hat{\beta}}+M-4}K_{31} - \frac{7e^{7\hat{\beta}}+3e^{3\hat{\beta}}+2e^{\hat{\beta}}}{e^{7\hat{\beta}}+e^{3\hat{\beta}}+2e^{\hat{\beta}}+M-4}K_{32}$$

$$-\frac{8e^{8\hat{\beta}}+2e^{2\hat{\beta}}+2e^{\hat{\beta}}}{e^{8\hat{\beta}}+e^{2\hat{\beta}}+2e^{\hat{\beta}}+M-4}K_{33} - \frac{9e^{9\hat{\beta}}+3e^{\hat{\beta}}}{e^{9\hat{\beta}}+3e^{\hat{\beta}}+M-4}K_{34} - \frac{6e^{3\hat{\beta}}+6e^{2\hat{\beta}}}{2e^{3\hat{\beta}}+3e^{2\hat{\beta}}+M-5}K_{35}$$

$$-\frac{9e^{3\hat{\beta}}+2e^{2\hat{\beta}}+e^{\hat{\beta}}}{3e^{3\hat{\beta}}+e^{2\hat{\beta}}+e^{\hat{\beta}}+M-5}K_{36} - \frac{4e^{4\hat{\beta}}+8e^{2\hat{\beta}}}{e^{4\hat{\beta}}+4e^{2\hat{\beta}}+M-5}K_{37} - \frac{4e^{4\hat{\beta}}+3e^{3\hat{\beta}}+4e^{2\hat{\beta}}+e^{\hat{\beta}}}{e^{4\hat{\beta}}+e^{3\hat{\beta}}+2e^{2\hat{\beta}}+e^{\hat{\beta}}+M-5}K_{38}$$

$$-\frac{4e^{4\hat{\beta}}+6e^{3\hat{\beta}}+2e^{\hat{\beta}}}{e^{4\hat{\beta}}+2e^{3\hat{\beta}}+2e^{\hat{\beta}}+M-5}K_{39} - \frac{8e^{4\hat{\beta}}+2e^{2\hat{\beta}}+2e^{\hat{\beta}}}{2e^{4\hat{\beta}}+e^{2\hat{\beta}}+2e^{\hat{\beta}}+M-5}K_{40} - \frac{5e^{5\hat{\beta}}+6e^{2\hat{\beta}}+e^{\hat{\beta}}}{e^{5\hat{\beta}}+3e^{2\hat{\beta}}+e^{\hat{\beta}}+M-5}K_{41}$$

$$-\frac{5e^{5\hat{\beta}}+3e^{3\hat{\beta}}+2e^{2\hat{\beta}}+2e^{\hat{\beta}}}{e^{5\hat{\beta}}+e^{3\hat{\beta}}+e^{2\hat{\beta}}+2e^{\hat{\beta}}+M-5}K_{42} - \frac{5e^{5\hat{\beta}}+4e^{4\hat{\beta}}+3e^{\hat{\beta}}}{e^{5\hat{\beta}}+e^{4\hat{\beta}}+3e^{\hat{\beta}}+M-5}K_{43} - \frac{6e^{6\hat{\beta}}+4e^{4\hat{\beta}}+2e^{\hat{\beta}}}{e^{6\hat{\beta}}+2e^{2\hat{\beta}}+2e^{\hat{\beta}}+M-5}K_{44}$$

$$-\frac{6e^{6\hat{\beta}}+3e^{3\hat{\beta}}+3e^{\hat{\beta}}}{e^{6\hat{\beta}}+e^{3\hat{\beta}}+3e^{\hat{\beta}}+M-5}K_{45} - \frac{7e^{7\hat{\beta}}+2e^{2\hat{\beta}}+3e^{\hat{\beta}}}{e^{7\hat{\beta}}+e^{2\hat{\beta}}+3e^{\hat{\beta}}+M-5}K_{46} - \frac{8e^{8\hat{\beta}}+4e^{\hat{\beta}}}{e^{8\hat{\beta}}+4e^{\hat{\beta}}+M-5}K_{47}$$

$$-\frac{12e^{2\hat{\beta}}}{6e^{2\hat{\beta}}+M-6}K_{48} - \frac{3e^{3\hat{\beta}}+8e^{2\hat{\beta}}+e^{\hat{\beta}}}{e^{3\hat{\beta}}+4e^{2\hat{\beta}}+e^{\hat{\beta}}+M-6}K_{49} - \frac{6e^{3\hat{\beta}}+4e^{2\hat{\beta}}+2e^{\hat{\beta}}}{2e^{3\hat{\beta}}+2e^{2\hat{\beta}}+2e^{\hat{\beta}}+M-6}K_{50}$$

$$-\frac{9e^{3\hat{\beta}}+3e^{\hat{\beta}}}{3e^{3\hat{\beta}}+3e^{\hat{\beta}}+M-6}K_{51} - \frac{4e^{4\hat{\beta}}+6e^{2\hat{\beta}}+2e^{\hat{\beta}}}{e^{4\hat{\beta}}+3e^{2\hat{\beta}}+2e^{\hat{\beta}}+M-6}K_{52} - \frac{4e^{4\hat{\beta}}+3e^{3\hat{\beta}}+2e^{2\hat{\beta}}+3e^{\hat{\beta}}}{e^{4\hat{\beta}}+e^{3\hat{\beta}}+e^{2\hat{\beta}}+3e^{\hat{\beta}}+M-6}K_{53}$$

$$-\frac{8e^{4\hat{\beta}}+4e^{\hat{\beta}}}{2e^{4\hat{\beta}}+4e^{\hat{\beta}}+M-6}K_{54} - \frac{5e^{5\hat{\beta}}+4e^{2\hat{\beta}}+3e^{\hat{\beta}}}{e^{5\hat{\beta}}+2e^{2\hat{\beta}}+3e^{\hat{\beta}}+M-6}K_{55} - \frac{5e^{5\hat{\beta}}+3e^{3\hat{\beta}}+4e^{\hat{\beta}}}{e^{5\hat{\beta}}+e^{3\hat{\beta}}+4e^{\hat{\beta}}+M-6}K_{56}$$

$$-\frac{6e^{6\hat{\beta}}+2e^{2\hat{\beta}}+4e^{\hat{\beta}}}{e^{6\hat{\beta}}+e^{2\hat{\beta}}+4e^{\hat{\beta}}+M-6}K_{57} - \frac{7e^{7\hat{\beta}}+5e^{\hat{\beta}}}{e^{7\hat{\beta}}+5e^{\hat{\beta}}+M-6}K_{58} - \frac{10e^{2\hat{\beta}}+2e^{\hat{\beta}}}{5e^{2\hat{\beta}}+2e^{\hat{\beta}}+M-7}K_{59}$$

$$-\frac{3e^{3\hat{\beta}}+6e^{2\hat{\beta}}+3e^{\hat{\beta}}}{e^{3\hat{\beta}}+3e^{2\hat{\beta}}+3e^{\hat{\beta}}+M-7}K_{60} - \frac{6e^{3\hat{\beta}}+2e^{2\hat{\beta}}+4e^{\hat{\beta}}}{2e^{3\hat{\beta}}+e^{2\hat{\beta}}+4e^{\hat{\beta}}+M-7}K_{61} - \frac{4e^{4\hat{\beta}}+4e^{2\hat{\beta}}+4e^{\hat{\beta}}}{e^{4\hat{\beta}}+2e^{2\hat{\beta}}+4e^{\hat{\beta}}+M-7}K_{62}$$

$$-\frac{4e^{4\hat{\beta}}+3e^{3\hat{\beta}}+5e^{\hat{\beta}}}{e^{4\hat{\beta}}+e^{3\hat{\beta}}+5e^{\hat{\beta}}+M-7}K_{63} - \frac{5e^{5\hat{\beta}}+2e^{2\hat{\beta}}+5e^{\hat{\beta}}}{e^{5\hat{\beta}}+e^{2\hat{\beta}}+5e^{\hat{\beta}}+M-7}K_{64} - \frac{6e^{6\hat{\beta}}+6e^{\hat{\beta}}}{e^{6\hat{\beta}}+6e^{\hat{\beta}}+M-7}K_{65}$$

$$-\frac{8e^{2\hat{\beta}}+4e^{\hat{\beta}}}{4e^{2\hat{\beta}}+4e^{\hat{\beta}}+M-8}K_{66} - \frac{3e^{3\hat{\beta}}+4e^{2\hat{\beta}}+5e^{\hat{\beta}}}{e^{3\hat{\beta}}+2e^{2\hat{\beta}}+5e^{\hat{\beta}}+M-8}K_{67} - \frac{6e^{3\hat{\beta}}+6e^{\hat{\beta}}}{2e^{3\hat{\beta}}+6e^{\hat{\beta}}+M-8}K_{68}$$

$$-\frac{4e^{4\hat{\beta}}+2e^{2\hat{\beta}}+6e^{\hat{\beta}}}{e^{4\hat{\beta}}+e^{2\hat{\beta}}+6e^{\hat{\beta}}+M-8}K_{69} - \frac{5e^{5\hat{\beta}}+7e^{\hat{\beta}}}{e^{5\hat{\beta}}+7e^{\hat{\beta}}+M-8}K_{70} - \frac{6e^{2\hat{\beta}}+6e^{\hat{\beta}}}{3e^{2\hat{\beta}}+6e^{\hat{\beta}}+M-9}K_{71}$$

$$-\frac{3e^{3\hat{\beta}}+2e^{2\hat{\beta}}+7e^{\hat{\beta}}}{e^{3\hat{\beta}}+e^{2\hat{\beta}}+7e^{\hat{\beta}}+M-9}K_{72} - \frac{4e^{4\hat{\beta}}+8e^{\hat{\beta}}}{e^{4\hat{\beta}}+8e^{\hat{\beta}}+M-9}K_{73} - \frac{4e^{2\hat{\beta}}+8e^{\hat{\beta}}}{2e^{2\hat{\beta}}+8e^{\hat{\beta}}+M-10}K_{74}$$

$$-\frac{3e^{3\hat{\beta}}+9e^{\hat{\beta}}}{e^{3\hat{\beta}}+9e^{\hat{\beta}}+M-10}K_{75} - \frac{2e^{2\hat{\beta}}+10e^{\hat{\beta}}}{e^{2\hat{\beta}}+10e^{\hat{\beta}}+M-11}K_{76} - \frac{12e^{\hat{\beta}}}{12e^{\hat{\beta}}+M-12}K_{77} = 0$$

$$(2)$$

Three important points about the proposed equation should be emphasized here. First, each one of the 77 terms of the pseudo-likelihood equation is composed by a product of two factors: a fraction and a K_i value. The first factor is nothing more than the contribution of the respective contextual configuration pattern to the pseudo-likelihood equation, while the second one is the number of times this pattern occurs along the image. Another important issue is related to the validity of the proposed equation for an arbitrary M (number of classes or states). For a reduced number of classes (tipically, $M = 3$, $M = 4$), the equation is further simplified, since many $K_i's$, $i = 1, 2, \ldots, \lambda$, are zero, simply because many contextual patterns are physically impossible to occur. Therefore, in practical terms, a reduction on the number of clasees in the classification problem (M) implies in reduction of the computational cost of the Potts MRF model parameter estimation. It has been shown by Markov Chain Monte Carlo (MCMC) simulation that this pseudo-likelihood equation produces estimates that are equivalent to the real parameter values [10, 11].

4.2   GMRF MPL Estimation

As there is no dependency between the hyperparameters from different image bands, it is quite reasonable to perform MPL estimation in each band independently. Assuming this hypothesis and considering a second-oder neighborhood system, the pseudo-likelihood function is given by [18]:

$$\log PL\left(\theta, \mu, \sigma^2\right) = \sum_{(i,j)\in\Omega} \left\{ -\frac{1}{2}\log\left(2\pi\sigma^2\right) \right. \tag{3}$$
$$\left. -\frac{1}{2\sigma^2}\left[y_{ij} - \theta^T\psi_{ij} - \mu\left(1 - 2\theta^T I\right)\right]^2 \right\}$$

where Ω denotes the entire random field, ψ_{ij} is a 4-D vector where each element is defined as the sum of the two neighboring pixels in the horizontal, vertical and both diagonal directions, respectively. The expression for the MPL estimator of $\hat{\theta}$ is given by:

$$\hat{\theta} = \left\{ \left[\sum_{(i,j)\in\Omega}(y_{ij} - \hat{\mu})\,\tilde{\psi}_{ij}^T\right]\left[\sum_{(i,j)\in\Omega}\tilde{\psi}_{ij}\tilde{\psi}_{ij}^T\right]^{-1}\right\} \tag{4}$$

where $\hat{\mu}$ is the sample mean of the image pixels, $\tilde{\psi}_{ij} = \psi_{ij} - \frac{1}{N}\sum_{(k,l)\in\Omega}\psi_{ij}$ and N is the number of image pixels.

5   Experiments and Results

In order to test and evaluate the the combination of iterative combinatorial optimization algorithms in contextual classification, we show some experiments using NMR images of *marmoset* brains, a monkey species often used in medical experiments. These images were acquired by the CInAPCe project, an abbreviation for the Portuguese expression "Inter-Institutional Cooperation to Support Brain Research" a Brazilian research project that has as main purpose the establishment of a scientific network seeking the development of neuroscience research through multidisciplinary approaches. In this sense, pattern recognition can contribute to the development of new methods and tools for processing and analyzing magnetic resonance imaging and its integration with other methodologies in the investigation of epilepsies. Figure 2 shows the bands PD, T1 and T2 of a marmoset NMR multispectral brain image. Note the significant amount of noise in the images, which makes classification an even more challenging task.

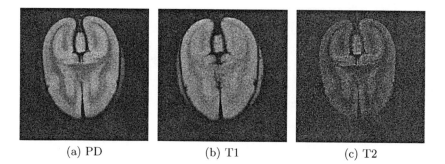

| (a) PD | (b) T1 | (c) T2 |

Fig. 2. PD, T1 and T2 NMR noisy image bands of the multispectral *marmoset* brain image

Combining Classifiers. Let $x \in \Re^n$ be a feature vector and $G = \{1, 2, \ldots, C\}$ be the set of class labels. Each classifier D_i in the ensemble $D = \{D_1, \ldots, D_L\}$ outputs c degrees of support. Without loss of generality we can assume that all c degrees are in the interval $[0, 1]$, that is, $D_i : \Re^n \longrightarrow [0, 1]^c$. Denote by $d_i(x)$ the support that classifier D_i gives to the hypothesis that x comes from the j-th class. The larger the support, the more likely the class label j. In the proposed method, the degree of support for each classifier is a decision rule that combines both spectral and spatial information, as indicated by equation 1. The L classifier outputs for a particular input x can be organized in a decision profile ($DP(x)$) as a matrix [9]. Figure 3 illustrates the structure of a *decision profile*.

Simple nontrainable combiners calculate the support for class ω_j using only the j-*th* column of $DP(\mathbf{x})$ by:

$$\mu_j(x) = \Im [d_{i,j}, \ldots, d_{L,j}] \tag{5}$$

where $\Im$ is a combination function. The class label of x is found as the index of the maximum $\mu_j(x)$. In this work, besides the majority vote, we chose five different rules. They are summarized in Table 1.

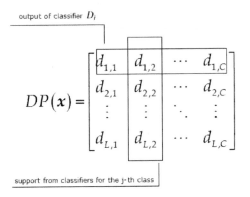

Fig. 3. The structure of a *Decision Profile*

Table 1. Classifier combination functions for soft decision fusion

Sum	$\mu_j(\boldsymbol{x}) = \sum_{i=1}^{L} d_{i,j}(\boldsymbol{x})$
Product	$\mu_j(\boldsymbol{x}) = \prod_{i=1}^{L} d_{i,j}(\boldsymbol{x})$
Minimum	$\mu_j(\boldsymbol{x}) = min_i\{d_{i,j}(\boldsymbol{x})\}$
Maximum	$\mu_j(\boldsymbol{x}) = max_i\{d_{i,j}(\boldsymbol{x})\}$
Median	$\mu_j(\boldsymbol{x}) = median_i\{d_{i,j}(\boldsymbol{x})\}$

The experiments were conducted to experimentally verify the effect of the use of multiple initial conditions in the combinatorial optimization algorithms ICM, MPM and GSA on both second (8 nearest neighbors) and third order (12 nearest neighbors) neighborhood systems. In all experiments along this paper, we used 300 training samples for each class (white matter, gray matter and background), numbering approximately only 1% of the total image pixels. The classification errors and confusion matrix are estimated by the *leave-one-out cross validation* method. For both ICM and GSA algorithms, convergence was considered by achieving one of two conditions: less than 0.1% of the pixels are updated in the current iteration, or the maximum of 5 iterations is reached. For the MPM algorithm, the number of random samples generated in the MCMC simulation was fixed to 50, with a 'burn-in' window of size 10.

To produce different initializations to the combinatorial optimization algorithms we used seven statistical pattern classifiers: Quadratic (QDC) and Linear Discriminant Analysis (LDC), Parzen windows (PARZENC), K-Nearest-Neighbor (KNNC), Logistic Discrimination (LOGLC), Nearest Mean (NMC) and Decision Trees (TREEC).

Quantitative statistical analysis was performed by meand of the Cohen's Kappa coefficients [2], a statistical measure of agreement between the *ground truth* and the classifier output. The higher the Kappa (at a maximum value of one), the better the results. To analyse the obtained results, we used the T statistic to test the difference between mean performances on second (k_1) and third order systems (k_2). This statistc is distribuited according a t_{n-1} law, where n is the number of samples, and is defined as $T = \frac{\bar{k}}{\sigma_d/\sqrt{n}}$, where $\bar{k}$ is the difference between the group means ($\bar{k} = k_1 - k_2$) and σ_d is the standard deviation of the punctual differences. The higher the difference between the means (numerator), the higher the chance of having two distinct groups. But also, the higher the variability of the observed results (denominator), the harder the discrimination in two groups. Considering a significance level $\alpha = 0.05$, the critical value is $t_c = -1.943$, which means that, for $T < t_c$ we should reject the hipothesis that nothing changed. In other words, the average performances are significantly different.

Table 2 presents the Kappa coefficients obtained by the combination of second order MRF-based contextual classifiers applying the functions described in Table 1, while Table 3 shows the results of the combination of third order MRF-based contextual classifiers. Analyzing the results, it is possible to conclude that, in all cases, the use of higher-order systems significanlty improved the classification performance. For the ICM algorithm, we have a $T = 26.8337$, that is far above the critical value $t_c = 2.0105$ (from a t_5 distribution table), indicating the significance of the results. Moreover, the same conclusions hold for both GSA and MPM algorithms, since we have $T = 4.6967$ and $T = 2.8305$, respectively. For more details concerning the results obtained using only second-order systems the reader is refered to [11].

A final observation that its worth mentioning here is that a Kappa coefficient equal to one does not mean a perfect classification result. As this measure is computed only over the training and testing samples, that is, over a restricted area of the image, it means that the classification method had a total agreement with the groud truth in these selected regions (which here are rectangles of 300 samples for each class).

Finally, to illustrate the results, some qualitative results are presented in the following. Figure 4 shows classification maps for the best classification results for four different situations. As we go from figure a.) to d.) more information is included in the decision rule: the first image shows the result of a pointwise classifier, the second one is the result of traditional contextual classification (using second order system and a single initial condition), the third one is the result of the combination of the second-order MRF-based contextual classifiers and the fourth one is the result of combining third-order MRF-based contextual classifiers. As expected, it is clear that the amount of available information is directly related to the classification performance. The more information, the better are the results. An interesting note regarding the processing time for the generation of the solutions is that, when using multiple initializations (all 7 initial conditions), the elapsed times for GSA, ICM and MPM were 298, 370 and 3991 seconds, respectively, against 17, 16 and 503 seconds when using a single initial condition. Therefore, the obtained results show that the proposed MAP-MRF approach is capable of improving classification performance, keeping a reasonable

Table 2. Kappa coefficients and variances for ICM, GSA and MPM classifications on second order systems using all seven initializations with different combination strategies

	Rule-Based Combiner	Kappa	Variance
ICM	MAX	0.9850	0.000024743
	MIN	0.9850	0.000024743
	SUM	0.9767	0.000038257
	PRODUCT	0.9767	0.000038257
	VOTE	0.9683	0.000051597
	MEDIAN	0.9683	0.000051597
MPM	MAX	0.9818	0.000030169
	MIN	0.9833	0.000027463
	SUM	0.9983	0.0000027747
	PRODUCT	0.9800	0.000032872
	VOTE	0.9983	0.0000027747
	MEDIAN	0.9967	0.0000055431
GSA	MAX	0.9950	0.000008305
	MIN	0.9757	0.000082813
	SUM	0.9479	0.00017344
	PRODUCT	0.9618	0.00012868
	VOTE	0.9444	0.00018445
	MEDIAN	0.9549	0.00015120

Table 3. Kappa coefficients and variances for ICM, GSA and MPM classifications on third order systems using all seven initializations with different combination strategies

	Rule-Based Combiner	Kappa	Variance
ICM	MAX	1.0	0.0
	MIN	1.0	0.0
	SUM	0.9933	0.000011061
	PRODUCT	0.9933	0.000011061
	VOTE	0.9867	0.000022020
	MEDIAN	0.9867	0.000022020
MPM	MAX	1.0	0.0
	MIN	1.0	0.0
	SUM	1.0	0.0
	PRODUCT	1.0	0.0
	VOTE	1.0	0.0
	MEDIAN	1.0	0.0
GSA	MAX	0.9983	0.0000027747
	MIN	0.9983	0.0000027747
	SUM	1.0	0.0
	PRODUCT	1.0	0.0
	VOTE	1.0	0.0
	MEDIAN	1.0	0.0

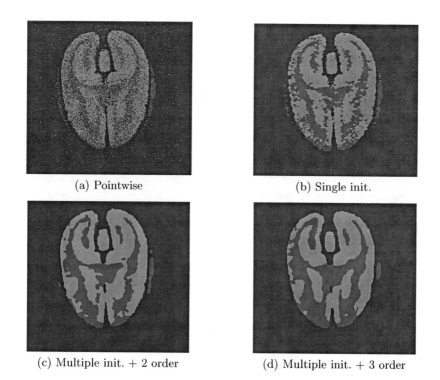

(a) Pointwise

(b) Single init.

(c) Multiple init. + 2 order

(d) Multiple init. + 3 order

Fig. 4. Classification maps for several situations: as we go from a.) to d.) more information is included in the decision rule

tradeoff between quality of the results and computational cost, defining a promising alternative to *Simulated Annealing* in image labeling applications.

6   Conclusions

In this paper we proposed an approach for MAP-MRF contextual classification by combining iterative suboptimal combinatorial optimization algorithms, making use of multiple initializations and information fusion rules. In the proposed model, the Potts MRF model parameter plays the role of a regularization parameter, controlling the tradeoff between data fidelity and prior knowledge. To estimate this parameter, a maximum pseudo-likelihood equation is applied, avoiding manual adjustments. The obtained results indicate that the method is robust against the presence of noise in the observed data and significantly improves the classification performance while keeping a reasonable computational cost.

Acknowledgments

We would like to thank FAPESP for the finantial support through Alexandre L. M. Levada scholarship (n. 06/01711-4).

References

1. Besag, J.: Spatial interaction and the statistical analysis of lattice systems. Journal of the Royal Statistical Society B 36(2), 192–236 (1974)
2. Congalton, R.G.: A review of assessing the accuracy of classifications of remotely sensed data. Remote Sensing of Enviroment 37, 35–46 (1991)
3. Duda, R.O., Hart, P.E., Stork, D.G.: Pattern classification, 2nd edn. John Wiley & Sons, New York (2001)
4. Fukunaga, K.: Introduction to Statistical Pattern Recognition, 2nd edn. Academic Press, New York (1990)
5. Gaetano, R., Scarpa, G., Poggi, G.: Hierarchical texture-based segmentation of multiresolution remote-sensing images. IEEE Transactions on Geoscience and Remote Sensing 47(7), 2129–2141 (2009)
6. JENSEN, J.L., KÜNSH, H.R.: On asymptotic normality of pseudo likelihood estimates for pairwise interaction processes. Annals of the Institute of Statistical Mathematics 46(3), 475–486 (1994)
7. Kittler, J., Hatef, M., Duin, R.P., Matas, J.: On combining classifiers. IEEE Transactions on Pattern Analysis and Machine Intelligence 20(3), 226–239 (1998)
8. Kolmogorov, V., Zabih, R.: What energy functions can be minimized via graph cuts? IEEE Transactions on Pattern Analysis and Machine Intelligence 26(2), 147–159 (2004)
9. Kuncheva, L.I.: Combining Pattern Classifiers: Methods and Algorithms. Wiley Interscience, Hoboken (2004)
10. Levada, A.L.M., Mascarenhas, N.D.A., TannÚs, A.: Pseudo-likelihood equations for potts mrf model parameter estimation on higher order neighborhood systems. IEEE Geoscience and Remote Sensing Letters 5(3), 522–526 (2008)
11. Levada, A.L.M., Mascarenhas, N.D.A., Tannús, A.: A novel map-mrf approach for multispectral image contextual classification using combination of suboptimal iterative algorithms. Pattern Recognition Letters 31(13), 1795–1808 (2010)
12. Li, M., Wu, Y., Zhang, Q.: Sar image segmentation based on mixture context and wavelet hidden-class-label markov random field. Computers & Mathematics with Applications 57(6), 961–969 (2009)
13. Nikos, K., Tziritas, G., Paragios, N.: Performance vs computational efficiency for optimizing single and dynamic mrfs: Setting the state of the art with primal-dual strategies. Computer Vision and Image Understanding 112(1), 14–29 (2008)
14. Scarpa, G., Gaetano, R., Haindl, M., Zerubia, J.: Hierarchical multiple markov chain model for unsupervised texture segmentation. IEEE Transactions on Image Processing 18(8), 1830–1843 (2009)
15. Theodoridis, S., Koutroumbas, K.: Pattern Recognition, 3rd edn. Academic Press, New York (2006)
16. Tzikas, D.G., Likas, A.C., Galatsanos, N.P.: The variational approximation for bayesian inference. IEEE Signal Processing Magazine 25(6), 131–146 (2008)
17. Webb, A.: Statistical Pattern Recognition, 2nd edn. Arnold, London (2002)

18. Won, C.S., Gray, R.M.: Stochastic Image Processing. Kluwer Academic/Plenum Publishers (2004)
19. Woolrich, M.W., Behrens, T.E.: Variational bayes inference of spatial mixture models for segmentation. IEEE Transactions on Medical Imaging 25(10), 1380–1391 (2006)
20. Yamazaki, T., Gingras, D.: A contextual classification system for remote sensing using a multivariate gaussian mrf model. In: Proceedings of the XXIII International Symposium on Circuits and Systems (ISCAS), vol. 2, pp. 648–651. IEEE, Atlanta (1996)
21. Yin, X., Chen, S., Hu, E., Zhang, D.: Semi-supervised clustering with metric learning: An adaptive kernel method. Pattern Recognition 43(4), 1320–1333 (2010)
22. Yuan, C., Neubauer, C.: A variational bayesian approach for classification with corrupted inputs. In: Proceedings of the 7th International Conference on Computer Vision and Pattern Recognition, CVPR, pp. 1–8. IEEE, Minneapolis (2007)
23. Zeng, Y., Samaras, D., Chen, W., Peng, Q.: Topology cuts: A novel min-cut/max-flow algorithm for topology preserving segmentation in n d images. Computer Vision and Image Understanding 112(1), 81–90 (2008)
24. Zhu, X., Goldberg, A.: Introduction to Semi-Supervised Learning. Morgan & Claypool, Princeton (2009)

Integrated Cooperative Framework for Project Resources Allocation

Mihaela Brut, Jean-Luc Soubie, and Florence Sèdes

IRIT - Research Institute in Computer Science, Toulouse, France
{Mihaela.Brut,Jean-Luc.Soubie,Florence.Sedes}@irit.fr

Abstract. The present paper presents a generic, flexible and robust framework for decision support in cooperative systems in charge with human resources allocation for various project tasks. Considering a knowledge database where people and projects are characterized through the task and competences binomial, the particularity of this frameworks consists in integrating inside the cooperative systems the benefits of complex user modeling and of personalization handled by the adaptive hypermedia systems, as well as the benefits of knowledge management with the support of semantic Web technologies.

Keywords: collaborative systems, ontology-oriented knowledge databases, user profile, task modelling.

1 Introduction

Intelligent support provided automatically to the users while using a system (accomplishing specific tasks) is a key challenge for knowledge management research, considered by multiple disciplines, and especially by the semantic Web, cooperative knowledge based systems [1], knowledge-based systems [2], or adaptive systems [3], [4]. Essential and common in all such approaches is to consider a conceptualization of the considered domain [5].

The present approach exploits all these achievements in the context of cooperative systems, where task decomposition in multiple layers, according a hierarchical structure, enables to acquire such a granularity level where a sub-task could be associated with a specific competence. In addition, the idea of developing a library of problem models promoted by the cooperative systems is capitalized in the context of ontology-oriented knowledge databases.

The backbone of the present approach is to adopt an ontology set in order to *semantically model people, documents, and services*, but also for a flexible modelling of operative *functionalities*, expressed especially in terms of *tasks*. This enables to provide support during task execution in the form of personalized recommendation of useful resources. For this purpose, it is necessary to integrate inside the cooperative systems the benefits of complex user modelling and of personalization handled by the adaptive hypermedia systems, as well as the benefits of knowledge management with the support of semantic Web technologies.

E.R. Hruschka Junior et al. (Eds.): INTECH 2011, CCIS 165, pp. 40–49, 2011.
© Springer-Verlag Berlin Heidelberg 2011

In the next section we will present the existing approaches in modelling users and tasks in terms of competences with the support of ontologies. Section 3 expose how this models are exploited by the recommender systems. Section 4 will outline the approaches that lead to transition from decision to cooperation with the support of knowledge. Section 5 will present our framework, while conclusions and further work directions will be outlined in the final.

2 Competence-Oriented User and Task Modelling

The double perspective of modelling both user and his tasks in terms of competences has few predecessors in the literature. [6] introduce the notion of enterprise models, where the activity inside institution is described in terms of processes and activities, but also in terms of key concepts, user skills, or enterprise organizational structure. As well, the idea of "competency questions" is introduced as model evaluation criterion, which specify which queries a model should be able to answer.

The notion of enterprise models was re-considered by [7] and extended by [8] in the form of the Integrating Modelling Methodology (IMM), where three sub-models are defined:

- *Task model*: identifies, group and describe the flow between tasks that the system users can perform;
- *Domain model* describes semantically and logically domain topics and the relation between them;
- *Skill model* connects the domain and the task model: a skill is the knowledge about a specific domain topic together with the ability to apply this knowledge within the specified task.

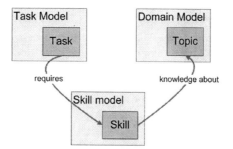

Fig. 1. IMM models (according [8])

We illustrate further how the ontologies could be adopted in order to express competences and to model users and tasks.

2.1 User Modeling

User modeling is a specific issue of the adaptive hypermedia systems domain. It adopts a feature-based modeling technique, considering some important characteristics of the user as an individual: knowledge, interests, goals, background, and individual traits [9].

The idea of developing competency-based user models expressed through one or more ontologies was explored in multiple systems. The CommOn framework uses self-defined competence schemes, organized as ontology, in order to develop Competency-Based Web Services dedicated to Human Resource Management [10]. The project CommonCV applies the framework for CV development and search. In [11] is presented an information system for storing, evaluating and reasoning about competencies of students at universities, based on a fine-grained representation of skills and a competence ontology. However, the competency management remains the major goal of such approaches, while task allocation or task accomplishment is not considered.

In [12] we developed a user model defined in terms of technical competences in a specific area, expressed through domain ontology such as ACM topic hierarchy[1] enriched with three relation types. The model was used as support for developing personalized recommendations.

2.2 Task Modeling

In the context of adaptive hypermedia systems, user tasks are sometimes considered for developing personalized recommendations inside e-commerce Web sites, where the path to commending a product is considered a desired task. [13] adopts the proposed task-oriented user modeling approach in the context of Web pages recommendations development. The relations between the common navigational "tasks" and Web pages or users are characterized through the Probability Latent Semantic Analysis (PLSA) model.

A consistent effort in task modeling was accomplished in the context of intelligent tutoring systems, when modeling the educational tasks to be accomplished by the students. [14] proposes an ontology-based modeling framework for instructional and learning theories, which is also compliant with the e-learning standards.

In the framework of I*Teach project[2] [15], a Wiki-based Web repository of educational scenarios and tasks was developed. For their annotations, taxonomy of ICT-enhanced competencies was used. The repository could be viewed as an example of the competency taxonomy-based annotations of the educational materials. It includes support for retrieving scenarios and tasks based on taxonomy concepts. Particular class-based data organization was adopted.

There are also some approaches for task-based modeling of agents with focus on the cooperation between agents while adopting a hierarchical tasks' decomposition [16].

As well, the Web services orchestration support developed in the context of the WSMO (Web Service Modeling Ontology) framework constitutes a task-based Web services modeling approach [17]. WSMO provides the conceptual underpinning and a formal language for semantically describing all relevant aspects of Web services accessible through a Web service interface in order to facilitate the automatization of discovering, combining and invoking services over the Web. In [18] we developed a solution for Web services orchestration in the context of multimedia-distributed systems, considering the WSMO approach.

---

[1] http://acm.rkbexplorer.com/ontologies/acm
[2] http://i-teach.info.uaic.ro/

2.3 Personalized Recommendation Techniques

In order to recommend pertinent resources to users in accordance with their current activity, two main approaches were developed: content-based recommendations and collaborative filtering. Various algorithmic solutions are adopted by the recommendation techniques: the decisional trees, classification algorithms such as the k nearest neighbors (knn) algorithm, the Rochio algorithm, the probabilistic approach based on Bayesian networks [19]. As well, the development of hybrid techniques and the integration of semantic Web technologies could enhance the quality of recommendations [20].

The essential approach of any recommendation technique is to analyze the user's navigational activity (by using some consecrated data mining algorithms). Some "higher" abstraction level approaches considered the concept-based navigation (where each concept and page is a navigation hub, as in the KBS Hyperbook system), document cluster level navigation [21] or task-oriented navigation [13].

In [22] we proposed a recommendation approach whose novelty consists in supervising the user conceptual navigation through the ontology instead of his/her site navigation: for each visited document, its annotations are considered in order to define user fingerprints through ontology concepts; as well, by adopting a measure of similarity between concepts, the ontology-based domain knowledge is integrated into the recommendation algorithm. We developed further multiple enhancement of the recommendation technique [23].

3 From Decision to Cooperation with the Support of Knowledge

A Decision Support System (DSS) supports and helps decision makers in their decision process for a better effectiveness [24]. A decision solution is the result of successive interactions between the user and the system [25], which build decision support based on a knowledge database.

In the area of knowledge-based systems, the manner of building the knowledge databases evolved in time from an accurate reproduction of the human experts reasoning to the development of generic models libraries where the quality is mainly measured in terms of performance in solving specific problem types [26]. The European project KADS [27] was a pioneer in this advancement.

[28] proposed to advantage in this quality evaluation the support provided to potential user when accomplishing his tasks (the quality of the collaboration between system and user).

This approach was implemented in multiple projects. The MACAO project [29] was focused on integrating multiple knowledge databases (corresponding to different expertise domains) and in developing a generic framework for solving different problem types (belonging to different domains). The methodology required developing progressively a domain model, a reasoning model for controlling the problem resolution into a particular domain, as well as the validation schema. As applications, the domain ontologies from the Common-KADS library where used [30], alongside with the problem types proposed by the KADS project [27]. This methodology evolved to a generic approach for cooperative problem solving known as CKBS - Cooperative Knowledge Based Systems [1], whose architecture is based upon three models:

- *Application model*: a knowledge base implementing the functionalities of the system in the domain of problem solving;
- *Cooperation model*: knowledge base of the task assignment according to the organizational constraints,
- *User model* is a representation of the user point of view on the common task, on the task assignment.

All the knowledge bases are hierarchically modeled according to the task/method paradigm. The notion of task is recursively defined at least by its goal, its entries and/or prerequisites, and its methods. The task refers to *what* (what must be done), the methods refer to *how* (the ways to do that). According to the requirements of the system, it could be useful to know *who* (the agent in charge of the task), *with what* (prerequisite elements for the task performance), or *why* (explanation about the role of this task in the problem solving process).

4   Integrated Cooperative Framework for Project Resources Allocation

We present further our cooperative framework that illustrates how could be integrated inside the Cooperative Knowledge Based Systems architecture a project knowledge database and the recommendation functionality in order to provide the project managers with decision support.

Considering the *task & competences* binomial in order to characterize people and projects, but also other enterprise resources, our framework aims to facilitate the decision support for human resources managers and for project managers when they have to establish the project teams, to re-configure the teams and/or the project specifications in the case of failure or conflicts or to locate the other useful resources.

Ontologies are considered for a more refined modeling of resources (users, documents, and services), but also for a flexible modeling of functionalities, especially in terms of tasks. Thus, the personalized recommendations of useful resources are accompanied by the task-oriented decision support.

Our framework is organized according the three main components of a cooperative knowledge-based system (see Figure 2):

- *User model:* is constituted by the representation adopted by the two main addressees of our approach, namely the project manager (that operates with a task-oriented representation) and human resources manager (that operates with a competency-oriented representation).

  The people profiles (named further, more generic, "user profiles") and the project models should be developed for this purpose, according the adopted tasks & competences perspective.

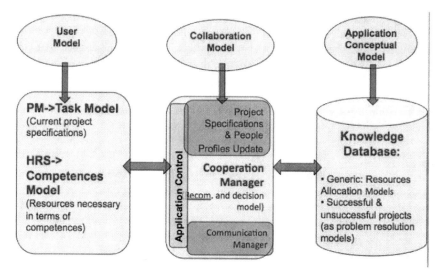

Fig. 2. Architecture of the proposed cooperative framework

- *Application model*: consists mainly into a knowledge database to be exploited when implementing decision support and personalization. Its core will concern the knowledge about projects, including generic models and project instances (the previous projects, either successful or not, are considered as an important knowledge source).

  As supplementary knowledge, the collections of people profiles, services descriptions and documents models are also considered.
- *Cooperation model*: represents the knowledge database where the organization policies and constraints are considered in order to develop solutions for the current project execution, including personalized recommendations and decision support.

4.1 User Model

The user model is based on the tasks and competences binomial and is defined through a two-layers modeling:

- *Task level*: allocated tasks in different projects, effectively accomplished tasks and potential tasks, for which the user express his will to be involved;
- *Competences level*: certified competences according the obtained diplomas, practiced competences during the execution of effective tasks, and foreseen competences as a matter of personal development program.

For acquiring a flexible **task modeling**, a possible solution is to consider as starting point existing heavyweight ontology Omnibus[3], which is built according the theory of role. It provides a complex modeling of user characteristics and activities as well, mainly in the framework of tutoring systems, thus exploiting and formalizing

---

[3] http://edont.qee.jp/omnibus/

the theories on learning styles and educational strategies. The formal models developed for task-oriented educational scenarios could be capitalized and adapted in the framework of the project management. The perspective from the cooperative systems approach could be adopted, where tasks are decomposed in multiple layers, according a hierarchical structure, until the granularity level where a sub-task could be associated with a specific competence.

For **modeling user profile**, the reference model promoted by the semantic Web through the semantic desktop framework could be adopted: PIMO, Personal Information Model[4]. It includes a personal level and a group level, and enables to describe general information about users [31].

The **user competences** could be expressed in terms of technical competences in the computer science domain, by adopting the recently elaborated computing ontology[5]. The perspective of a domain model as covering the totality of competences in a specific area is considered with this respect. The methodology for developing a competency-based user profile based on a given model (such as PIMO) and expressed through ontological constructs (based, for example, on the computing ontology) is presented in [12], where the IEEE Personal and Private Information (PAPI) user model and ACM topic hierarchy were considered.

4.2 Application Model

The main purpose of the application model is to develop a knowledge database that will be exploited when implementing decision support and personalization. Following the practice from cooperative systems, this knowledge database consists mainly into a library of models and instances of the problems to be solved. Thus, the knowledge about projects (our focused problem type) consist in generic project models and in project instances representing finished projects, either successful or not. Such concrete projects gather significant knowledge about solutions for (individual and group) human resources allocation according project specifications, including solutions adopted in critical situations that required resources re-allocation or tasks re-allocation, etc.

The **project knowledge database** is organized according the presented framework for task modeling, namely based on multiple ontologies including support for functional properties description.

Alongside with the project knowledge database, an **additional knowledge database** is constituted by the collections of *people profiles* (including information about competences and tasks), the *software agents' descriptions* (following for example the WSMO framework (see [18]) and the *documents models* (developed through automatic ontology-based annotation techniques, extending the approach presented in [32]). We consider the software agents and the documents as functionalities and resources available across the different projects that could be exploited when providing support to users.

---

[4] http://www.semanticdesktop.org/ontologies/
[5] http://what.csc.villanova.edu/twiki/bin/view/Main/TheComputingOntology

4.3 Cooperation Model

The cooperation model aims to develop the *effective decision support* for the specific problem to be currently solved. It represents the knowledge database where the organization policies and constraints are considered in order to develop solutions for the current project execution, including personalized recommendations, decision support for nominal situations and decision support for critical situations.

Personalized recommendations during task accomplishment (project execution) consist in recommending documents, services, collaborators and other resources at each project step according the context (e.g. team characteristics, project technical aspects, personal development needs). In [33] we presented the applied methodology for developing such recommendations in the case when all the resources are modeled in terms of ontological constructs, as the present framework involves as well.

In order to acquire **intelligent decision support in resources allocation**, the flexible allocation strategies should be adopted that consider the available resources in terms of required competences, people profile evolution, people collaboration history, as well as the team collaboration strategy adopted in the current project.

5 Conclusions and Further Work

We presented a framework for decision support in cooperative systems in charge with human resources allocation for various project tasks that integrated technologies from multiple areas such as cooperative knowledge based systems, adaptive hypermedia systems, semantic Web.

As a challenge for our future work, we propose to practically capitalize and integrate into such a framework the technical achievements from two already developed applications.

The first application is a tool that helps decision makers in critical situations and that adopts the modeling approach typical to cooperative knowledge based systems. It is based on a Task/Method paradigm, and it enables to take into account collateral effects of tasks in order to support decision makers in a critical context [34].

The second application is a recommender system for students, which combines user activity tracking with the exploitation of the semantic annotations associated with resources [33]. The developed recommendation approach based on the conceptual navigation tracking will be further refined from the current perspective of user tasks modeling alongside with his competences. Thus, the tasks semantic descriptions could be tracked alongside with the semantic description of the accessed resources.

References

1. Soubie, J.L., Zarate, P.: Distributed Decision Making: A Proposal of Support Through Cooperative Systems. Group Decision and Negotiation 14, 147–158 (2005)
2. Liebowitz, J.: The Handbook of Applied Expert Systems, 1st edn. CRC Press, Inc., Boca Raton (1997)
3. Jameson, A.: Adaptive interfaces and agents. In: Jacko, J.A. (ed.) Human Computer Interaction Handbook, 2nd edn., pp. 305–330. Erlbaum Mahwah, NJ (2008)

4. Brusilovsky, P., Millán, E.: User models for adaptive hypermedia and adaptive educational systems. In: Brusilovsky, P., Kobsa, A., Nejdl, W. (eds.) Adaptive Web 2007. LNCS, vol. 4321, pp. 3–53. Springer, Heidelberg (2007)
5. Gruber, T.R.: Toward principles for the design of ontologies used for knowledge sharing. International Journal of Human-Computer Studies 45, 907–928 (1995)
6. Fox, M.S., Grüninger, M.: Enterprise Modeling. AI Magazine 19(3), 109–121 (1998)
7. Angele, J., Fensel, D., Studer, R.: Domain and Task Modelling in MIKE. In: Proceedings of the IFIP WG8.1/13.2 Joint Working Conference on Domain Knowledge for Interactive System Design, Hall, pp. 8–10 (2006)
8. Rospocher, M., Ghidini, C., Serafini, L., Kump, B., Pammer, V., Lindstaedt, S.N., Faatz, A., Ley, T.: Collaborative Enterprise Integrated Modelling. In: SWAP CEUR Workshop Proceedings CEUR-WS.org, vol. 426 (2008)
9. Brusilovsky, P., Millán, E.: User models for adaptive hypermedia and adaptive educational systems. In: Brusilovsky, P., Kobsa, A., Nejdl, W. (eds.) Adaptive Web 2007. LNCS, vol. 4321, pp. 3–53. Springer, Heidelberg (2007)
10. Trichet, F., Leclère, M.: A Framework for Building Competency-Based Systems Dedicated to Human Resource Management. In: Zhong, N., Raś, Z.W., Tsumoto, S., Suzuki, E. (eds.) ISMIS 2003. LNCS (LNAI), vol. 2871, pp. 633–639. Springer, Heidelberg (2003)
11. Dorn, J., Pichlmair, M.: A Competence Management System for Universities. In: Proceeding of the European Conference on Artificial Intelligence, St. Gallen (2007)
12. Brut, M., Sedes, F., Jucan, T., Grigoras, R., Charvillat, V.: An Ontology-Based Modeling Approach for Developing a Competencies-Oriented Collective Intelligence. In: Proceedings of the ED-L2L Conference, Word Computer Congress (WCC 2008), Springer, Milano (2008)
13. Jin, X., Zhou, Y., Mobasher, B.: Task-Oriented Web User Modeling for Recommendation. In: Ardissono, L., Brna, P., Mitrović, A. (eds.) UM 2005. LNCS (LNAI), vol. 3538, pp. 109–118. Springer, Heidelberg (2005)
14. Hayashi, Y., Bourdeau, J.: Ontological Support for a Theory-Eclectic Approach to Instructional and Learning Design. In: The Programming Language Ada. LNCS, pp. 155–169. Springer, Heidelberg (2006)
15. Brut, M., Buraga, S., Dumitriu, S., Grigoras, G., Girdea, M.: An Ontology-Based Modeling Approach for Adaptive E-Learning Systems. In: Proceedings of ICIW 2008, IEEE Computer Society Press, Athens (2008)
16. Lopes, A.L., Botelho, L.M.: Task Decomposition and Delegation Algorithms for Coordinating Unstructured Multi Agent Systems. In: Proc.of the International Conference on Complex, Intelligent and Software Intensive System, IEEE Computers Society Press, Los Alamitos (2007)
17. Roman, D., Keller, U., Lausen, H., De Bruijn, J., Lara, R., Stollberg, M., Polleres, A., Feier, C., Bussler, C., Fensel, D.: Web Service Modeling Ontology. Applied Ontology Journal 1(1), 77–106 (2005)
18. Brut, M., Sèdes, F., Manzat, A.-M.: A Web Services Orchestration Solution for Semantic Multimedia Indexing and Retrieval. In: Barolli, L., Xhafa, F., Hsu, H.-H. (eds.) Proc. CISIS 2009. IEEE Computer Society, Fukuoka (2009)
19. Pazzani, M.J., Billsus, D.: Content-Based Recommendation Systems. In: Brusilovsky, P., Kobsa, A., Nejdl, W. (eds.) Adaptive Web 2007. LNCS, vol. 4321, pp. 325–341. Springer, Heidelberg (2007)
20. Burke, R.: Hybrid Web Recommender Systems. In: Brusilovsky, P., Kobsa, A., Nejdl, W. (eds.) Adaptive Web 2007. LNCS, vol. 4321, pp. 377–408. Springer, Heidelberg (2007)

21. Henze, N., Nejdl, W.: Adaptation in open corpus hypermedia. Int. J. of Artificial Intelligence in Education 12(4), 325–350 (2001)
22. Brut, M., Sèdes, F., Zayani, C.: Ontology-Based User Competencies Modeling for E-Learning Recommender Systems. In: Chevalier, M., Julien, C., Soulé-Dupuy(Eds, C. (eds.) Collaborative and Social Information Retrieval and Access: Techniques for Improved User Modeling, vol. VI, pp. 119–138. IGI Global (2008)
23. Brut, M., Sèdes, F.: Ontology-Based Solution for Personalized Recommendations in E-Learning Systems. Methodological Aspects and Evaluation Criterias. In: Jemni, M., Sampson, D. (eds.) IEEE International Conference on Advanced Learning Technologies (ICALT 2010), IEEE Computer Society, Sousse (2010)
24. Keen, P.G.W., Scott Morton, M.S.: Decision Support Systems: An organisational perspective. Addison-Wesley, Reading (1978)
25. Sprague, R.H., Carlson, E.D.: Building Effective Decision Support Systems. Prentice Hall, Inc., Englewood Cliffs (1982)
26. Zaraté, P., Soubie, J.-L.: An overview of Supports for Collective Decision Making. Journal of Decision Systems, Hermès / Lavoisier 13(2), 221–221 (2004)
27. Schreiber, G.B., Wielinga, B., Breuker, J.A. (eds.): KADS: a Principled Approach to Knowledge Based System Development. Academic Press, New York (1993)
28. Chabaud, C., Aussenac-Gilles, N., Soubie, J.-L.: A validation method of the validity of artificial intelligence as a work aid. In: Queinnec, Y., Daniellou, F. (eds.) Proceedings of IEA'91 International Ergonomics Association, pp. 619–621. Taylor & Francis, London (1991)
29. Aussenac, N., Soubie, J.-L., Frontin, J.: A knowledge acquisition tool for expertise transfer. In: Proceedings of EKAW 1988 (European Knowledge Acquisition Workshop), GMD Studien 143, Bonn, RFA, pp 8.1-8.12 (1998)
30. Wielinga, B., Van De Velde, W., Schreiber, G., Akkermans, H.: The CommonKADS Framework for Knowledge Modelling, Report of ESPRIT KADS-II project (1992)
31. Sauermann, L., Van Elst, L., Dengel, A.: Pimo - a framework for representing personal information models. In: Pellegrini, T., Schaffert, S. (eds.) Proceedings of I-Semantics 2007, JUCS, pp. 270–277 (2007)
32. Brut, M., Dumitrescu, S., Sedes, F.: A Semantic-Oriented Approach for Organizing and Developing Annotation for E-learning. IEEE Transactions on Learning Technologies (99) (2010), doi:10.1109/TLT.2010.40
33. Broisin, J., Brut, M., Butoianu, V., Sedes, F., Vidal, P.: A Personalized Recommendation Framework based on CAM and Document Annotations. In: Proceedings of RecSysTel, Procedia Computer Science. Elsevier, Amsterdam (2010)
34. Camilleri, G., Soubie, J.-L., Zaraté, P.: Critical Situations for Decision Making: A Support Based on a Modelling Tool. Group Decision and Negotiation 14(2), 159–171 (2005)

SNPs Classification: Building Biological High-Level Knowledge Using Genetic Algorithms

Andre Bevilaqua, Fabricio Alves Rodrigues, and Laurence Rodrigues do Amaral

Computer Science Departament, UFG Jatai, GO - Brazil
lramaral@yahoo.com.br, laurence@jatai.ufg.br

Abstract. Computational approaches have been applied in many different biology application domains. When such tools are based on conventional computation, their approach has shown limitations when dealing with complex biological problems. In the present study, a computational evolutionary environment (GASNP) is proposed as a tool to extract classification rules from biological dataset. The main goal of the proposed approach is to allow the discovery of concise, and accurate, high-level rules (from a biological database named dbSNP - Database Single Nucleotide Polymorphism) which can be used as a classification system. More than focusing only on the classification accuracy, the proposed GASNP model aims at balancing prediction precision, interpretability and comprehensibility. The obtained results show that the proposed GASNP has great potential and is capable of extracting useful high-level knowledge that could not be extracted by traditional classification methods such as Decision Trees, One R and the Single Conjunctive Rule Learner, among others, using the same dataset.

Keywords: Bioinformatic, Machine Learning, Evolutionary Computation, Genetic Algorithms, SNPs.

1 Introduction

Molecular Biology field has interesting areas that allows the development and application of computer techniques [1]. Due to the great amount and complexity of the involved information, tools based on conventional computation have shown to be limited when dealing with complex biological problems. Computational intelligence techniques, such as genetic algorithms, have been increasingly used to solve problems in Molecular Biology. The applicability of these techniques comes from their capacity to learn automatically, processing initially a great volume of data and based on it producing useful hypotheses [2]. Identifying the genes conferring susceptibility or resistance to common human diseases should become increasingly feasible with improved methods for finding DNA sequence variants on a genome-wide scale. To locate genes affecting these rare disorders, researchers perform linkage analysis on families, which requires 300 to 500 highly informative genetic markers spanning the entire human genome. However, it has been considerably harder to locate the genes contributing to the risk of common diseases such as diabetes, heart disease, cancers,

E.R. Hruschka Junior et al. (Eds.): INTECH 2011, CCIS 165, pp. 50–58, 2011.

and psychiatric disorders, because these phenotypes are affected by multiple genes, each with small effect; environmental contributions are also important. Instead of linkage analysis on families or classes it may be much more efficient to perform association analysis on many affected and unaffected individuals, which would require hundreds of thousands of variants spread over the entire genome. About 90% of sequence variants in humans are differences in single bases of DNA, called single nucleotide polymorphisms (SNPs) and these SNPs can be in the coding regions of genes or in regulatory regions [11]. New techniques for the large-scale identification of SNPs in the human population [12] are resulting in an exponential expansion in the number known, and already the National Institute of Health (NIH) SNP database (http://www.ncbi.nlm.nih.gov/SNP) contains approximately 2.8 million cases. There are high hopes that knowledge of an individuals SNP genotype will provide a basis for assessing susceptibility to disease and the optimal choice of therapies [13]. A major challenge in realizing these expectations is understanding how and when the variants cause disease [14]. Thus, the study of the SNPs and these variants will allow researchers to identify the genetic basis for common diseases and to improve the efficacy of drugs and other therapies [11]. In the present study, the main objective is to mine accurate and short high level rules that will be associated to each class individually, reducing the problem to few features per class. Also, a value will be associated to each feature that composes the rule. The results generated in this work may help researchers to understand the alteration mechanisms in the SNP of *Anopheles gambiae*. A Genetic Algorithm was elaborated to obtain IF-THEN rules from dbSNP database of *A. gambiae*.

2   Evolutionary Environment

2.1   Genetic Algorithms (GA)

GA are computational search methods based on natural evolution and genetic mechanisms, simulating the Darwins's natural selection theory [3]. The GA implemented in our evolutionary environment was adapted from [9]. GA in [9] was elaborated with the goal of obtaining IF-THEN classification rules in clinical databases. Another evolutionary environment, also based on [9], was applied in cancer cells gene expression database [6], measured by microarray [5].

2.2   Individual Representation

The individual used on our GA is composed by six (6) genes. The first gene of the individual corresponds to the orientation SNP scaffold, the second corresponds to the SNP position, the third corresponds to the value of allele 1, the fourth corresponds to the number of observations of allele 1, the fifth corresponds to the value of allele 2 and the sixth corresponds to the number of observations of allele 2. The individual is illustrated in Figure 1.

$Gene_1$			...	...	$Gene_6$		
W_1	O_1	V_1	...	...	W_6	O_6	V_6

Fig. 1. Individual representation

All genes of the GA individual is subdivided into three fields: weight (W_i), operator (O_i) and value (V_i), as illustrated in Figure 1. Each GA gene corresponds to one condition in the antecedent part of the rule (IF) and the whole individual is the previous rule. The weight field is an integer variable and its value is between 0 (zero) and 10 (ten). It is important to say that this weight field determines the insertion or exclusion of the correspondent gene in the previous rule. If this value is lesser than a boundary-value, this gene will not appear in the rule, otherwise the gene appears. In this work, the value 7 (seven) was used as the boundary-value. The operator field can be < (minor), > (larger), = (equal) or ! (diferent). The value of orientation SNP scaffold is + (forward) or - (reverse). The value of SNP position is an integer variable which can vary between the minor and the larger value found in the database. The value of alleles 1 and 2 are: A (adenine), G (guanine), C (cytosine) or T (thymine). The value that represents the number of observations of allele 1 and 2 is an integer number that can vary between the minor and the larger value found in the database.

2.3 Genetic Operators and Parameters

Stochastic tournament with Tour of size 3 was used as the selection method for crossover. One-point crossover with probability equal to 100% is applied to each couple of selected individuals, generating two new ones. Mutation is applied to the new individuals. A specific mutation operator is used to each type of gene field with a rate of 30%. During the mutation of the weight field, the new value is given by the increment or the decrement of one unit to the original value. The mutation changes the current operator field to other valid operator. In this work we have used four operators (<, >, = or !). The population for the next generation is formed by selecting the best individuals among the components of parents and children populations. To define the best GA configuration, we chose the configuration that achieved the best test results for all classes.

We used 200 individuals, evaluated our GA per 200 generations and set the weight field to 7. This environment was obtained after testing various configurations, such as:

- Population size: 100, 200 and 400;
- Generations: 100 and 200;
- Selection method: Roulette and Stochastic tournament;
- Weight field: 6, 7 and 8;

To show that chosen configuration is robust, we ran 35 times using different random seeds and compared the obtained results considering a significance test using $\alpha = 0:05$. The Table 1 present these obtained results with 95% of significance. For the intergenic class, the lowest value obtained is 0.855842286, and the highest is

0.878957714 (with difference 1.8%). For the intronic class, the lowest value obtained is 0.800512661, and the highest is 0.818573053 (with difference 2.3%). The best result was obtained for the silent mutation class. The lowest value obtained is 0.75966427, and the highest is 0.772678587, with difference 1.3%.

Table 1. Significance Test

Seed	Intergenic	Intronic	Silent Mutation
1	0.795	0.888	0.783
2	0.795	0.892	0.768
3	0.79	0.789	0.761
4	0.79	0.892	0.785
5	0.86	0.787	0.783
6	0.795	0.888	0.795
7	0.795	0.89	0.705
8	0.866	0.897	0.761
9	0.854	0.897	0.807
10	0.79	0.892	0.751
11	0.795	0.854	0.756
12	0.871	0.892	0.797
13	0.822	0.816	0.761
14	0.795	0.865	0.772
15	0.862	0.892	0.795
16	0.79	0.876	0.768
17	0.795	0.892	0.761
18	0.809	0.876	0.763
19	0.82	0.796	0.776
20	0.795	0.892	0.745
21	0.822	0.875	0.759
22	0.79	0.892	0.745
23	0.795	0.863	0.761
24	0.795	0.847	0.757
25	0.786	0.876	0.766
26	0.795	0.868	0.745
27	0.79	0.897	0.779
28	0.79	0.853	0.756
29	0.866	0.885	0.771
30	0.822	0.892	0.785
31	0.83	0.81	0.776
32	0.795	0.882	0.77
33	0.795	0.882	0.771
34	0.784	0.789	0.737
35	0.795	0.885	0.745
SD	0.027257317	0.034886539	0.019641621
AV	0.809542857	0.8674	0.766171429
Significance	0.009030196	0.011557714	0.006507159
Low	0.800512661	0.855842286	0.75966427
High	0.818573053	0.878957714	0.772678587

2.4 Fitness Function

In general, the individual fitness quantifies its quality as a solution for the target problem. In this work, FF evaluates the quality of the rule associated to each individual. Some concepts must be explained before defining our FF. When a rule defined for the classification of a specific class C is applied to a known case, four different types of results can be observed, depending on the class predicted by the rule and the true class of the case [8]:

- True Positive (tp) - The rule classifies the case as class C and the case really belongs to class C;
- False Positive (fp) - The rule classifies the case as class C, but the case does not belong to class C;
- True Negative (tn) - The rule does not classify the case as class C and the case does not belong to class C;
- False Negative (fn) - The rule does not classify the case as class C, but the case really belongs to class C;

Based on the four possible results of a rule, the fitness function used in our evolutionary environment applies two indicators commonly used in medical domains, called Sensitivity (Se) and Specificity (Sp), which can be defined as follows:

$$Se = \frac{tp}{(tp + fn)} \tag{1}$$

$$Sp = \frac{tn}{(tn + fp)} \tag{2}$$

Using the sensitivity and specificity concepts, FF is defined as the combination of these two indicators, Se and Sp, as follows:

$$Fitness = (Se + Sp) / 2 \tag{3}$$

The goal is to maximize, at the same time, Se as well as Sp. In each execution, the GA works in a binary classification problem, that is, when the GA is searching for rules associated to a given class C, all the other classes are grouped in one unique class (not C).

2.5 Database

Sequence variants are differences in single bases of DNA, called single nucleotide polymorphisms (SNPs). Sequence variations exist at defined positions within genomes and are responsible for individual phenotypic characteristics, including a person propensity toward complex disorders such as heart disease and cancer [7]. The Single Nucleotide Polymorphism database (dbSNP) is a public-domain archive for a broad collection of simple genetic polymorphisms. This collection of polymorphisms includes single-base nucleotide substitutions (SNPs) [7]. This evolutionary environment was applied in SNP database (dbSNP) of *A. gambiae*.

The major goal is to search for relations between six fields (orientation SNP scaffold, SNP position, value of allele 1, number of observations of allele 1, value of allele 2 and number of observations of allele 2) and three types of SNP (intergenic, intronic and silent mutation). The database has 495 records (intergenic - 80%, intronic - 15.75% and silent mutation - 4.25%).

3   Results

We split the database in three partitions. All partitions have 165 records (132 records of intergenic class, 26 records of intronic class and 7 records of silent mutation class). In this work, we used two partitions in training and one partition in test. The Table II presents the best rules discovered by our GA and shows their evaluations in the training and test sets.

In Table 2, observe that our environment found a low number of attributes per class (only 3) and a low number of used attributes in all rules (only 4). Furthermore, the atributes number of obs of allele 1 and 2 appeared in all rules. The result obtained for intergenic class is very good because we found a test result better than a training result (0.864 against 0.795, a difference of 0.069 or 6,9%). The remaining results were good too. For the intronic and silent mutation classes, we obtained test results very near of the training result. For intronic class the difference was 0.073 or 7.3% and for silent mutation class the difference was 0.023 or 2.3%.

Table 2. Best rules discovered for each class

Type of SNP (class)	Rule	Fitness Training	Fitness Test
Intergenic	If(orientation SNP scaffold = +) AND (number of obs of allele 1 ! 7) AND (number of obs. of allele 2 > 6)	0.795	0.864
Intronic	If(orientation SNP scaffold = -) AND (SNP position < 9385) AND (number of obs. of allele 2 ! 8)	0.888	0.815
Silent Mutation	IF (SNP position < 2095) AND (number of obs of allele 1 ! 5) AND (number of obs. of allele 2 < 3)	0.783	0.76

We found an average fitness of 82.2% in the training set and an average fitness of 81.3% in the test set. This values shows that we found good fitness for all classes and shows that our method is very general, ie, it wasn't affected by overfitting. In order to better evaluate the empirical results obtained using our proposed AG, a comparative analysis was conducted considering the accuracy of other fourteen traditional classification algorithms present into Weka Suite [10]. They are: J48, BFTree, UserClassifier, DecisionStump, FT, OneR, ConjuctiveRule, Decision Table, DTNB, JRIP, NNge, PART, Ridor and ZeroR. All methods are used to build highlevel knowledge. This classification methods were divided in two groups: the first uses as output the trees and the second, rules. The tree group is: J48, BFTree, UserClassifier, DecisionStump and FT. The rule group is: OneR, ConjuctiveRule, Decision Table, DTNB, JRIP, NNge, PART, Ridor and ZeroR. The table III presents the comparison between our environment with others traditional classification algorithms. In all methods aforementioned, we used 3-fold cross validation.

Table 3. Comparison between our method and other traditional methods using the fitness function described by the expression (3)

Method	Intergenic	Intronic	Silent Mutation
GASNP	0.864	0.815	0.76
J48	0.885	0.535	0.875
BFTree	0.885	0.575	0.88
UserClassifier	0.5	0.5	0.5
Decision Stump	0.895	0.665	0.885
OneR	0.85	0.5	0.895
Conjuctive Rule	0.85	0.5	0.895
Decision Table	0.88	0.54	0.875
DTNB	0.9	0.58	0.905
JRIP	0.87	0.57	0.885
NNge	0.84	0.625	0.84
PART	0.9	0.695	0.895
Ridor	0.905	0.735	0.905
ZeroR	0.5	0.5	0.5

Our environment obtained the best result for the intronic class with difference of 0.08 or 8% for the second best result (Ridor method with 0.735). When we compared the three classes, intergenic, intronic and silent mutation, our environment is better than two methods: UserClassifier and ZeroR. Both methods obtained results of 0.5 in three classes. This happened because this methods obtained excellent results for specificity (100%) but obtained worst results for sensibility (0%) or vice versa. When we applied these results in (3) function, the result is not so good. For the intergenic class, our method is better than DecisionStump, OneR, ConjuctiveRule and ZeroR. Even to intergenic class, we obtained equivalent results with other 4 methods: J48, BFTree, Decision Table and JRIP. Although our results are worse, the knowledge built by our method is more interpretable and understandable than the one produced by those. J48 built a tree with 12 leaves and size 21. BFTree built a tree with size 37 and 19 leaf nodes. The Decision Table and JRIP built a rule set with 10 and 6 rules, respectively. Our rule set is composed by only 3 rules with 3 attributes, each. When we use this rule set as a black-box classifier, we used only 4 attributes.

When we project a classifier, it has to classify with high hit rates, but high hit rates only for some classes is not sufficient - it has to classify all classes with high hit rates.

The Table 4 shows the mean and standard deviation of methods evaluated in this work. Although our method has the fourth best average (only 0.04 or 4% worse than the best result), when we analyzed the standard deviation our environment had the best result. Thus, our method can be considered the most balanced, with good results in all three classes, unlike the other evaluated methods.

Table 4. Comparison between our method and other traditional methods using the fitness function described by the expression (3)

Method	Mean	Standard Deviation
GASNP	0.81	0.05
J48	0.77	0.20
BFTree	0.78	0.18
DecisionStump	0.75	0.22
FT	0.82	0.13
OneR	0.75	0.22
ConjuctiveRule	0.75	0.22
Decision Table	0.77	0.19
DTNB	0.8	0.19
JRIP	0.78	0.18
NNGE	0.77	0.12
PART	0.83	0.12
Ridor	0.85	0.1

4   Final Remarks

Many complex biological problems have received more attention from part of the computational intelligence community mainly because of the great amount of information available in electronic repositories and their complexity. In this work, we proposed an evolutionary environment to extract high-level knowledge (IF-THEN rules) from a specific SNP database subset. Considering that a classification system should go beyond prediction accuracy, we have implemented a fitness function based on features which can help obtaining comprehensible and interpretable results while keeping acceptable classification accuracy. In general the proposed method allowed to obtain simple classification rules with a low number of attributes per class. It obtained good convergence rates and presented more informative and comprehensive results than other traditional classification methods also used in our comparative analysis.

Therefore, it is possible to conclude that the use of the proposed evolutionary environment is indicated mainly when classifying real problems, where the discovery of high-level knowledge about the domain is crucial. The future for this area of research is bright. It is clear from the initial research efforts that bioinformatics methods that predict molecular effects of mutation will continue to improve. A word of caution must be added, however, that bioinformatic scientists building these methods will have the most success if they choose their learning tools carefully and their training sets to best represent the spectrum of predictions they will be making [15]. As future works, we hope to improve the results obtained for the three classes, especially silent mutation, vastly increasing the competitiveness of our environment.

References

1. Setbal, J.C., Meidanis, J.: Introduction to Computacional Molecular Biology. PWS Publishing Company, Boston (1997)
2. Baldi, P., Brunak, S.: Bioinformatics: the Machine Learning approach. MIT Press, Cambridge (2001)

3. Goldberg, D.E.: Genetic Algorithms in Search, Optimization and Machine Learning. Adison-Wesley, Reading (1989)
4. Fidelis, M.V., Lopes, H.S., Freitas, A.A.: Discovery Comprehensible Classification Rules with a Genetic Algorithm. In: Proceedings of the Congress on Evolutionary Computation, CEC 2000 (2000)
5. Amaral, L.R., Sadoyama, G., Espindola, F.S., Oliveira, G.M.B.: Oncogenes Classification Measured by Microarray using Genetic Algorithms. In: IASTED International Conference on Artificial Intelligence and Applications, AIA 2008 (2008)
6. Ross, D.T., Scherf, U., Eisen, M.B., Perou, C.M., Rees, C., Spellman, P., Iyer, V., Jeffrey, S.S., Van de Rijn, M., Waltham, M., Pergamenschikov, A., Lee, J.C.F., Lashkari, D., Shalon, D., Myers, T.G., Weinstein, J.N., Botstein, D., Brown, P.O.: Systematic variation in gene expression patterns in human cancer cell lines. Nature Genetics (2000)
7. Kitts, A., Sherry, S.: The NCBI Handbook. The National Library of Medicine (2002)
8. Lopes, H.S., Coutinho, M.S., Lima, W.C.: An evolutionary approach to simulate cognitive feedback learning in medical domain. In: Genetic Algorithms and Fuzzy Logic Systems, World Scientific, Singapore (1997)
9. Fidelis, M.V., Lopes, H.S., Freitas, A.A.: Discovery comprehensible classification rules with a genetic algorithm. In: Congress on Evolutionary Computation, CEC 2000 (2000)
10. Holmes, G., Donkin, A., Witten, I.H.: Weka: A machine learning workbench. In: Proceedings of the Second Australia and New Zealand Conference on Intelligent Information Systems (1994)
11. Collins, F.S., Brooks, L.D., Chakravarti, A.: A DNA Polymorphism Discovery Resource for Research on Human Genetic Variation. Genome Research (1998)
12. Wang, D.G., Fan, J.B., Siao, C.J., Berno, A., Young, P., Sapolsky, R., Ghandour, G., Perkins, N., Winchester, E., Spencer, J., Kruglyak, L., Stein, L., Hsie, L., Topaloglou, T., Hubbell, E., Robinson, E., Mittmann, M., Morris, M.S., Shen, N., Kilburn, D., Rioux, J., Nusbaum, C., Rozen, S., Hudson, T.J., Lander, E.S., Lipshutz, R., Chee, M.: Large-scale identification, mapping, and genotyping of single-nucleotide polymorphisms in the human genome, Science (1998)
13. Masood, E.: As consortium plans free SNP map of human genome. Nature (1999)
14. Wang, Z., Moult, J.: SNPs, Protein Structure, and Disease. Human Mutation (2001)
15. Mooney, S.: Bioinformatics approaches and resources for single nucleotide polymorphism functional analysis. Briefings in Bioinformatics (2005)

A Comparison of Clustering Algorithms for Data Streams

Cássio M.M. Pereira* and Rodrigo F. de Mello

University of São Paulo, Institute of Mathematical and Computer Sciences,
São Carlos SP 13566-590, Brazil
{cpereira,mello}@icmc.usp.br

Abstract. In this paper we present a comparative study of three data stream clustering algorithms: STREAM, CluStream and MR-Stream. We used a total of 90 synthetic data sets generated from spatial point processes following Gaussian distributions or Mixtures of Gaussians. The algorithms were executed in three main scenarios: 1) low dimensional; 2) low dimensional with concept drift and 3) high dimensional with concept drift. In general, CluStream outperformed the other algorithms in terms of clustering quality at a higher execution time cost. Our results are analyzed with the non-parametric Friedman test and post-hoc Nemenyi test, both with $\alpha = 5\%$. Recommendations and future research directions are also explored.

1 Introduction

Recently, advances in hardware and software have enabled a significant increase in the capacity of generating and storing data in the most diverse segments of society [1]. Everyday life tasks, such as using a credit card or browsing web sites, result in personal information being automatically recorded. According to Gantz et al. [10], the digital universe in 2007 was estimated in 281 exabytes and is expected to be 10 times larger in 2011. That amount of gathered data is not useful by itself, requiring processing in order to extract relevant and useful information for further analysis by a domain specialist. These requirements have motivated the research field of data streams mining [1, 9].

We can formalize the notion of a data stream as a possibly infinite sequence of multi-dimensional instances $(\overline{X}_1, \ldots, \overline{X}_i, \ldots)$, arriving at time stamps $(T_1, \ldots, T_i, \ldots)$. Each $\overline{X}_i$ is a multi-dimensional instance containing d dimensions, which are denoted by $\overline{X}_i = (x_i^1 \ldots x_i^d)$. Two of the most important characteristics of a data stream are that: 1) as the stream is possibly infinite, algorithms should make one pass over data; 2) there is an inherent temporal component associated with a stream mining process, as data may evolve over time. This is a property known as *temporal locality* [1] and makes simply extending one-pass mining algorithms to data streams not as effective as designing algorithms that

---

* This work has been funded by FAPESP (Fundação de Amparo à Pesquisa do Estado de São Paulo) under grant 2010/05062-6.

E.R. Hruschka Junior et al. (Eds.): INTECH 2011, CCIS 165, pp. 59–74, 2011.

take this property into account. This property, by which the concepts in a stream evolve over time, is also called *concept drift*.

Among the many research topics in data streams mining, *clustering* has been one of the main discussed areas. The non-supervised characteristic of clustering is especially attractive in the data stream scenario, as it is not trivial to make human experts supervise continuously arriving instances of a stream. One of the main challenges in this area is in adapting arbitrary clustering algorithms to data streams, because of the one-pass constraints on the data set.

Because of the inherent subjectivity of a clustering task [14], as part of exploratory data analysis, one can pose the problem under different views. One can define a metric space and consider instances as data points in such space. Clustering can then be viewed as a problem of *partitioning* the instances into groups of nearby points, according to some distance, such as Euclidean distance. An objective function of a clustering algorithm could target the minimization of intra-cluster variance (distance from points to their cluster mean) and maximize inter-cluster distances [13]. Another view of clustering may not seek to simply output a partition of the given input instances, but a *hierarchy* of such partitions, which indicate the relative proximity of the instances being joined together in a cluster. Still another view could be one related to the *density* of points. One can define a certain radius and consider the number of points inside the multi-dimensional region of space defined within such radius. Connected regions of space which are relatively more dense are considered as groups, separated by regions with a lower density of points [8].

All of these approaches have been the basis for algorithms proposed in the literature. One issue remains though, comparing how these different methods perform in relation to one another over a well-defined class of problems. This paper fills this gap by providing a comparison among three algorithms, each one being a well-known representative of one of the clustering views previously discussed.

This paper is organized as follows. In the next section, we review selected algorithms in the data streams clustering literature. In Section 3, we define the comparison methodology employed in this study. Section 4 presents experimental results of the algorithms under different data sets. Finally, in Section 5, we present our conclusions and recommendations.

2   Clustering Algorithms for Data Streams

We can broadly divide the existing algorithms for data streams clustering in three categories: partitional, hierarchical and density based. Note however that some algorithms present characteristics from more than one of these categories, e.g. CluStream uses K-Means as a procedure during its offline stage.

In the first category, partitional, K-Means [13] has been the most influential algorithm. It is based in the idea of minimizing intra-cluster variance, which is used as its objective function. K-Means is the inspiration for STREAM [18], which is actually based on K-Medians (a variation of K-Means). STREAM is the first clustering algorithm to formally address the data stream model.

In the second category, hierarchical, BIRCH (Balanced Iterative Reducing and Clustering using Hierarchies) [24] has been the most influencing algorithm, and was proposed in the context of very large databases. It has inspired important algorithms in the data streams clustering literature, such as CluStream [2], HPStream [3] and E-Stream [20].

Lastly, in the third category, the density-based clustering algorithm DBSCAN [8] has been the main inspiration for the subsequent algorithms. It aims at finding arbitrarily shaped clusters, which are typically viewed as dense regions of objects in the data space, separated by regions of low density (regarded as noise) [11]. DBSCAN defines a cluster as a maximal set of density-connected points. Every object that is not part of a cluster is regarded as noise. DBSCAN has inspired clustering algorithms in the data streams literature such as DenStream [4], D-Stream [5] and MR-Stream [23].

In this work we have selected three algorithms, one of each category, to be evaluated and compared. The partitional algorithm selected was STREAM, as it was the first one proposed to address the clustering task in a data stream. The second algorithm chosen was CluStream, considered to be the reference algorithm to cluster data streams [6]. Lastly, we selected MR-Stream as it is one of the most recently proposed methods and represents the density-based class of algorithms.

2.1 STREAM

This algorithm is based on local approximations that tend to incrementally find a better clustering. It uses the following view of clustering. Let $k \in \mathbb{Z}^+$ and N be a collection of n points in a metric space. The objective is to find k medians such that each point in N is assigned to the closest cluster center. Given this view, one can define the quality of a partition as the squared sum of the distance of each point to its assigned cluster. Finding an optimal solution to the k medians problem is known to be NP complete [16], so several heuristics have been proposed, among them is the well-known K-Means, which only guarantees a local optimum [18].

STREAM uses the concept of facility location, which is a Lagrangian relaxation of the K-Medians problem. Instead of restricting the number of clusters to be found to k, a cost is associated with every cluster center (facility) created. This cost prevents the output from being the trivial solution (one cluster per data instance).

The facility location problem can be formally defined as follows. Let N be a collection of n points in a metric space, a distance function $d : N \times N \rightarrow \mathbb{R}^+$ and a parameter z, which defines the cost per center. For any choice of $C = \{c_1, c_2, \ldots, c_k\}$ of k centers, define a partition of N in $N_1, N_2, \ldots, N_k$, such that N_i contains all the closest points to center c_i than any other center. The objective is selecting a value of k and a set of C centers to minimize the facility cost function (FC) displayed in Equation 1.

$$FC(N, C) = z|C| + \sum_{i=1}^{k} \sum_{\overline{X} \in N_i} d^2(\overline{X}, c_i) \tag{1}$$

The facility location problem is NP complete as well and several theoretical approximations are known [15]. The STREAM algorithm is based on an incremental search for a better solution. Initially, it weighs the set of points by the number of their occurrences in each block. The points are then clustered using the procedure LOCALSEARCH, which outputs the set of centers found. The points are then discarded, remaining only the centers.

The procedure LOCALSEARCH selects a subset of points to serve as centers. The main step in this routine is evaluating the gain, as defined in Equation 2. The gain defines what is the advantage (in terms of cost) in case a center was created at point $\overline{X}$. To compute that, it must be taken into account the cost z of creating a center at $\overline{X}$, in case it does not exist already. Next, the points which are currently more distant to their centers than to $\overline{X}$ must be re-assigned to $\overline{X}$. That results in a gain t and may leave centers with no assigned points, which must be closed. In case u centers are closed, that represents a gain of uz. There may also be some centers such that the points assigned to them, if moved to $\overline{X}$, would yield a larger gain than the cost to keep those centers open. If that is the case, then consider the number of such centers v. The gain obtained by closing them is $vz - a$, where a is the additional cost of assigning the points to $\overline{X}$.

$$gain(\overline{X}) = -z + t + uz + vz - a \tag{2}$$

STREAM incrementally evaluates the net cost of opening and closing centers, searching for a solution closest to the optimal. It has some limitations, such as not considering the evolution of data (temporal locality property) or temporal granularity in clustering. A user may want to examine the clusters found in the horizon of one day of the stream, or one week, or a year. The clusters found can be significantly different if other time horizons are considered. This limitation led to the proposal of the CluStream algorithm.

2.2   CluStream

CluStream is an algorithm designed to overcome some limitations of STREAM, such as not allowing the user to specify a time horizon for clustering. The main idea is to divide the clustering task into two stages, the first one being online (microclustering) and the second one offline (macroclustering). It uses many of the concepts present in BIRCH with extensions for the data streams scenario.

The summary statistics computed during the online stage are placed in microclusters. Given a set of n d-dimensional points $\overline{X_{i_1}}, \ldots, \overline{X_{i_n}}$, with time stamps $T_{i_1}, \ldots, T_{i_n}$, a microcluster is defined as the tuple $(\overline{CF2^x}, \overline{CF1^x}, CF2^t, CF1^t, n)$ of dimension $2d + 3$. The vector $\overline{CF1^x} = \sum_{j=1}^{n} \overline{X_{i_j}}$ is the linear sum of the elements in the microcluster, while $\overline{CF2^x} = \sum_{j=1}^{n} (\overline{X_{i_j}})^2$ is their squared sum. The microcluster tuple used in CluStream is an extension of the one originally proposed in BIRCH. The added elements are the temporal values $CF1^t$ (linear sum of the time stamps) and $CF2^t$ (squared sum of the time stamps).

The information maintained in the microclusters, updated during the online stage, are periodically stored to disk in the form of snapshots. CluStream uses a model called tilted time frame, where the moment of storing the snapshots is defined in a logarithmic scale. The data are saved to disk when the current time clock t_c is divisible by α^i, where $\alpha \in \mathbb{Z}^+$ is defined by the user, and i is the order of the snapshot. The maximum order at any moment varies from 1 to $\log_\alpha t_c$.

The greater the order, the more space the intervals to take snapshots become. The intuition behind this tilted time frame is that, in general, one wishes to keep more information about recent events than older ones, so snapshots of a lower order are taken more frequently and snapshots of greater order are taken at more spaced intervals. At any moment only the last $\alpha + 1$ snapshots are kept on disk.

Initially, the algorithm maintains a total of q microclusters, $M_1, \ldots, M_q$, where q is a user defined parameter larger than the natural number of clusters k. As new points arrive on the stream, they must be absorbed by existing microclusters or form a new one. The criteria for absorption is based on the maximum frontier of each microcluster. If the point is within this frontier, then it is absorbed, otherwise a new microcluster is created with the point. In this latter case there are two options: 1) removing the oldest existing microcluster according to a parameter δ defined by the user or 2) merge the two closest microclusters by using the additive property. That makes the memory usage not exceed a certain threshold.

The offline stage, also called macroclustering, clusters the microclusters obtained during the online stage. The algorithm allows the user to explore clusters in the stream over different time horizons. Given an input h by the user, corresponding to the desired time horizon, and the number k of desired clusters, the algorithm finds k high level clusters in the specified horizon. To accomplish that, it initially finds the first snapshot prior to $t_c - h$, from which the existing microclusters are identified to be subtracted from the current microclusters. The result of this difference operation is then used as input to the K-Means algorithm, ending up with the k desired clusters.

One of the greatest advantages of CluStream is the ability to obtain groups of a data stream at different time resolutions, which can help to understand how clusters evolve over time. This feature has made the algorithm one of the most popular in the data streams clustering literature, being considered even as a reference in the area [6].

CluStream also has some limitations. One of its problems is in dealing with high dimensional data. In high dimensions all pairs of points tend to be approximately equidistant. This makes it hard for CluStream, which uses at its base Euclidean distance, to find meaningful clusters. This limitation led to the development of HPStream, an algorithm that tries to find the best subset of dimensions where meaningful clusters can be extracted.

Another limitation of CluStream, also present in its originating algorithm BIRCH, is the inability to find arbitrarily shaped clusters. This led to the development of several density-based clustering algorithms for data streams. One of the most recently proposed in this category is MR-Stream.

2.3 MR-Stream

MR-Stream (Multiple Resolution Clustering for Data Streams) adopts a density-based technique to find clusters.

Consider a data stream formed by points in an n-dimensional space S. A point in this stream is a multi-dimensional vector $\overline{X}_i \in S$. The algorithm MR-Stream divides the space S in cells. Each cell C can be partitioned again in 2^n subcells, in case each dimension is divided into two parts. The result is a recursive partitioning of S in cells contained in various levels of granularity.

A tree structure is used to represent the partitioning into cells. Each node of the tree corresponds to a cell. A user defined parameter H is used to control the levels of partitioning, such that the height of the tree is no more than H. Each dimension is then divided in 2^H intervals. The root of the tree contains a synopsis of the entire space S. Each node of the tree at height $h < H$ stores synopsis information of S at granularity h.

As each point $\overline{X}_i$ arrives in the stream it receives a weight, which decreases with time if $\overline{X}_i$ does not appear again in the stream. The intuition behind this is that points which appear frequently in the stream should have more weight than rare ones. The initial weight of a point is 1. At time t_j the weight of a point is determined by its weight over time $t_i : (j > i) : w(\overline{X}_i, t_j) = w(\overline{X}_i, t_i)f(t_j - t_i)$, where f is a fading function and defined as $f(t) = \lambda^{-at}$, with $\lambda > 1$ and $a > 0$.

The weight of a cell j at time t is defined as $w(g, t) = \sum_{\overline{X}_i \in g} w(\overline{X}_i, t)$, where $w(\overline{X}_i, t)$ is the weight of the point $\overline{X}_i$ at time t. Let $S(t)$ be the set of points in space S at time t. The total weight of the cells in S is $\sum_{\overline{X}_i \in S(t)} w(\overline{X}_i, t) \leq 1/(1 - \lambda^{-a})$ for $t = 1, 2, \ldots$. At the limit where $t \to \infty$, the total weight of the cells in S equals $1/(1 - \lambda^{-a})$.

The density of a cell is defined as the quotient of its weight by the volume it occupies. At time t, the density of a cell g is $D(g, t) = w(g, t)/2^{n(H-h)}$. The mean density of the space S, which is the density of the root node, is defined according to Equation 3.

$$D(S) = \frac{w(S, t)}{V(S)} = \frac{1}{2^{n(H-h)}(1 - \lambda^{-a})} \tag{3}$$

Two cells g_1 and g_2 are neighbor cells if $distance(g_1, g_2) < d$, where d is a distance value. Considering $[a_i^1, b_i^1]$ the range of g_1 and $[a_i^2, b_i^2]$ the range of g_2 on dimension $1 \leq i \leq n$, we compute the distance between the two cells as the sum of the nearest distance between these two cells in all dimensions (Equation 4). If the data are normalized in the range $[0, 1]$ then a suggested distance threshold is $d = \epsilon 2^{-H}$, where ϵ is a user defined parameter.

$$distance(g_1, g_2) = \sum_{i=1}^{n} min(|a_i^1 - b_i^2|, |b_i^1 - a_i^2|)^2 \tag{4}$$

The algorithm is divided into two stages, online and offline, following the same idea as CluStream. During the online stage, as each point arrives in the stream the tree T is updated. At each interval t_p a pruning operation is executed, starting at the root node.

The offline stage consists in the selection of a set of nodes of the tree at height h for clustering at that resolution. It determines all reachable dense cells at a distance d and marks them as one cluster.

3   Comparison Methodology

In order to compare how the three algorithms performed against a well defined class of problems we chose to generate clusters following multivariate Gaussian distributions. This choice was made as this type of distribution is well understood, mathematically simple to work with and has been shown to fit many scenarios [19]. With this purpose we used the algorithm proposed in [14] to create a collection of 30 synthetic data sets for the first experiment set. The algorithm generates samples from a spatial point process in which spherically shaped Gaussian clusters are located randomly in the sampling window. The algorithm also ensures that the generated clusters do not overlap more than a specified amount, provides a minimum number of points per cluster, and allows the specification of the number of clusters to be generated.

In the first set of experiments we have generated 100K 2-dimensional points distributed in three clusters, without the presence of concept drift. A sample data set is shown in Figure 2, which illustrates one of the simpler cases. Other data sets have more complex structures, where clusters have a degree of overlap with one another.

For the second and third set of experiments we used clusters generated from mixtures of two Gaussian distributions. Equation 5 presents the probability density function for a point x, where $\mathcal{N}$ is a Gaussian parametrized by a mean vector μ and covariance matrix Σ. In our experiments we generated Gaussians with independent attributes, so our covariance matrices were identity matrices. Equation 6 shows the density function for the i-th n-dimensional Gaussian.

The value π_i in Equation 5 represents the corresponding weight of the i-th Gaussian of the mixture. For these experiments (II and III), we simulated concept drift as a change in the mean of the Gaussian distribution. The two multivariate means were sampled within unity interval and the weights of the Gaussians were adapted over time according to a sigmoid function (Equation 7), which is parametrized by t, the current time instant, s, a smoothness parameter which controls how abrupt is the change (higher values cause more abrupt changes) and t_c or time of change, a point in time which determines the moment when the second Gaussian starts to have more weight than the first. The sigmoid function is used to compute the weight of the second Gaussian, while the weight of the first one is given by $\pi_1 = 1 - \pi_2$. For our purposes we have found that $10/t_c$ returns adequate values for the smoothness parameter s, by which there is a

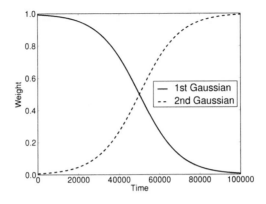

Fig. 1. Weights over time of two Gaussians which composed the mixture for one cluster

gradual change in the distribution of the data. Figure 1 presents an example of the weights of two Gaussians along time.

$$p(x) = \sum_{i=1}^{2} \pi_i \mathcal{N}(x|\mu_i, \Sigma_i) \tag{5}$$

$$\mathcal{N}(x|\mu_i, \Sigma_i) = \frac{1}{\sqrt{(2\pi)^n det(\Sigma_i)}} e^{-1/2(x-\mu_i)^T \Sigma_i^{-1}(x-\mu_i)} \tag{6}$$

$$weight(t, s, t_c) = \frac{1.0}{1.0 + e^{-s(t-t_c)}} \tag{7}$$

In the second set of experiments we also generated 100K 2-dimensional points distributed over three clusters. A sample data set is illustrated in Figure 3. Observe how the points move towards a new mean as time increases. For example, the points of the triangles cluster start the stream distributed over $\mu = [0.7, 0.7]^T$ and at the end are located around $\mu = [0.4, 0.3]^T$.

The third set of experiments targeted a more realistic scenario, thus the 100K points were distributed according to a 4-dimensional multivariate Gaussian mixture spread along 3 clusters with the presence of concept drift. We also added 4 more dimensions to every point. Two of those dimensions were redundant attributes, created as linear combinations of the attributes which composed the Gaussian mixture. The other 2 attributes simulated noise, so they were uniformly sampled within unity interval. Thus, in the third set of experiments the data was 8-dimensional.

In each set of experiments, we have generated 30 data sets, resulting in a total of 90 data sets considering all three sets.

In this study we have evaluated the algorithms with respect to three main aspects: execution time, memory usage and quality of clustering. Execution time is an important characteristic for data streams algorithms, as they must be efficient (preferably linear or sublinear complexity) with respect to input size.

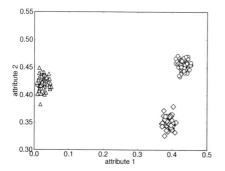

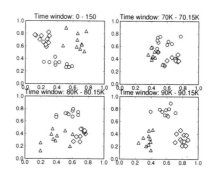

Fig. 2. Points sampled from 3 clusters of one of the streams in the first experiment set.

Fig. 3. Points sampled from 3 clusters of one of the streams in the second experiment set. Observe that the points move towards a new mean as time increases.

As a stream is possibly infinite, the algorithms should be quick enough to keep up with the new instances continuously arriving. Another important issue is the amount of memory used. Again, as a data stream is possibly infinite, it is impossible to keep all the instances stored in memory for processing. The third aspect evaluated in this study, quality, has been defined by the use of two measures, the Normalized Mutual Information (NMI) [17], an information theoretical measure, and the well-known Adjusted Rand Index (ARI) [12].

We have seen in the literature several papers [3, 20, 23] using Purity as a measure of quality for the clusterings obtained. Purity can be defined as in Equation 8, where Ω is the set of clusters, C is the set of classes, N is the number of objects, k an iterator through all the clusters and j the index of an arbitrary class. The problem in using Purity is that many of the algorithms to group data streams generate a different number of clusters when presented with a set of objects and Purity is easy to achieve for the trivial solution, when there is one cluster per data object. In light of this limitation to compare in a fair manner different clustering algorithms, we have opted to use two other measures which take the number of clusters into account. The first one is the Normalized Mutual Information (Equation 9), which computes the mutual information I (Equation 10) among clusters obtained and known classes, while using a normalization factor (denominator) based on the entropy $\mathcal{E}$ (Equation 11) of both. When there is a large number of clusters, the entropy tends to increase, so there is a penalty for creating clusters. This index stays in the range $[0, 1]$, so it facilitates comparison.

$$\text{purity}(\Omega, C) = \frac{1}{N} \sum_k \max_j |\omega_k \cap c_j| \tag{8}$$

$$\text{NMI}(\Omega, C) = \frac{I(\Omega, C)}{[\mathcal{E}(\Omega) + \mathcal{E}(C)]/2} \tag{9}$$

$$I(\Omega, C) = \sum_k \sum_j P(\omega_k \cap c_j) \log \frac{P(\omega_k \cap c_j)}{P(\omega_k)P(c_j)} \tag{10}$$

$$\mathcal{E}(\Omega) = -\sum_k P(\omega_k) \log P(\omega_k) \tag{11}$$

The second index used is the Adjusted Rand Index (ARI), which is based upon counting the pairs of points on which two partitions agree or disagree [21]. Any pair of points can be in one of four categories: (1) they are in the same cluster in both partitions (N_{11}), (2) they are in different clusters in both partitions (N_{00}), (3) they are in the same cluster in the first partition but in different ones in the second (N_{10}) and (4) they are in different clusters in the first partition and in the same cluster in the second partition (N_{01}). The values N_{11} and N_{00} can be seen as measures of agreement between the two partitions, while N_{10} and N_{01} as measures of disagreement. Given two partitions of a set S of N objects, let $U = \{U_1, U_2, \ldots, U_R\}$ be the first partition with R clusters and $V = \{V_1, V_2, \ldots, V_C\}$ the second partition with C clusters. Also let $\cap_{i=1}^R U_i = \cap_{j=1}^C V_j = \emptyset, \cup_{i=1}^R U_i = \cup_{j=1}^C V_j = S$. We can create a $R \times C$ contingency matrix where each element n_{ij} is the number of objects that are common to clusters U_i and V_j. The Adjusted Rand Index, assuming the generalized hypergeometric distribution as the model of randomness, takes values close to zero for two random partitions, and close to one when the partitions are mostly the same. It can be computed as described in Equation 12, where n_{ij} is an element of the contingency matrix, a_i is the sum of the i-th row and b_j the sum of the j-th column.

$$\text{ARI} = \frac{\sum_{ij} \binom{n_{ij}}{2} - [\sum_i \binom{a_i}{2} \sum_j \binom{b_j}{2}]/\binom{N}{2}}{\frac{1}{2}[\sum_i \binom{a_i}{2} + \sum_j \binom{b_j}{2}] - [\sum_i \binom{a_i}{2} \sum_j \binom{b_j}{2}]/\binom{N}{2}} \tag{12}$$

After obtaining the results for all data sets we proceeded with a statistical test to evaluate if the differences found among the clustering algorithms were statistically significant. As the variances of the measurements for the algorithms were not the same we did not use ANOVA [22], but opted instead for the non-parametric Friedman test [7] along with the Nemenyi post-hoc test, both with $\alpha = 5\%$.

All of the algorithms were implemented in the Java programming language and executed under the OpenJDK Runtime Environment (IcedTea6 1.9.1) in an Intel(R) Core(TM) i7 CPU with 2 GiB of RAM and the Fedora GNU/Linux 14 operating system.

4   Experimental Results

All of the experimental results discussed below are summarized in Table 1.

4.1   Experiment Set I

In the first experiment set we generated 30 data sets consisting of 100K 2-dimensional points, distributed along 3 clusters. The algorithms were measured with respect to memory usage, time of execution, NMI and ARI at every 150 points of the stream, which they were asked to cluster.

We executed the STREAM algorithm with the following parameters: $kmin = 2$ (minimum number of clusters) and $kmax = 4$ (maximum number of clusters). The CluStream algorithm was executed with $\alpha = 2.0$ (controls intervals of snapshots), $\delta = 512$ (controls the amount of time needed to consider a microcluster outdated), $t = 2$ (multiplicative factor for computing the maximum boundary of a cluster), $InitPts = 150$ (number of points for initially running K-Means and generating microclusters), $q = 100$ (maximum number of microclusters at any time) and $K = 3$ (number of desired macroclusters).

The MR-Stream algorithm was executed with $Ch = 3.0$ (density parameter), $Cl = 0.8$ (sparsity parameter), $\epsilon = 0.05$ (maximum distance between two neighbor cells is ϵ interval distance), $\mu = 5$ (minimum size of a real cluster), $\beta = 0.5$ (minimum weight of a cluster), $\lambda = 1.002$ (fading parameter) and $a = 1.0$ (part of the exponent of the fading parameter). The values for t_p (cell inspection time gap) and H (max height of the tree) parameters have been set as $t_p = (1/a)\log_\lambda(Ch/Cl)$ and $H = \log_2(C_l(1 - \lambda^{-at_p})/(1 - \lambda^{-a}))$, as explained in the original paper of MR-Stream. All algorithms were executed with $speed = 30$, which controls the time increment.

It is interesting to observe in Table 1 that in absolute terms the results obtained with respect to NMI and ARI agree, CluStream has the best performance, STREAM an intermediary performance and MR-Stream the worst.

Using the ranks of the algorithms in each data set as input, we employed the Friedman test to check if the means were statistically different or not. The best algorithms have lower ranks, e.g. the best has rank 1, the second best has rank 2, and so on. The p-values obtained for all measurements allowed us to reject the null hypothesis (that the algorithms have the same means). To find which of the specific differences were statistically significant we used the post-hoc Nemenyi test. Table 1 presents the test results using the following notation. A ⇑ means that the algorithm in the i-th row has a statistically significant lower mean rank than the algorithm in the j-th column, thus it is better than the other algorithm according to that measurement. A ⇓ means it has a higher rank (worse) and ⇔ means they are not statistically different. Note that for the tables presenting memory usage and execution times, the algorithms that have lower ranks (thus up arrows) are also the ones with the faster execution time and lower memory usage.

From the results presented, we observe that CluStream has (with statistical significance) the best clustering quality according to both NMI and ARI. However, it has the longest execution time, which can be partially attributed to its need to write snapshots to disk, an operation significantly more costly (with respect to time) than the others which operate only on main memory, as is the case of all of the operations of the other algorithms. The statistical test did not find a relevant difference between STREAM and MR-Stream with respect to ARI and NMI, indicating that for data streams with Gaussian clusters residing in low dimensional spaces without concept drift, both techniques have similar results.

In terms of memory usage, CluStream had a detectable statistical advantage over both STREAM and MR-Stream. It is important to notice, however, that this measurement is only taking RAM usage into account. Although CluStream also uses space in permanent storage to record snapshots, we do not consider it as a critical variable to measure, as the most important (costly) impact of this characteristic is already reflected in the longer execution time of the algorithm.

4.2   Experiment Set II

In the second experiment set, we also used 30 data sets consisting of 100K 2-dimensional points distributed over 3 clusters. However, in this experiment we added concept drift, which was simulated as an adaptation of the weights of the Gaussians in the mixture, as explained in Section 3. The effect was a gradual spatial rearrangement of the points over time.

The parameters used for the algorithms were the same as in experiment set I, except for parameter δ of CluStream, which was set to 5 instead of 512. This was done because it allows CluStream to consider microclusters within a smaller time window as outdated. This is important for the algorithm to be able to keep up with the concept drift that was added.

We can observe from the results in Table 1 that all algorithms had a drop in its values of both NMI and ARI, which was expected, as the concept drift that was added increased the difficulty in the clustering task. While CluStream also had a worse behavior than previously, it still outperformed both STREAM and MR-Stream. The results obtained by the CluStream algorithm only remained better than the other algorithms due to the change in the parameter δ. We executed experiment set II without this modification and CluStream had very poor results, reaching ARI values close to zero. This confirms the importance of considering the temporal property of clusters in an evolving stream.

In terms of execution time, CluStream once again had the longest execution time, while MR-Stream was the fastest algorithm, followed by STREAM. With regards to space usage, CluStream had a lower memory consumption than the other two.

4.3   Experiment Set III

In the third experiment set, we generated 30 data sets of 100K points each with concept drift added as well, but this time the data was 8-dimensional. Four of those dimensions consisted of a Gaussian mixture, two of linear combinations of the first four and the last two dimensions were noise, uniformly sampled. This experiment aimed at simulating a more realistic stream, which generally resides in higher dimensions, presents concept drift, with noise and redundant attributes.

The parameters for this experiment were set the same as in experiment set II, except for fading parameter λ of MR-Stream, which was set to 1.2, so that the weights of older points faded more quickly.

Table 1. Experimental Results

| | | Experiment set I | | | |
| | | Results | Statistical Comparison | | |
		mean ± stdev	STREAM	CluStream	MR-Stream
STREAM	NMI	00.73 ± 0.02	⇔	⇓	⇔
	ARI	00.58 ± 0.04	⇔	⇓	⇔
	Space (MiB)	06.46 ± 2.61	⇔	⇓	⇔
	Time (s)	01.66 ± 0.09	⇔	⇑	⇓
CluStream	NMI	00.90 ± 0.01	⇑	⇔	⇑
	ARI	00.85 ± 0.02	⇑	⇔	⇑
	Space (MiB)	03.78 ± 0.52	⇑	⇔	⇑
	Time (s)	15.94 ± 0.31	⇓	⇔	⇓
MR-Stream	NMI	00.61 ± 0.33	⇔	⇓	⇔
	ARI	00.53 ± 0.32	⇔	⇓	⇔
	Space (MiB)	06.54 ± 2.34	⇔	⇓	⇔
	Time (s)	01.26 ± 0.03	⇑	⇑	⇔
		Experiment set II			
STREAM	NMI	00.32 ± 0.13	⇔	⇓	⇔
	ARI	00.27 ± 0.11	⇔	⇓	⇔
	Space (MiB)	08.24 ± 4.74	⇔	⇓	⇔
	Time (s)	02.04 ± 0.11	⇔	⇑	⇓
CluStream	NMI	00.40 ± 0.16	⇑	⇔	⇑
	ARI	00.37 ± 0.16	⇑	⇔	⇑
	Space (MiB)	03.72 ± 3.72	⇑	⇔	⇑
	Time (s)	12.47 ± 0.19	⇓	⇔	⇓
MR-Stream	NMI	00.33 ± 0.13	⇔	⇓	⇔
	ARI	00.26 ± 0.13	⇔	⇓	⇔
	Space (MiB)	06.42 ± 2.55	⇔	⇓	⇔
	Time (s)	01.32 ± 0.06	⇑	⇑	⇔
		Experiment set III			
STREAM	NMI	00.12 ± 0.06	⇔	⇓	⇓
	ARI	00.10 ± 0.05	⇔	⇔	⇔
	Space (MiB)	05.49 ± 3.94	⇔	⇓	⇑
	Time (s)	06.61 ± 0.16	⇔	⇑	⇑
CluStream	NMI	00.16 ± 0.09	⇑	⇔	⇓
	ARI	00.13 ± 0.08	⇔	⇔	⇑
	Space (MiB)	04.07 ± 1.51	⇑	⇔	⇑
	Time (s)	17.39 ± 0.37	⇓	⇔	⇓
MR-Stream	NMI	00.35 ± 0.05	⇑	⇑	⇔
	ARI	00.08 ± 0.03	⇔	⇓	⇔
	Space (MiB)	13.24 ± 9.72	⇓	⇓	⇔
	Time (s)	07.89 ± 1.33	⇓	⇑	⇔

We observe in Table 1 that the quality in terms of ARI of all algorithms dropped. It is interesting to notice, however, that the value of NMI for MR-Stream increased marginally. For this set of experiments MR-Stream generated, in general, more clusters than in experiment set II. This leads to an increase in the entropy of the clusters, represented by the factor $H(\Omega)$ in Equation 9, which decreases the value of NMI. However, we noticed that the mutual information (term $I(\Omega, C)$ in Equation 9) had increased for experiment set III. That means a larger amount of information, by which our knowledge of the classes increases, when we know the clusters of the objects. Thus, the value of NMI was marginally higher than in experiment set II.

The time and space results for all algorithms remained similar to the ones in experiment set II, except that MR-Stream took more time and space than STREAM to execute.

We observe with this experiment that more dimensions do cause an impact on the quality of the data stream clustering algorithms analyzed. Efficient subspace clustering algorithms, which can find the most relevant dimensions (in our simulations the first four) may be an interesting option in these scenarios.

One example in this direction is the HP-Stream (High Dimensional Projected Stream) clustering algorithm, which is a variant of CluStream that does subspace clustering.

5   Conclusion

In this paper we have compared three different clustering algorithms designed for data streams. The contributions of this paper are: firstly to compare representative clustering algorithms in the data streams literature under an important class of problems. Secondly, the use of a new methodology for comparing clustering algorithms in the data streams literature, employing NMI and ARI instead of Purity, which does not impose a penalty in the number of clusters generated. And thirdly, giving a recommendation of which type of algorithm to use depending on the scenario at hand.

In our experiments we have found that CluStream delivers the best clustering quality at a higher execution time cost. These results can be attributed to two factors. The first one is that CluStream copes with concept drift by computing differences among clusters over a user defined time horizon. This allows the quality of the clustering to remain good as the stream progresses, because old points are disregarded in favor of new ones in the user defined horizon. The second factor is that in order to do this, CluStream has to store snapshots of the clusters to disk at intervals which follow a logarithmic scale. This increases the execution time of the algorithm, although it is important to maintain the clustering quality. On the other hand, this operation is alleviated by the logarithmic scale at which the writes to disk have to be performed.

We thus recommend that when dealing with a stream in the presence of concept drift, CluStream is the best algorithm with respect to clustering quality. If execution time is a critical factor, then STREAM is a fast choice while providing a relatively good clustering quality. In our experiments MR-Stream had, in general, a worse clustering quality than the other ones, although it was one of the fastest.

It must be stressed that the results obtained in our experiments are for Gaussian clusters, and cannot be generalized to other data distributions. Thus, MR-Stream, which is a density based algorithm, may have superior performance for arbitrarily shaped clusters than CluStream and STREAM, although this was not investigated in this paper.

An important issue that remains open is the definition of parameters for the algorithms. CluStream alone had a total of 6 parameters, while MR-Stream had a total of 7. STREAM had the fewest parameters. This shows that while superior performance can be achieved, such as in the case of CluStream, it is necessary to know about the stream prior to the execution of the algorithm, which is also the case for MR-Stream. While this is ok for some scenarios, finding the optimum settings for all parameters remains a difficult task which requires experience.

References

[1] Aggarwal, C.C.: Data Streams: Models and Algorithms (Advances in Database Systems). Springer, Secaucus (2006)

[2] Aggarwal, C.C., Han, J., Wang, J., Yu, P.S.: A framework for clustering evolving data streams. In: VLDB 2003: Proceedings of the 29th International Conference on Very Large Data Bases. pp. 81–92. VLDB Endowment (2003)

[3] Aggarwal, C.C., Han, J., Wang, J., Yu, P.S.: A framework for projected clustering of high dimensional data streams. In: VLDB 2004: Proceedings of the Thirtieth International Conference on Very Large Data Bases. pp. 852–863. VLDB Endowment (2004)

[4] Cao, F.: Density-based clustering over an evolving data stream with noise. In: Proc. Sixth SIAM Intl Conf. Data Mining (2006)

[5] Chen, Y., Tu, L.: Density-based clustering for real-time stream data. In: KDD 2007: Proceedings of the 13th ACM SIGKDD International Conference on Knowledge Discovery and Data Mining, pp. 133–142. ACM Press, New York (2007)

[6] Csernel, B., Clerot, F., Hébrail, G.: Streamsamp – datastream clustering over tilted windows through sampling. In: Proceedings of the International Workshop on Knowledge Discovery from Data Streams, IWKDDS 2006 (2006)

[7] Demšar, J.: Statistical comparisons of classifiers over multiple data sets. J. Mach. Learn. Res. 7, 1–30 (2006)

[8] Ester, M., Kriegel, H., Sander, J., Xu, X.: A density-based algorithm for discovering clusters in large spatial databases with noise. In: Proc. KDD, vol. 96, pp. 226–231 (1996)

[9] Gaber, M.M., Zaslavsky, A., Krishnaswamy, S.: Mining data streams: a review. SIGMOD Rec. 34(2), 18–26 (2005)

[10] Gantz, J., Reinsel, D., Chute, C., Schlichting, W., McArthur, J., Minton, S., Xheneti, I., Toncheva, A., Manfrediz, A.: The expanding digital universe: A forecast of worldwide information growth through 2010. Tech. rep., IDC (2007)

[11] Han, J., Kamber, M.: Data mining: concepts and techniques. Morgan Kaufmann Publishers Inc., San Francisco (2000)

[12] Hubert, L., Arabie, P.: Comparing partitions. Journal of Classification 2, 193–218 (1985), doi:10.1007/BF01908075

[13] Jain, A.K.: Data clustering: 50 years beyond K-means. In: Daelemans, W., Goethals, B., Morik, K. (eds.) ECML PKDD 2008, Part I. LNCS (LNAI), vol. 5211, pp. 3–4. Springer, Heidelberg (2008)

[14] Jain, A.K., Dubes, R.C.: Algorithms for clustering data. Prentice-Hall, Inc., Upper Saddle River (1988)

[15] Jain, K., Vazirani, V.V.: Primal-dual approximation algorithms for metric facility location and k-median problems. In: FOCS 1999: Proceedings of the 40th Annual Symposium on Foundations of Computer Science, p. 2. IEEE Computer Society Press, Washington, DC, USA (1999)

[16] Kaufman, L., Rousseeuw, P.: Finding groups in data; an introduction to cluster analysis. Wiley Series in Probability and Mathematical Statistics. Applied Probability and Statistics Section. EUA (1990)

[17] Manning, C.D., Raghavan, P.: Schutze: Introduction to Information Retrieval, 1st edn. Cambridge University Press, Cambridge (2008)

[18] O'Callaghan, L., Meyerson, A., Motwani, R., Mishra, N., Guha, S.: Streaming-data algorithms for high-quality clustering. In: Data Engineering, International Conference on, vol. 0, p. 0685 (2002)

[19] Tan, P.N., Steinbach, M., Kumar, V.: Introduction to Data Mining. Addison-Wesley Longman Publishing Co., Boston (2005)

[20] Udommanetanakit, K., Rakthanmanon, T., Waiyamai, K.: E-stream: Evolution-based technique for stream clustering. In: Alhajj, R., Gao, H., Li, X., Li, J., Zaïane, O.R. (eds.) ADMA 2007. LNCS (LNAI), vol. 4632, pp. 605–615. Springer, Heidelberg (2007)

[21] Vinh, N.X., Epps, J., Bailey, J.: Information theoretic measures for clusterings comparison: is a correction for chance necessary? In: ICML 2009, pp. 1073–1080. ACM Press, New York (2009)

[22] Walpole, R., Myers, R., Myers, S., Ye, K.: Probability and statistics for engineers and scientists. Prentice-Hall, Upper Saddle River (1998)

[23] Wan, L., Ng, W.K., Dang, X.H., Yu, P.S., Zhang, K.: Density-based clustering of data streams at multiple resolutions. ACM Trans. Knowl. Discov. Data 3(3), 1–28 (2009)

[24] Zhang, T., Ramakrishnan, R., Livny, M.: Birch: an efficient data clustering method for very large databases. SIGMOD Rec. 25(2), 103–114 (1996)

Approach Space Framework for Image Database Classification*

Sheela Ramanna[1,2] and James F. Peters[1]

[1] Department of Applied Computer Science
University of Winnipeg
Winnipeg, Manitoba R3B 2E9, Canada
s.ramanna@uwinnipeg.ca
[2] Computational Intelligence Laboratory,
Department of Electrical & Computer Engineering, University of Manitoba,
75A Chancellor's Circle, Winnipeg, Manitoba R3T 5V6, Canada
jfpeters@ee.umanitoba.ca

Abstract. This article considers the problem of how to formulate a framework for classifying digital images in large-scale image databases. The solution to this problem stems from recent work on near tolerance rough sets and from the realisation that collections of images can be viewed in the context of approach spaces. A nonempty set equipped with a distance function satisfying certain conditions is an example of an approach space. In approach spaces, the notion of distance is closely related to the notion of nearness. Approach merotopies provide a means of determining the similarity between a query image and a collection of images. An application of approach space-based image classification is given in terms of collections of hand-finger movement images captured during therapeutic gaming system exercises.

Keywords: Approach space, framework, image database, merotopy, near sets, tolerance rough sets.

1 Introduction

Numerous applications that employ image database classification (IDC) techniques include medical imaging, surveillance, remote sensing and searching large image databases. Image database classification is comprised of three main tasks: feature extraction (image representation), training (classifier design) and testing (classification). Classifier designs are either parametric or nonparametric. For example, parametric classifiers require intensive learning such things as parameters for support vector machines (SVM) [4]. The most common non-parametric

---

* Many thanks to Som Naimpally and Christopher Henry for their suggestions and insights concerning topics in this paper. This research has been supported by the Natural Science & Engineering Research Council of Canada (NSERC) grants 185986, 194376, Manitoba Centre of Excellence Fund, and Canadian Arthritis Network grant SRI-BIO-05.

E.R. Hruschka Junior et al. (Eds.): INTECH 2011, CCIS 165, pp. 75–89, 2011.

methods rely on Nearest-Neighbor (NN) distance estimation. It has been shown that NN-based image classifiers require no training time and have other favorable properties [2]. Within NN classifiers, one can use either image-to-image distance, or image-to-class distance. Our approach to classifier design is non-parametric and stems from recent work on near sets [28,26,29,43] and from the realisation that collections of images can be viewed in the context of approach spaces [1,16,17,40,30,31]. In general, this is made possible by considering a nonempty set X equipped with a distance function $\rho : \mathcal{P}X \times \mathcal{P}X :\rightarrow [0, \infty)$ satisfying certain conditions. The set of all subsets of X is denoted by $\mathcal{P}X$. The pair (X, ρ) is called an approach space.

Our approach is akin to the one in [3], where a feature descriptor distribution is approximated using NN-distances in a descriptor space without resorting to quantization or feature selection. In approach spaces, the notion of distance is closely related to the notion of nearness [13]. A collection $\mathcal{A} \subset \mathcal{P}X$ (*i.e.*, a set containing subsets of the powerset $\mathcal{P}X$) is **near** when $\nu_\rho(\mathcal{A}) \doteq \inf_{B \subset X} \sup_{A \in \mathcal{A}} \rho(B, A) = 0$ and **weakly near** when $\nu_\rho(\mathcal{A}) \leq \varepsilon$ for $\varepsilon \in [0, 1]$. The function $\nu_\rho(\mathcal{A})$ is an example of an approach merotopy [17,40]. This particular form of an approach merotopy was introduced in [30]. In the context of the form of IDC introduced in this article, only weak nearness between a set (query image) and a collection (image database) will be considered. This works well for an approach space framework for IDC, since values of $\nu_\rho(\mathcal{A})$ close to zero are satisfactory in establishing the approximate closeness of a query image region to database images. In this work, preprocessing in the form of the determination of tolerance classes in an image cover is carried out prior to the onset of IDC.

After determining a cover on a pair of images (query image representing a category and test image from a database), it is then possible to measure the nearness of a pair of images considered in the context of approach spaces and tolerance rough sets (TRSs). Tolerance rough sets were first introduced in [18]. From a time complexity point of view, this approach is advantageous. That is, it is only necessary to select a representative element of each class in a cover (since all of the other elements in the same class have similar descriptions) to carry out a comparison between a query image and a representative element of each class in a test image cover.

This paper has the following organization. A brief survey of works related to the proposed approach to image database classification is given in Sect. 2. Then, in Sect. 3, a brief introduction to tolerance rough sets is given. The basics of approach spaces are presented in Sect. 4. A brief introduction to descriptively near sets is given in Sect. 5. Finally, in Sect. 6, an overview of an application environment for this research is given in terms of an integrated motion tracking telerehabilitation system followed by analysis of hand-finger motion images in Sect. 7.

2   Related Works

A review of rough sets and near sets in medical imaging can be found in [7]. Papers related to the foundations and applications of fuzzy sets, rough sets and near sets approaches in image analysis can be found in S.K. Pal and J.F. Peters [23]. In solving the image correspondence problem, each image is viewed as a set of points and then the distance between images (sets) is measured. In the approach to IDC introduced in this paper, approach spaces and approach merotopies are defined in terms of the distance between sets and collections. In approach space theory, the distance between points and sets is probably the most appealing structure, intuitively [16]. A number of distance functions have been introduced recently to classify images, *e.g.*, [7,33,32,10,11,12,9,23]: tolerance nearness measure(tNM), tolerance Hausdorff distance nearness measure (tHD) [33,32,10,11,12,9,23], tolerance Hamming distance nearness measure (tHM) [33,32,12], generalized Mahalanobis nearness measure (gMNM) [36,33], Peters-Wasilewski tolerance class intersection nearness measure (tiNM) [26,27], tolerance class overlap distribution (TOD) [20,19], tolerance histogram measure (HSM) [20,19]). Image similarity measurement with tolerance near sets was introduced in [35]. In [35], measures based on tolerance class intersection and statistical comparison of overlaps between tolerance classes were considered. Also, the measures were applied to standard images drawn from SIMPLIcity database [1]. In this paper, the focus is on the experimental results obtained within the context of approach spaces and approach merotopies defined in terms of three distance functions in classifying image databases containing hand movement images, namely, tNM, tHM and tHD.

3   Tolerance Rough Sets

A nonempty set X is a rough set if, and only if the approximation boundary of X is nonempty. Rather than the usual partition of X with the indiscernibility relation introduced by Z. Pawlak [24], set approximation is viewed in the context of a cover of X defined by an tolerance relation τ_Φ, where Φ is a set of features of objects $x \in X$ [18]. Let $A \subset X$ and let $\tau_\Phi(x)$ denote a tolerance class containing the set of all objects $x \in A, y \in X$ such $x \ \tau_\Phi \ y$. The upper approximation of A is denoted by $\Phi^* A$, the set of all such tolerance classes $\tau_\Phi(x)$ that have a nonempty intersection with A, *i.e.*, $\tau_\Phi(x) \cap A \neq \emptyset$. The lower approximation of A (denoted $\Phi_* A$) is the set of all tolerance classes $\tau_\Phi(x)$ contained in A, *i.e.*, $\tau_\Phi(x) \subset A$. The set A is a **tolerance rough set** if, and only if the set $Bnd_\tau A = \Phi_* A \ - \ \Phi^* A$ (boundary of approximation of A) is empty.

Example 1. By way of illustration of near TRSs, consider the greyscale images of the Mona Lisa and Lena in Fig. 1.1 and Fig. 1.2, respectively. Let M, L denote a pair of digital images and let p denote the number of pixels on an edge for a $p \times p$ subimage s in either M or L. In this example, $p = 5$. The region surrounding the Mona Lisa's eyes and nose is denoted by a sample set X in Fig. 1.3. Similarly, a sample set Y for the region containing the eyes and nose of Lena is shown in Fig. 1.4. For simplicity, put $\Phi = \{gr : gr : X \rightarrow \Re$ where, $gr(x) =$ avg grey level of subimage $x\}$, a single feature set representing

---

[1] http://wang.ist.psu.edu/docs/related/

1.1: Mona Lisa (ML)   1.2: Lena (L)   1.3: ML class X, $p = 5, \varepsilon = 0.01$ 1.4: L class Y, $p = 5, \varepsilon = 0.01$

Fig. 1. Sample Near TRSs

by the probe function gr. After selecting B, a cover of Im is determined by a tolerance relation τ_Φ. Using the NEAR system [11], it is possible to use a mouse to click on one part of a pair images with covers and NEAR will then display (1) image location where one has clicked (indicated with a tiny dark square ■, *e.g.*, lower righthand corner of Mona Lisa's eye in Fig. 1.3) and (2) all of the other subimages with similar feature values in the same tolerance class for both images. It can be observed that there are a number shaded subimages both inside and outside X in Fig. 1.3). This indicates that X is a tolerance rough set, since at least one tolerance class in image M is entirely contained inside X. Similarly, it can be observed that Y is a tolerance rough set. Since X and Y contain subimages with similar average grey levels, it is also the case that X and Y are near TRSs. A more detailed discussion of the functionality of the NEAR system is given in Sec. 7.2.

4   Approach Spaces

The collection of subsets of a nonempty set X is denoted by $\mathcal{P}X = 2^X$ (power set). For $B \subset X, A \subset X$, $B^{(\varepsilon)} = \{A : \rho(A, B) \leq \varepsilon\}$ for a distance function $\rho : \mathcal{P}X \times \mathcal{P}X :\to [0, \infty)$. An **approach space** [17,1] is a nonempty set X equipped with a distance function ρ if, and only if, for all nonempty subsets $A, B, C \subset \mathcal{P}X$, conditions (A.1)-(A.4) are satisfied.

(A.1) $\rho(A, A) = 0$,
(A.2) $\rho(A, \emptyset) = \infty$,
(A.3) $\rho(A, B \cup C) = min\{\rho(A, B), \rho(A, C)\}$,
(A.4) $\rho(A, B) \leq \rho(A, B^{(\varepsilon)}) + \varepsilon$.

For a nonempty subset $A \subset X$ and a nonempty set $B \subset X$, define the **gap functional** $D_{\rho_{\|\cdot\|}}(A, B)$ [14], where

$$D_{\rho_{\|\cdot\|}}(A, B) = \begin{cases} \inf\{\rho_{\|\cdot\|}(a, b) : a \in A, b \in B\}, & \text{if } A \text{ and } B \text{ are not empty,} \\ \infty, & \text{if } A \text{ or } B \text{ is empty.} \end{cases}$$

Let $\rho_{\|\cdot\|}$ denote $\|\cdot\|: X \times X :\rightarrow [0, \infty)$ denote the norm on $X \times X$ defined by $\rho_{\|\cdot\|}(\boldsymbol{x}, \boldsymbol{y}) = \| \boldsymbol{x} - \boldsymbol{y} \|_1 = \sum_{i=1,n} |x_i - y_i|$.

Lemma 1. *Suppose X is a metric space with distance function ρ, $x \in X$ and $\mathcal{A} \in \mathcal{P}^2 X$. Then*

$$\rho(x, \bigcup \mathcal{A}) = inf\{\rho(x, A) : A \in \mathcal{A}\}.$$

Proof. The proof appears in [38, p. 25]. □

Lemma 2. $D_{\rho_{\|\cdot\|}} : \mathcal{P}X \times \mathcal{P}X \rightarrow [0, \infty)$ *satisfies (A.1)-(A.4).*

Proof. (A.1)-(A.2) are immediate from the definition of $D_{\rho_{\|\cdot\|}}$. For all $A, B, C \subset X$, $D_{\rho_{\|\cdot\|}}$ satisfies (A.3), since, from Lemma 1, we have

$$D_{\rho_{\|\cdot\|}}(A, B \cup C) = inf\{D\rho_{\|\cdot\|}(A, B), D\rho_{\|\cdot\|}(B, C)\}.$$

$D_{\rho_{\|\cdot\|}}$ satisfies (A.4), since

$$D_{\rho_{\|\cdot\|}}(A, B) \leq D_{\rho_{\|\cdot\|}}(A, B^\varepsilon) + \varepsilon. \qquad □$$

Theorem 1. $(X, D_{\rho_{\|\cdot\|}})$ *is an approach space.*

5   Descriptively Near Sets

Descriptively near sets are disjoints sets that resemble each other. Feature vectors (vectors of numbers represented feature values extracted from objects) provide a basis for set descriptions (see, *e.g.*, [28,26,21,22]). A feature-based gap functional defined for the norm on a set X is introduced by J.F. Peters in [29]. Let $\Phi_n(x) = (\phi_1(x), \ldots, \phi_n(x))$ denote a **feature vector**, where $\phi_i :\rightarrow \Re$. In addition, let $\Phi_X = (\Phi_1(x), \ldots, \Phi_{|X|}(x))$ denote a set of feature vectors for objects $x \in X$. In this article, a description-based gap functional $D_{\Phi_X, \rho_{\|\cdot\|}}$ is defined in terms of the Hausdorff lower distance [8] of the norm on $\mathcal{P}\Phi_X \times \mathcal{P}\Phi_Y$ for sets $X, Y \subset \mathcal{P}X$, *i.e.*,

$$D_{\Phi_X, \rho_{\|\cdot\|}}(A, B) = \begin{cases} inf\,\{\rho_{\|\cdot\|}(\Phi_A, \Phi_B)\}, & \text{if } \Phi_X \text{ and } \Phi_Y \text{ are not empty,} \\ \infty, & \text{if } \Phi_X \text{ or } \Phi_Y \text{ is empty.} \end{cases}$$

Theorem 2. $(X, D_{\Phi_X, \rho_{\|\cdot\|}})$ *is an approach space.*

Proof. Immediate from the definition of $D_{\Phi_X, \rho_{\|\cdot\|}}$ and Lemma 2. □

Given an approach space (X, ν_ρ), define $\nu_\rho : \mathcal{P}(\mathcal{P}X) :\rightarrow [0, \infty]$ by

$$\nu_\rho(\mathcal{A}) = \inf_{x \in X} \sup_{A \in \mathcal{A}} \rho(x, A). \qquad (1)$$

The collection $\mathcal{A} \in \mathcal{P}^2 X$ is **near** if, and only if $\nu(\mathcal{A}) = 0$ for some element $x \in X$ [17]. The function ν is called an **approach merotopy** [40]. In the sequel, rewrite (1), replacing $x \in X$ with $B \subset X$ and ρ with $D_{\Phi_X, \rho_{\|\cdot\|}}$, then, for a selected $B \subset X$,

$$\nu_{D_{\Phi_X, \rho_{\|\cdot\|}}}(\mathcal{A}) = \inf_{B \subset X} \sup_{A \in \mathcal{A}} D_{\Phi_X, \rho_{\|\cdot\|}}(B, A). \tag{2}$$

Then the collection $\mathcal{A} \subset \mathcal{P}X$ is Φ-**near** if, and only if $\nu_{D_{\Phi_X, \rho_{\|\cdot\|}}}(\mathcal{A}) = 0$ for some $B \subset X$.

Definition 1. Near Tolerance Rough Sets
Assume every $A \subset X$ is a tolerance rough set relative to a cover on X defined by tolerance relation τ_Φ. Given an approach space $(X, D_{\Phi_X, \rho_{\|\cdot\|}}))$, sets $A, B \subset X$ are near if, and only if $D_{\Phi_X, \rho_{\|\cdot\|}}(A, B) = 0$. When it is clear from the context, ρ concisely denotes $D_{\Phi_X, \rho_{\|\cdot\|}}$.

Theorem 3. *Put X equal to a nonempty set of tolerance rough sets. Given an approach space (X, ρ), a collection $\mathcal{A} \in \mathcal{P}^2 X$ is Φ-near if, and only if $\rho(A, B) = 0$ for some $B \subset X$ and for every subset $A \in \mathcal{A}$.*

Proof.
$\Rightarrow$ Given that a collection $\mathcal{A} \in \mathcal{P}^2 X$ is Φ-near, then $\nu_\rho(\mathcal{A}) = 0$. Hence, for some $B \subset X$, $\rho(A, B) = 0$.
$\Leftarrow$ Given that $\rho(A, B) = 0$ for some $B \subset X$ and for every $A \in \mathcal{A}$, it follows from the definition of $\nu_\rho(\mathcal{A})$ that the collection $\mathcal{A} \in \mathcal{P}^2 X$ is Φ-near. □

Example 1. Sample hand images
A digital image can be viewed as a set of points.

In this case, a point is either a picture element (pixel) or $p \times p, p \in [1, 255]$ subimage. In this example, an approach space (X, ν_ρ) is defined in terms of a set of hand images X and distance $\nu_\rho(\mathcal{A})$. Let B denote the set of subimages contained in the hand section for a client (lefthand side in Fig. 2) and let $\mathcal{A} \subset \mathcal{P}X$ denote a collection of subsets containing subimages of a second client (the righthand image in Fig. 2). Basically, the description of each subimage in B = 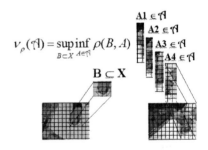 in Fig. 2 is compared with the description of subimages in $\mathcal{A}$ such as (a portion of $A4$ in Fig. 2).

$$\nu_\rho(\mathcal{A}) = \sup_{B \subset X} \inf_{A \in \mathcal{A}} \rho(B, A)$$

Fig. 2. Φ-Near Collection

For simplicity, we consider subimage description in terms of feature values extracted from a subimage using a single probe function. That is, let $\Phi(x) = (\phi_{eo}(x))$ contain a single probe function $\phi_{eo}(x)$ (average edge orientation of pixels in a subimage x). A method that can be used to determine edge orientation is given in [5, 708-710] and not repeated, here. It is a straightforward task to verify that each $B \subset X, A \in \mathcal{A}$ in Fig. 2 are examples of tolerance rough sets (see, *e.g.*, [34]). In that case, the similarities in the orientations of parts of the two hands in Fig. 2 leads to $\nu_\rho(\mathcal{A}) = 0$ for some $B \subset X$ and $\mathcal{A} \in \mathcal{P}^2 X$. Hence, in each case, B, A are examples of near TRSs.

6 Application Environment: Integrated Motion Tracking Telerehabilitation System

This section briefly describes a telerehabilitation (TR) system (shown in Fig. 3) that integrates wireless hand-finger motion tracking during therapeutic gaming system exercises, store and feed forward hand images and gaming signal data to a remote registry and automates on-demand image database classification within the context of an approach space framework. The proposed approach to rehabilitation hand-finger motion tracking grew out of work on TR in a pervasive computing environment [25,32]. Since rehabilitation often requires continued efforts on the part of patients over longer time periods, a less expensive means to practice therapeutic movements remotely using a telerehabilitation system to allow patients to continue therapy at home and in most cases unassisted has become important. The particular Canadian Arthritis Network (CAN) TR arthritis care registry reported in [25,15] and designed for our TR system consists of a web-based front-end allowing registered users to login and gain access to hand-finger motion image database, videos, data and tools for classifying, processing uploaded data from therapeutic exercise gaming sessions as well as on-demand report generation. What follows is an overview of the TR system, devices and components used in our experiments and data collection.

6.1 Telerehabilitation System Overview

In Fig. 3, a client holds an object (ex: top hat) that has been instrumented to record hand movements while playing a video game. The least expensive and simplest approach for a home based motion tracking system was found in readily available commercial, off-the-shelf devices based around the Nintendo Wii^{TM}. This system encourages its users to become more active during the gaming process using a combination of an infrared position-detection scheme, accelerometers and Bluetooth-based remotes [41,42]. The hand-finger motions are recorded using an IR camera shown in Fig. 4. The IR camera has a resolution of 1024x768 pixels and can track up to four targets simultaneously. The camera is located in the remote, thus eliminating the need for patients to purchase the entire console system. During TR game play, all of the events and coordinates of on-screen objects are recorded to a log file that can then be subsequently stored and uploaded to a secure server as a game option. A TR gaming server listens for data from gaming sessions along with a separate health registry that is able to gather the data into an active database and provide analysis tools for registered users to login and examine performance parameters of individual patients.

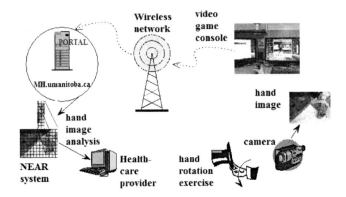

Fig. 3. Arthritis Care Motion Tracking Telerehabilitation System

The TR system runs on Windows Vista so communication devices and drivers had to be compatible. IOGEAR, GBU221 dongle were selected as they satisfied our criteria for a home-based system. This included using the WID-COMM Bluetooth stack which was stable with the remote and provided a robust connection with the chosen device and desktop system. This is of particular interest for home-based therapy as the data is uploaded through secure servers and then released to healthcare providers for remote monitoring.

Fig. 4. Camera and emitter

Clients are required to move the controller in different patterns to achieve specific goals during gameplay. Through the combination of measuring acceleration in the X, Y and Z directions and monitoring position using infrared (IR) camera to obtain X and Y coordinates with some degree of depth in the Z-direction (16 steps), programmers are able to simulate movement as users manipulate the remote. A detailed description is given in [15]. TR system gaming data includes hand-finger motion images which is fed to the NEAR system (shown in Fig. 3). The NEAR system makes it possible to perform image database classification. The focus of this paper is on analysis of such images.

7   Analyzing Hand-Finger Motion Images with NEAR System

Before we describe the application of the approach space framework for classifying images, we give a brief introduction to approach merotopies using three different distance functions.

7.1 Approach Merotopies

We are interested in measuring the distance between digital images (a digital image is viewed as a set of points). Let us define an approach space (X, ν_ρ), where X is a set of tolerance rough sets and ρ is a distance function that measures the nearness of pairs of TRSs. A particular choice of ρ gives rise to a particular approach merotopy defined in terms of a subset $B \subset X$ and a collection $\mathcal{A} \subset \mathcal{P}X$. Assume $I1, I2$ denote query image and test image, respectively. Put $X = I_1 \cup I_2$ and assume that subset B resides in image I_1 and collection $\mathcal{A}$ resides in test image $I2$. Let A denote an element of the collection $\mathcal{A}$. The experimental results using three distance functions from [11] are reported here, namely,

(distance.1) $tNM(B, A)$ (tolerance nearness measure),
(distance.2) $tHD(B, A)$ (tolerance Hausdorff measure),
(distance.3) $tHM(B, A)$ (tolerance Hamming measure).

A detailed explanation of the each of these distance functions is given in [10,12] and not repeated here.

Example 2. Sample tNM-based Approach Space Merotopies
Assume $A \in \mathcal{A}$. Define a merotopy $\nu_\rho(\mathcal{A})$ in terms of the distance function $\rho_{tNM} : \mathcal{P}X \times \mathcal{P}X :\to [0, \infty)$

$$\rho_{tNM}(B, A) = \begin{cases} 1 - tNM(B, A), & \text{if } B \text{ and } A \text{ are not empty,} \\ \infty, & \text{if } B \text{ or } A \text{ is empty.} \end{cases}$$

Then, by definition, $(X, \nu_{\rho_{tNM}})$ is an approach space and $\nu_{\rho_{tNM}}(\mathcal{A})$ is a tNM-based approach merotopy, where

$$\nu_{\rho_{tNM}}(\mathcal{A}) = \inf_{B \subset X} \sup_{A \in \mathcal{A}} \rho_{tNM}(B, A).$$

Similar merotopies arise from two additional approach spaces, $(X, \nu_{\rho_{tHD}})$, $(X, \nu_{\rho_{tHM}})$, namely, the Hausdorff-based merotopy $\nu_{\rho_{tHD}}(\mathcal{A})$ and the Hamming distance-based merotopy $\nu_{\rho_{tHM}}(\mathcal{A})$. What follows in a description of the NEAR system used in our experiments.

7.2 NEAR System

The NEAR system is designed to demonstrate applications of the near set theory and implements various nearness measures [11]. Currently, the system shown in Fig. 5 performs a number of major tasks, namely, displaying equivalence and tolerance classes for an image, segmentation evaluation, measuring the nearness of pairs of images, image retrieval on a selected image database using individual probe functions, displaying the output of processing an image and storing the results of an image analysis session. Probe functions provide a basis for describing and discerning images. Image features are represented by probe functions in the NEAR system in a separate panel (see Fig. 5.2). A selection of probe functions is given in Table 1.

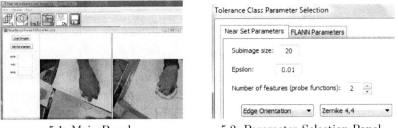

5.1: Main Panel   5.2: Parameter Selection Panel

Fig. 5. NEAR system GUI [11]

Table 1. Sample set of probe functions implemented in the NEAR system: $\mathcal{B} = \{\phi_1, \phi_2, ..., \phi_{25}\}$

Feature	Description
Colour	Average grey level of pixels
Colour	Red, Green and Blue colour components
Shape	Average edge intensity, Edge Orientation, Zernike Moments
Texture	Entropy of the greylevel values
Texture	Contrast, Correlation, Uniformity, Homogeneity

7.3   Analysis of Results

The results reported here represent sequences of images of hand-finger motions during rehabilitation exercise. These images can be downloaded from[2]. The degree of resemblance between of what would be considered normal hand-finger motion and arthritic hand-finger motion can be measured. Image sequences from 4 clients (subjects) with a total of 115 images (18 for client A, 29 for client B, 30 for client C, 38 for client D) have been used in this work. Figure 6 shows query image for each client used in measuring the distance between hand images for these clients. Out of these, one image sequence belonging to Client C is arthritic and the rest are normal clients.

Several probe functions were used in the experiments. However, only the features that resulted in the lowest approach merotopy values are reported in Table 2, namely, $\Phi = \{eo\}$ (edge orientation eo) and $\Phi = \{eo, Z\}$ (edge orientation eo and Zernike moment Z). The average nearness measure values(tNM, tHD and tHM) for the five best hand images are reported. In Table 2, p represents the subimage size, Db represents the size of the image database for each client (in other words, hand-finger movement sequence) and, $TestImg$ represents the test image that is closest to the query image. It can also be observed from the nearness measurements in Table 2, that tNM measure values are close to 1 or $\rho_{tNM}(A, B)$ is almost 0 in cases when the query image of a client's hand is being

---

[2] http://wren.ece.umanitoba.ca

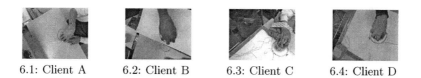

6.1: Client A   6.2: Client B   6.3: Client C   6.4: Client D

Fig. 6. Sample Hand Movement Query Images obtained during rehabilitation exercise

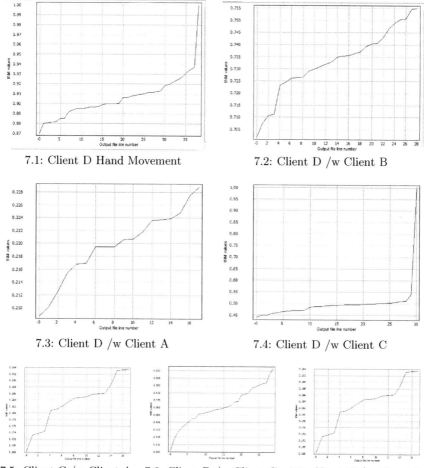

7.1: Client D Hand Movement   7.2: Client D /w Client B

7.3: Client D /w Client A   7.4: Client D /w Client C

7.5: Client C /w Client A   7.6: Client B /w Client C   7.7: Client C /w Client C

Fig. 7. Image retrieval results with tNM and edge-orientation features

Table 2. Semantically Coherent Images, $\varepsilon = 0.099$

Query	$\nu_{P_{tNM}}$	$\nu_{P_{tHD}}$	$\nu_{P_{tNM}}$	Φ	p	Db	$TestImg$	Classification
	0.069	0.001	0.271	eo	20	38		**near**
	0.077	0.001	0.856	eo,Z	10	38		**near**
	0.248	0.001	0.385	eo	20	29		far
	0.756	0.001	0.174	eo	20	18		far
	0.809	0.001	0.284	eo	20	18		far
	0.492	0.001	0.531	eo	20	30		far
	0.417	0.001	0.517	eo	10	30		far
	0.092	0.001	0.36	eo	10	30		**near**

compared with its own hand movements (see Client D in row 1, 2 and Client C in row 8). tHD nearness measure values simply do not discriminate between the *same* client's hand movements vs. other client's hand movements. tHM nearness values are somewhat more discriminatory than tHD, but not as good as tNM measure values. In these experiments, $\varepsilon = 0.099$ in determining if a query image is Φ^ε-near a test image. For a merotopy value $\nu_{P_{tNM}}(\mathcal{A}) < \varepsilon$, a query image and test image are considered *near* (see the last column of Table 2). Otherwise, the query image is classified as *far* from a particular test image.

Figure 7 shows tNM measure values for each client compared with other client hand movements (115 in total) in the entire data base. For example, $1 - tNM$ values shown in Figures 7.1 and 7.7 are very close to 0 whereas $1 - tNM$ values for Figures 7.2 through 7.6 are quite far from being close to 0. These results demonstrate the efficacy of the tNM measure values in that it is able to distinguish subtle hand movements of the same hand as compared to hand movements of a different hand.

8 Conclusion

This article introduces a framework for classifying image databases in the context of approach spaces. The separation of digital images into groups of similar images is a natural outcome of the fact the notion of distance between sets in approach space is closely related to notion of nearness of sets. The nearness of sets is ascertained with an approach merotopy. In this article, Φ-nearness found in [30] is replaced by Φ^ε-nearness, since images that are found to be close enough (within some small ε) is sufficient to classify the images as similar.

Tolerance rough sets work well in determining the nearness of sets in approach spaces, since we already know that the objects in a class are similar. Hence, we need only representatives of classes rather than all of the objects in a class in determining the nearness of disjoint sets. The main contribution of this article is the introduction of a complete framework that combines approach spaces, merotopies and TRSs in classifying digital images. We have demonstrated an application of this framework to images captured during an actual rehabilitation exercise. The NEAR system which is part of the integrated Motion Tracking Telerehabilitation System makes it possible to obtain nearness measures. Our experiments and analyses have shown that an approach merotopy defined in terms of the tolerance nearness measure (tNM) is effective in distinguishing hand movements of various clients (both normal and arthritic).

Future work on classifying image databases will take into account approach merotopies defined in terms of other distance functions such as the Earth Movers Distance(EMD) [37] and Proportional Transportation Distance (PTD) was introduced by Giannopolus and Veltkamp in [6]. PTD is interesting because it is a pseudo-metric that is invariant under rigid motion, respects scaling and obeys triangle inequality. This is in contrast to EMD that does not satisfy the triangle inequality for sets of unequal total weight.

References

1. Banaschewski, B., Lowen, R., Olmen, C.V.: Regularity in approach theory, Acta Math. Hungarica 115(3), 183–196 (2007)
2. Boiman, O.: Inference by Composition, Ph.D. Thesis, supervisor: Michal Irani, Department of Electrical & Computer Engineering, The Weizmann Institute of Science (2009)
3. Boiman, O., Shechtman, E.: Defense of Nearest-Neighbor Based Image Classification. In: Proceedings of CVPR 2008, pp. 1–10 (2008)
4. Bosch, A., Zisserman, A., Munoz, X.: Representing shape with a spatial pyramid kernel. In: Proceedings of CIVR, pp. 401–408 (2007)
5. Gonzalez, R.C., Woods, R.E.: Digital Image Processing, 3rd edn. Prentice-Hall, NJ (2008)
6. Giannopoulos, P., Veltkamp, R.C.: A Pseudo-Metric for Weighted Point Sets. In: Heyden, A., Sparr, G., Nielsen, M., Johansen, P. (eds.) ECCV 2002. LNCS, vol. 2352, pp. 715–730. Springer, Heidelberg (2002)
7. Hassanien, A.E., Abraham, A., Peters, J.F., Schaefer, G., Henry, C.: Rough sets and near sets in medical imaging: A review. IEEE Trans. Info. Tech. in Biomedicine 13(6), 955–968 (2009), doi:10.1109/TITB.2009.2017017
8. Hausdorff, F.: Grundzüge der Mengenlehre, Veit and Company, Leipzig, pp. viii + 476 (1914)
9. Henry, C., Peters, J.F.: Perception based image classification. Int. J. of Intell. Computing & Cybernetics 3(3), 410–430 (2010)
10. Henry, C., Peters, J.F.: Near set evaluation and recognition (NEAR) system V2.0, UM CI Laboratory Technical Report TR–2010–017, Computational Intelligence Laboratory, University of Manitoba (2010),
   http://wren.ee.umanitoba.ca/images/ci_reports/reportci-2010-17.pdf

11. Henry, C., Peters, J.F.: Near set evaluation and recognition (NEAR) system V2.0, http://wren.ee.umanitoba.ca/
12. Henry, C.: Near sets: Theory and Applications, Ph.D. Thesis, supervisor: J.F. Peters, Department of Electrical & Computer Engineering, University of Manitoba (2010), http://wren.ee.umanitoba.ca/
13. Khare, M., Tiwari, S.: Approach merotopological spaces and their completion. Int. J. of Math. and Math. Sciences, 1–16 (1994), doi:10.1155/2010/409804
14. Leader, S.: On clusters in proximity spaces. Fundamenta Mathematicae 47, 205–213 (1959)
15. Lockery, D., Peters, J.F., Taswell, C.: CTGaming: A problem-oriented registry for clinical telegaming rehabilitation and intervention. J. of Emerging Technologies in Web Intelligence (2010) (in press)
16. Lowen, R.: Approach spaces: The missing link in the Topology-Uniformity-Metric triad. Oxford Univ. Press, Oxford (1997)
17. Lowen, R., Sioen, M., Vaughan, D.: Competing quasi-metric spaces. An alternative approach. Houston J. Math. 29(1), 113–136 (2003)
18. Marcus, S.: Tolerance rough sets, Čech topologies, learning processes. Bull. Polish Academy of Sciences, Technical Sciences 42(3), 471–487 (1994)
19. Meghdadi, A.-H., Peters, J.F.: Perceptual systems approach to measuring image resemblance. In: Pal, S., Peters, J. (eds.) Rough Fuzzy Image Analysis, pp. 8.1-8.23. CRC Press, Boca Raton (2010)
20. Meghdadi, A.H., Peters, J.F., Ramanna, S.: Tolerance Classes in Measuring Image Resemblance. In: Velásquez, J.D., Ríos, S.A., Howlett, R.J., Jain, L.C. (eds.) KES 2009. LNCS, vol. 5712, pp. 127–134. Springer, Heidelberg (2009), doi:10.1007/978-3-642-04592-916.
21. Naimpally, S.A.: Near and far. A centennial tribute to Frigyes Riesz. Siberian Electronic Mathematical Reports 2, 144–153 (2009)
22. Naimpally, S.A.: Proximity Approach to Problems in Topology and Analysis. Oldenbourg Verlag, Munich, pp. xiv+206 (2009); ISBN 978-3-486-58917-7
23. Pal, S., Peters, J.: Rough Fuzzy Image Analysis. Foundations and Methodologies. CRC Press, Taylor & Francis Group (2010); ISBN 13: 978-1-4398-0329-5
24. Pawlak, Z.: Rough sets. Int. J. Comp. Inform. Science 11, 341–356 (1982)
25. Peters, J.F., Szturm, T., Borkowski, M., Lockery, D., Ramanna, S., Shay, B.: Wireless adaptive therapeutic telegaming in a pervasive computing environment. In: Pervasive Computing, ser. Computer Communications and Networks, ch. 1, pp. 3–28. Springer, London (2009)
26. Peters, J.F., Wasilewski, P.: Foundations of near sets. Inf. Sci. 179(18), 3091–3109 (2009), http://dx.doi.org/10.1016/j.ins.2009.04.018
27. Wasilewski, P., Peters, J.F., Ramanna, S.: Perceptual tolerance intersection. Trans. on Rough Sets XIII, 159–174 (2011)
28. Peters, J.F.: Near sets. General theory about nearness of objects. Applied Mathematical Sciences 1(53), 2609–2629 (2007)
29. Peters, J.F.: Metric spaces for near sets. Applied Mathematical Sciences 5(2), 73–78 (2011)
30. Peters, J.F., Naimpally, S.A.: Approach spaces for near families. General Mathematics Notes 2(1), 159–164 (2011)
31. Peters, J.F., Tiwari, S.: Approach merotopies and near filters. Theory and application. Gen. Math. Notes 2 (2011) (in press)
32. Peters, J.F., Puzio, L., Szturm, T.: Measuring nearness of rehabilitation hand images with finely-tuned anisotropic wavelets. In: Int. Conf. on Image Processing & Communication, CD, pp. 12.50–13.15 (2009)

33. Peters, J.F., Puzio, L.: Image analysis with anisotropic wavelet-based nearness measures. Int. J. of Computational Intell. Systems 2(3), 168–183 (2009)
34. Ramanna, S., Peters, J.F., Wu, W.-Z.: Content-Based Image Retrieval: Perceptually Near Tolerance Rough Set Approach. Journal of Zhejiang Ocean University (Natural Science) 29(5), 462–471 (2010) ISSN 1008-830X
35. Ramanna, S.: Discovering image similarities: Tolerance near set approach. In: Pal, S., Peters, J. (eds.) Rough Fuzzy Image Analysis, pp. 12.1–12.15. CRC Press, Boca Raton (2010)
36. Ramanna, S.: Perceptually near Pawlak partitions. Trans. on Rough Sets XII, 170–191 (2010)
37. Rubner, Y.: Perceptual Metrics for Image Database Navigation, Ph.D. Thesis, Stanford University (1999)
38. Searóid, M.Ó.: Metric Spaces. Springer, Berlin (2007)
39. Thron, W.J.: Topological Structures. Holt, Rinehart and Winston, NY (1966)
40. Tiwari, S.: Some Aspects of General Topology and Applications. Approach Merotopic Structures and Applications, Supervisor: M. Khare, Ph.D. thesis, Mathematics Dept., Allahabad Univ, pp. vii + 112 (2010)
41. WiiBrew.: (August 2009), http://wiibrew.org/
42. WiiLi.: (December 2007), http://www.wiili.com/
43. Wolski, M.: Perception and classification. A note on near sets and rough sets. Fundamenta Informaticae 101, 143–155 (2010), doi:10.3233/FI-2010-281

Learning Temporal Interval Relations Using Inductive Logic Programming

Maria do Carmo Nicoletti, Flávia O.S. de Sá Lisboa,
and Estevam Rafael Hruschka Jr.

CS Dept., UFSCar, Rod. Washington Luiz km 235, S. Carlos, SP, Brazil
carmo@dc.ufscar.br, flavia@ifsc.usp.br, estevam@dc.ufscar.br

Abstract. The notion of time permeates every single aspect of the world around us and, as such, it should be taken into account when developing automatic systems that implement many of its processes. In the literature several proposals for representing the notion of time can be found. One of the most popular is the Allen's temporal interval, based on a set of 13 relations that may hold between two time intervals. The main goal of this work is to explore the automatic learning of several of temporal relations from data, using an inductive logic programming (ILP) system. The paper describes a set of automatic learning experiments whose main aims are (i) determining the impact of the negative training patterns on the induced relation (ii) evidencing the necessary background knowledge for inducing the exact expression of the target concept and (iii) investigate the viability of ILP as a learning mechanism in real-time systems.

Keywords: temporal modelling, temporal interval representation, automatic learning of temporal relations, ILP, FOIL.

1 Introduction

The representation of temporal knowledge aiming at implementing temporal reasoning is a recurrent problem in many knowledge areas, particularly in Artificial Intelligence (AI). The temporal aspect of situations and events is extremely relevant for implementing intelligent systems; the innumerous proposals to efficiently represent temporal information as well as surveys found in the literature are evidence of the importance of this issue (e.g. [1] [2] [3] [4] [5] [6] [7] [8] [9] [10]). As observed in [11], "[Temporal representation and reasoning] are becoming increasingly important with the advent of ubiquitous computing, grid computing and the Internet, where large amounts of information and processes are available, and where all these may be evolving in time".

Vila in [12] mentions a few different areas of AI where representing time and implementing temporal reasoning are essential for the development of reliable and robust systems: (i) medical diagnosis and explanation – information about when, in what sequence the symptoms have occurred and how long they have persisted are critical in prescribing the correct treatment; (ii) planning – in the development of a

E.R. Hruschka Junior et al. (Eds.): INTECH 2011, CCIS 165, pp. 90–104, 2011.

plan, not only the duration of its actions and tasks should be carefully considered but also how they can be appropriately temporally ordered considering their many possible interaction over time; (iii) industrial process supervision – the control of an industrial process involves many temporal aspects such as past states, variable values evolution over time, the point of time particular sub-processes start (or end) etc. (iv) natural language understanding – mainly focusing on the verb tense in a sentence. Particularly when the focus is on natural language-based information systems, as pointed out in [13], "Applications such as information extraction, question-answering, summarization, visualization and developments in the Semantic Web can all benefit from analysis and interpretation along the temporal dimension."

One of the most well-known and influential formalisms that deals with time representation is the Allen's temporal interval algebra [14] [15] [16] [17] [18] [19] [20] [21] [22] [23]. The main purpose of the work described in this paper is to explore how some of the temporal interval logic relations which have been stated as axioms, can be automatically learnt by a relational machine learning system. Of particular interest is to determine the influence of the negative examples on the induced concept. The FOIL (First Order Inductive Learner) system [24] [25], which uses Horn clauses as the language for representing and inducing knowledge, and one of the most successful ILP systems, was used in the experiments.

The paper is organized as follows: Section 2 briefly introduces the relational machine learning system FOIL in order to provide the basic knowledge for understanding how the system works and the information it requires. Section 3 presents some of the main concepts and the basic relations related to Allen's temporal intervals. Particularly, the learning of seven of Allen's 13 basic relations will be main goal to achieve when using the relational learning system FOIL, as described in Section 4. Finally in Section 5 comments about the work and a few directions into future work are presented.

2   The FOIL System – Main Aspects

As stated in [26], "Inductive Logic Programming (ILP) is the area of AI which deals with the induction of hypothesized predicate definitions from examples and background knowledge. Logic programs are used as a single representation for examples, background knowledge and hypotheses. ILP is differentiated from most other forms of Machine Learning (ML) both by its use of an expressive representation language and its ability to make use of logically encoded background knowledge."

FOIL is an ILP system which induces function-free Horn clause representations of relations. The inductive process implemented by FOIL is based on examples (positive and negative examples of the relation to be learnt) and a given background knowledge (BK), known as domain theory (a set of presumably known relations which are fed to the system in their extensional form, i.e., as ground facts). FOIL learns a description of the target relation represented in terms of the target and, eventually, of the other relations given as BK. So, given the positive and negative examples that define the relation to be learnt and the positive examples that define each of the relations that are part of the BK, FOIL's task is to learn a function-free Horn clause definition of the target relation.

"FOIL's definitions consist of ordered clauses. These clauses are extended forms of function-free Horn clauses in that the body literals may be negated, where the meaning of negation accords with the Prolog convention. There is an option to exclude such negated literals if the user wishes. The head of a clause is always a literal consisting of the target relation, with unique variables for each argument position. The literals in the body may be often forms (including negations), subject to various restrictions. Every literal must contain at least one variable bound by the head of the clause or a preceding body literal; such variables will be referred to as 'previously bound'. FOIL checks whether discrete types have constants in common and if so considers variables of such compatible types to satisfy type restrictions on relations" [25].

When learning a definition, FOIL uses a covering approach (an example is covered by a clause that proves it). FOIL repeatedly learns a clause and then removes the positive examples that are covered by it from the set of positive examples to be covered. Once the definition is complete (all the positive examples are covered), FOIL prunes out redundant clauses. The whole process is much more elaborated than the brief view given above. A detailed and in-depth description of FOIL can be found in [24], [25] [27]. As an example of how to use FOIL for learning a relation, consider the graph given in Figure 1. Suppose the relation *path(A,B)* (representing that there is a path between two nodes A and B of the graph) is the target relation whose general representation should be learnt by FOIL. Suppose also that examples of relations are known, such as (i) *arc(A,B)* (expressing that there is an arc from node A to B), (ii) *node(A)*, expressing that A is a node in the graph.

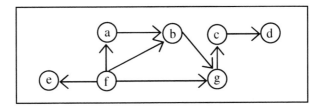

Fig. 1. A graph defined by 7 nodes and 8 arcs

Input data to FOIL shown in Figure 2 follows the required syntax where the header of a relation, other than the target relation, begins with an '*' and consists of the relation name, argument types and optional keys, followed by a sequence of lines containing examples. Each example consists of constants separated by commas (argument separator) and must appear in a single line. Due to space restriction, however, the convention of placing one example per line will not be followed in this paper. A line with the character '.' indicates the end of the extensional description of the corresponding relation. Note in Figure 2 that the negative examples of relation *path/2* have not been given – if all the positive examples are known, the negative examples can be generated under the CWA (Closed World Assumption). When referring to predicates, their arity (i.e., number of arguments) can be omitted for the sake of simplicity, when that does not introduce ambiguity.

X: a,b,c,d,e,f,g.	a,g	f,c	*arc(X,X)	f,e	b
	b,c	f,d	a,b	f,g	c
path(X,X)	b,d	f,e	b,g	c,d	d
a,b	b,g	f,g	g,c	.	e
a,c	c,d	g,c	f,a	*node(X)	f
a,d	f,a	g,d	f,b	a	g
	f,b	.			.

Fig. 2. Input for FOIL to learn relation *path/2* given two relations as BK. Due to space restriction the convention of having one example per line has been abolished. The information displayed in six columns above should be read from left to right, in sequence.

Considering the input file as described in Figure 2, FOIL induces the two clauses below which are a general description that can be used to find a path in any graph. Note that although the unary relation *node/1* has been given to FOIL as background knowledge, its contribution for representing the concept of path (in the given context) is not relevant enough and so, *node/1* is not part of the set of clauses induced by FOIL.

path(A,B) :- arc(A,B).
path(A,B) :- arc(A,C), path(C,B).

3   A Brief Overview of Allen's Temporal Interval Relations

The formalism known as Temporal Interval Relations (TIR) (or Allen's Interval Algebra), based on binary interval relations to represent and reason about temporal knowledge, was initially proposed by Allen in [14], [15]. Since then it has been the subject of several research works particularly related to its use in different domains and possible extensions it allows [2] [28] [29].

The information about TIR given next has been compiled from the many sources that discuss this formalism, particularly from [21]. TIR has a simple linear model of time, having one primitive object referred to as *time period* and one primitive relation named *meets/2*. A time period can be thought of as the time associated with some event occurring or some property holding in the world. Although the intuitive idea associated with the *meets/2* relation is very clear, its description as a formal concept (aiming at its implementation) is not trivial, since it involves a previous definition of the adopted granularity for time as well as the adopted representation for time interval.

Allen in [15] discusses the appropriateness of using time points as opposed to time intervals, as the basis for temporal representation and reasoning. As Mani and co-workers comment in [13], "Depending on the representation and the choice of primitive (intervals or instants, or both), a variety of different temporal relations between times can be defined."

In spite of TIR taking temporal intervals as primitive, the formalism contemplates the possibility of, assuming a model consisting of a fully ordered set of points of time, representing an interval T as an ordered pair of points of time $< t-, t+ >$, satisfying the pre-condition of the first point being lesser than the second, i.e., $t- < t+$. For the purposes of this paper this was the representation adopted, noted by $[t-, t+]$, in spite of some inconveniences it can bring, which have been vaguely described by Allen in [15] as "being too uniform and does not facilitate structuring the knowledge in a way which is convenient for typical temporal reasoning task". Vila in [12] presents a detailed discussion related to time representations (time points, intervals); Allen and Hayes in [17] and [18] consider extending TIR introducing the concept of time point.

Table 1 presents Allen's 5 basic binary temporal relations between intervals, namely *meets, before, overlaps, during,* and *equal*.

Table 1. Allen's 5 basic binary temporal interval relations and their equivalent relations assuming intervals (time periods) are defined by time points, i.e., A = [a−,a+] (a− < a+) and B= [b−, b+] (b− < b+), where {a−,a+, b−,b+} ⊆ ℜ. In the second column the default conditions (derived from the fact that for interval T, t− < t+ always holds) are also presented. The condition(s) in bold face are the ones that characterize the corresponding relation. Comma represents the logical 'and' and semi-colon the logical inclusive 'or'.

Interval Relation	Conditions of interval endpoints	Pictorial representation
meets(A,B)	a− < b−, a− < b+ **a+ = b−,** a+ < b+	AAAA BBBBBBB
before(A,B)	a− < b−, a− < b+ **a+ < b−,** a+ < b+	AAAA BBBBBBB
overlaps(A,B)	**a− < b−,** a− < b+ **a+ > b−,** a+ < b+	AAAA BBBBBBB
during(A,B)	**(a− > b−, a+ =< b+) ;** **(a− >= b−, a+ < b+)**	See Table 2
equal(A,B)	**a− = b−,** a− < b+ a+ > b−, **a+ = b+**	AAAAA BBBBB

The second column of Table 1 shows the equivalent relations on endpoints; the four conditions on time points are presented (although some of them can be logically entitled by others). According to Allen, the subdivision of the *during* relation into three others namely *starts, finishes* and a new *during*, provides a better computational model. The three new temporal interval relations are shown in Table 2. Considering the subdivision of *during* relation the number of basic temporal interval relations adds up to 7.

Reminding that if R is a binary relation, the converse (reversed) relation of R, written R⁻¹, is a relation such that yR⁻¹x if and only if xRy. The 7 basic relations shown in Table 1 and Table 2 can be expanded into 13, if their reversed relations are considered (the reversed relation of *equal* is itself). Table 3 names the reversed relations associated to 6 basic temporal interval relations (*equal* excluded).

Table 2. Subdividing the *during* relation from Table 1 into three new relations: *starts*, *finishes* and a new *during*. Notation and convention follow those established for Table 1.

Interval Relation	Conditions of interval endpoints	Pictorial representation
starts(A,B)	**a− = b−**, a− < b+ a+ > b−, **a+ < b+**	AAAA BBBBBBB
finishes(A,B)	**a− > b−**, a− < b+ a+ > b−, **a+ = b+**	AAAA BBBBBBB
during(A,B)	**a− > b−**, a− < b+ a+ > b−, **a+ < b+**	AAAA BBBBBBB

Table 3. Temporal basic interval relations, their correspondent reversed relations and the equivalence relation between each pair of them

Interval Relation	Reversed Relation	Equivalences
meets	met_by	meets(A,B) ≡ met_by(B,A)
before	after	before(A,B) ≡ after(B,A)
overlaps	overlapped_by	overlaps(A,B) ≡ overlapped_by(B,A)
starts	started_by	starts(A,B) ≡ started_by(B,A)
finishes	finished_by	finishes(A,B) ≡ finished_by(B,A)
during	contains	during(A,B) ≡ contains(B,A)

4 Learning Temporal Interval Relations with FOIL – The Basic Learning Cases

This section describes the necessary information (positive examples and BK) for using FOIL to learn each of Allen's 7 basic temporal relations shown in Table 1 and Table 2. For the experiments it was used the version 5.1 of FOIL downloaded from http://www.cs.cmu.edu/afs/cs/project/ai-repository/ai/areas/learning/systems/foil. The FOIL system runs on a Virtual Machine with Linux Ubuntu version 10 with gcc compiler.

For each relation a table containing the positive examples (PE), the background knowledge (BK) and the induced concept (IC) is presented. To ease the understanding of the information in each of the following tables a figure (contained in Figure 3) explicitly representing the given knowledge is presented. There was also an attempt to minimize the number of examples of the relation to be learnt as well as of the BK given to FOIL as input. The motivation for that was to determine the least possible amount of information to give to FOIL that would still allow the system to induce the proper expression of the relation, as described in Table 1. As mentioned before, in the following tables the knowledge will not be presented according to the syntax required by FOIL nor the combinations of different BK and sets of positive examples will be exhaustively covered. The main goal is to show how the basic temporal relations can be learnt and how the background knowledge and positive examples can influence the induced expression. In the experiments a time interval is represented by its two endpoints. As a consequence, Allen's binary relations are represented by four arguments - the first two define the first temporal interval and the last two, the second temporal interval. It is assumed that each of these pair of values defines a proper temporal interval, as discussed in Section 3, i.e., a valid temporal interval T is defined as an ordered pair of points of time <t−, t+>, satisfying the pre-condition of the first point being lesser than the second, i.e., t− < t+). For the experiments described in the following subsections, the pictorial examples of the respective relation, as shows Figure 2, have been used.

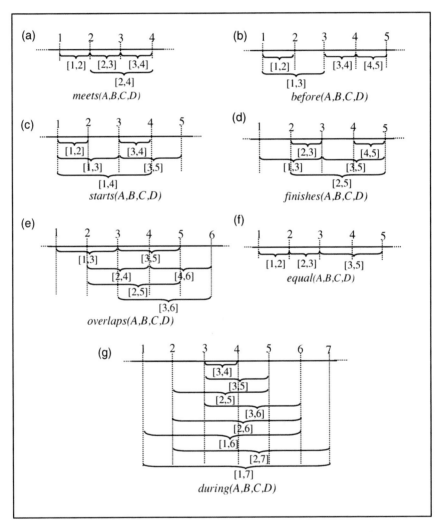

Fig. 3. Pictorial examples used for learning the 7 basic temporal relations

In the following tables: (a) LE identifies a number associated with a learning experiment; (b) due to space restrictions, the line with the character "." indicating the end of a listing of examples will be suppressed; (c) column PE lists the positive examples of the relation to be learnt; (d) column NE lists the negative examples – if none is provided by the user, FOIL automatically generates them under the CWA. When the CWA is used, the column informs the number of negative examples generated by FOIL; (e) the presence of *** in column IC means that FOIL was unable to induce an expression for the concepts represented by the positive examples, given the KB and NE examples shown in the corresponding line of the table; (f) FOIL requires the definition of the type of data the examples represent. For all the experiments, this request has been accomplished by having, at the beginning of the input file, the type definition: X:1,2,3,4 or X:1,2,3,4,5 or X:1,2,3,4,5,6 or X:1,2,3,4,5,6,7, depending on the relation to be learnt (see Figure 3).

4.1 Learning the *meets/4* Relation

Figure 3(a) pictorially shows the three positive examples of relation *meets/4* initially given to FOIL. Table 4 shows the learning results obtained by FOIL in three learning environments: #1: 3 positive examples, no negative examples and no BK; #2: 3 positive examples, 1 negative example and no BK; and #3: 2 positive examples, 1 negative example and no BK.

Table 4. Learning *meets/4* based on Figure 3(a) where X: 1,2,3,4 (for FOIL)

LE	PE (meets(X,X,X,X))		NE	BK	IC
#1	1,2,2,3 1,2,2,4	2,3,3,4	CWA (#NE: 253)	∅	***
#2	1,2,2,3 1,2,2,4	2,3,3,4	1,2,3,4	∅	meets(A,B,C,D) :- B=C.
#3	1,2,2,3 1,2,2,4		1,2,3,4 2,3,1,2	∅	meets(A,B,C,D) :- B=C.

In #1 no NEs were given and FOIL used the CWA to automatically generate 253 negative examples (all possible combinations with repeated elements of numbers 1,2,3,4, except for the three given as positive examples). Many of the negative examples were actually positive examples (e.g. 1,3,3,4 is considered a negative example under CWA, given the three positive examples). In #2 and #3 FOIL induced the condition that should be satisfied by the upper limit and lower limit of the first and the second temporal intervals respectively (i.e., B=C). Particularly #3 shows that it is possible to learn the concept with only 2 well-defined positive examples and 2 well-defined negative examples. For the learning of the *meets/4* relation no BK was required.

4.2 Learning the *before/4* Relation

Figure 3(b) pictorially shows the situations that inspired the positive examples of relation *before/4* initially given to FOIL. Table 5 shows the learning results obtained by FOIL in four learning environments described as: #1: 3 positive examples, no negative examples and no BK; #2: 3 positive examples, no negative examples and one relation as BK; #3: 3 positive examples, 2 negative examples and one relation as BK and finally #4: three positive examples, 3 negative examples and one relation as BK.

Table 5. Learning *before/4* based on Figure 3(b) where X: 1,2,3,4,5 (for FOIL)

LE	PE (before(X,X,X,X))		NE		BK	IC
#1	1,2,3,4 1,2,4,5	1,3,4,5	CWA (#NE: 622)		∅	***
#2	1,2,3,4 1,2,4,5	1,3,4,5	CWA (#NE: 622)		lessthan(X,X) 1,2 2,4 1,3 2,5 1,4 3,4 1,5 3,5 2,3 4,5	before(A,B,C,D) :- ¬lessthan(E,A), lessthan(B,C), lessthan(C,D), lessthan(E,B), ¬before(A,C,F,D).
#3	1,2,3,4 1,2,4,5	1,3,4,5	3,4,1,2 2,3,3,4		Same as #2	***
#4	1,2,3,4 1,2,4,5	1,3,4,5	3,4,1,2 2,3,3,4	1,3,2,5	Same as #2	before(A,B,C,D) :- lessthan(B,C).

Similarly to what happened with *meets/4*, the use of CWA by FOIL (since negative examples have not been given) generates false negatives - FOIL tries to generalize based on wrong information and does not succeed (see experiment #1). Considering that 3 positive examples were given, by the CWA the examples 1,2,3,5 and 2,3,4,5, for instance, are considered negative examples when they clearly are positive examples. In experiment #2 the CWA was maintained and the relation *lessthan/2* was given as BK. Although FOIL succeeds to induce an expression for relation *before/4*, that definitely is not a good representation of the concept, since it rules out many positive examples that, due to the use of the CWA, have been considered as negative examples. The input to FOIL in #3 and #4 differs only in relation to an extra negative example given to the system in #4 which, definitely, is critical for the system to induce the expected representation of the concept.

4.3 Learning the *equal/4* Relation

The learning of relation *equal/4* was based on the situation displayed in Figure 3(f). The information given to FOIL in the experiments is described in Table 6. The four experiments were conducted with the same positive examples and no BK. They vary in relation to the negative examples given. In #1: no negative example; #2: 1 negative example; #3: 1 negative example and #4: 2 negative examples (those that were individually given in #2 and #3).

In #1 the use of CWA provoked many positive examples to be considered as negative (e.g. 1,3,1,3) and FOIL ended without learning any concept. Note that in #2 and #3 only one suitable negative example was given and only a partial definition of the concept was induced. However in #4, when the two negative examples are given, FOIL was provided with the necessary information to induce the conjunction of both conditions that represents the correct expression of *equal/4*.

Table 6. Learning *equal/4* based on Figure 3(f) where X: 1,2,3,4,5 (for FOIL)

LE	PE (equal(X,X,X,X))	NE	BK	IC
#1	1,2,1,2 3,5,3,5 2,3,2,3	CWA (#NE: 622)	∅	***
#2	Same as #1	1,3,2,3	∅	equal(A,B,C,D) :- A=C.
#3	Same as #1	1,2,1,4	∅	equal(A,B,C,D) :- B=D.
#4	Same as #1	1,2,1,4 1,3,2,3	∅	equal(A,B,C,D) :- A=C, B=D.

4.4 Learning the *starts/4* Relation

The information pictorially shown in Figure 3(c) has been used for learning the relation *starts/4* in four attempts, as described in Table 7. In experiment #1 the CWA was adopted by FOIL since no negative example was provided. Similarly to what happened in the three previous relations, many false negatives were created and FOIL failed to induce an expression for the concept. Experiments #2, #3 and #4 were conducted with the same set of positive examples and with the same relation given as BK. They vary in relation to the negative examples provided. The two negative examples given in #3 were unable to provide FOIL with sufficient information to induce a suitable expression of the concept; only when a few more negative examples are provided (#4) FOIL induces the expected representation for *starts/4*.

Table 7. Learning *starts/4* based on Figure 3(c) where X: 1,2,3,4,5,6 (for FOIL)

LE	PE (starts(X,X,X,X))	NE	BK	IC
#1	1,2,1,3 1,3,1,4 1,2,1,4 3,4,3,5	CWA (#NE: 621)	∅	***
#2	Same as #1	2,5,5,6	lessthan(X,X) 1,2 2,3 3,5 1,3 2,4 3,6 1,4 2,5 4,5 1,5 2,6 4,6 1,6 3,4 5,6	starts(A,B,C,D) :- A=C.
#3	Same as #1	2,5,5,6 2,5,2,3	Same as #2	starts(A,B,C,D) :- ¬lessthan(E,C).
#4	Same as #1	2,5,5,6 3,6,2,5 2,5,2,3 3,6,4,5 3,6,4,6 3,6,1,2 3,6,2,6	Same as #2	starts(A,B,C,D) :- A=C, lessthan(B,D).

4.5 Learning the *finishes/4* Relation

The *finishes/4* relation defines when two time intervals are such that the first starts after the second has started and both end at the same ending point. Figure 3(d) shows a diagram of the situation used as information to FOIL, to conduct the 7 learning experiments detailed in Table 8, all using the same set of four positive examples. The CWA was used by FOIL in #1 and, as expected, due to the many false negatives generated, FOIL failed to induce an expression for the concept. As the only negative example given in #2 was 2,5,2,3 when generalizing FOIL adds the literal A<>C in the body of the clause, since A=C in the negative example given. The two negative examples given in #3 direct FOIL to include literal *lessthan/2* in the induced expression. Note in #4 that given the five negative examples (the two from #3 plus three new ones), FOIL induces the same expression as in #3. Increasing the number of NE to 7, as in #5, FOIL includes a negative literal in the induced expression. If FOIL is instructed *via* command prompt, as in #6, to ignore negative literals, the expected expression for *finished/4* is obtained. The same expression, however, can be induced without instructing FOIL, by including a carefully chosen negative example, as done in #7.

Table 8. Learning *finishes/4* based on Figure 3(d) where X: 1,2,3,4,5,6 (for FOIL)

LE	PE(finishes(X,X,X,X))		NE		BK	IC
#1	2,3,1,3 4,5,2,5 4,5,3,5 3,5,2,5		CWA (#NE: 1292)		∅	***
#2	Same as #1		2,5,2,3		Same as #2 (Table 7)	finishes(A,B,C,D) :- A<>C.
#3	Same as #1		2,5,2,3 2,5,3,5		Same as #2 (Table 7)	finishes(A,B,C,D) :- lessthan(C,A).
#4	Same as #1		2,5,2,3 2,5,3,4 2,5,2,6 2,5,5,6 2,5,3,5		Same as #2 (Table 7)	finishes(A,B,C,D) :- lessthan(C,A).
#5	Same as #1		2,5,2,3 2,5,5,6 2,5,2,6 3,4,4,6 2,5,3,5 3,4,1,2 2,5,3,4		Same as #2 (Table 7)	finishes(A,B,C,D) :- B=D, ¬lessthan(A,C).
#6	Same as #1		Same as #5		Same as #2 (Table 7)	(*) finishes(A,B,C,D) :- B=D, lessthan(C,A).
#7	Same as #1		2,5,2,3 2,5,5,6 2,5,2,6 3,4,4,6 2,5,3,5 3,4,1,2 2,5,3,4 3,4,3,4		Same as #2 (Table 7)	finishes(A,B,C,D) :- B=D, lessthan(C,A).

* obtained with the –n argument when running FOIL. The parameter instructs FOIL not to consider negative literals.

4.6 Learning the *overlaps/4* Relation

As can be seen in Table 1, the definition of *overlaps/4* requires three conditions on interval endpoints; a careful analysis of the appropriate examples that can direct FOIL into the direction of inducing the proper definition should be conducted. As discussed before, the *overlaps* relation is true when the first temporal interval overlaps the second. Accordingly to the semantics associated with Allen's *overlaps* relation, the relation is true if (a) the first temporal interval starts earlier than the second, (b) the second starts while the first is still going on and (c) the first interval ends while the second is still going on.

Figure 3(e) is a diagram of the situations given as examples to FOIL in the eight experiments detailed in Table 9. Experiments #2 to #7 kept constant the number of positive examples and increased the number of negative examples starting with 1

(#2), followed by 2 (#3), 5 (#4), 7 (#5) and 12 (#6), when FOIL finally gathered enough information to induce the expected representation of *overlaps/4*, i.e., a conjunction of three conditions on time points of both intervals, as shown in Table 1.

The following experiments in Table 9 (i.e. #7 and #8) tried to reduce the number of positive examples used, maintaining the 12 negative examples. Experiment #7 differs from #6 in relation to the number of positive examples, which was decreased by one. FOIL still managed to induce the appropriate expression for the concept. However, when the number of positive examples dropped to 4, FOIL failed to find a representation for the concept consistent with the given examples and BK.

Table 9. Learning *overlaps/4* based on Figure 3(e) where X: 1,2,3,4,5,6 (for FOIL)

LE	PE(overlaps(X,X,X,X))		NE		BK	IC
#1	1,3,2,4 1,3,2,5 3,5,4,6	2,4,3,6 2,5,3,6 2,5,4,6	CWA (#NE: 1290)		∅	***
#2	Same as #1		3,6,4,6		Same as #2 (Table 7)	overlaps(A,B,C,D):- B<>D.
#3	Same as #1		3,6,4,6 3,6,2,6		Same as #2 (Table 7)	overlaps(A,B,C,D):- B<>D.
#4	Same as #1		3,6,4,6 3,6,2,6 3,6,2,5	3,6,4,5 3,6,1,2	Same as #2 (Table 7)	overlaps(A,B,C,D):- lessthan(B,D).
#5	Same as #1		3,6,4,6 3,6,2,6 3,6,2,5 3,6,4,5	3,6,1,2 1,2,2,4 1,2,3,5	Same as #2 (Table 7)	overlaps(A,B,C,D):- lessthan(B,D), lessthan(C,B).
#6	Same as #1		3,6,4,6 3,6,2,6 3,6,2,5 3,6,4,5 3,6,1,2 1,2,2,4	1,2,3,5 3,5,3,4 3,5,3,6 3,5,2,4 3,5,2,6 3,5,1,2	Same as #2 (Table 7)	overlaps(A,B,C,D):- lessthan(A,C), lessthan(B,D), lessthan(C,B).
#7	1,3,2,4 1,3,2,5 3,5,4,6	2,4,3,6 2,5,3,6	Same as #7		Same as #2 (Table 7)	overlaps(A,B,C,D):- lessthan(A,C), lessthan(B,D), lessthan(C,B).
#8	1,3,2,4 1,3,2,5	3,5,4,6 2,4,3,6	Same as #7		Same as #2 (Table 7)	***

4.7   Learning the *during/4* Relation

Figure 3(g) presents a diagram of the situations given as examples to FOIL as learning situations for relation *during/4*. Due to space restriction Table 10 only presents 5 out of the 7 conducted experiments. Also, the examples of *lessthan/2* given as BK are those already presented in Table 7, including the following pairs: 1,7 2,7 3,7 4,7 5,7 and 6,7 since X: 1,2,3,4,5,6,7.

The experiment where no negative examples were given, no BK was given and #PE=13, resulted in a set of 2388 automatically created negative examples (CWA) with FOIL ending without inducing any expression. The same strategy used before was adopted – to fix the number of positive examples and increase (per experiment) the number of negative examples. In all the experiments, except for the one described above, BK was represented by only one relation (*lessthan/2*) with 21 examples.

As can be seen in Table 10, FOIL was able to induce the expected concept in experiment #2, based on #PE=13 and #NE=10 (and on the BK *lessthan/2*). In the following experiment (#3) the number of negative examples was reduced to 6 and FOIL only induced a partial expression of the concept. In Experiment #4 the negative examples are back to 10 and a reduction in the number of positive examples was tried (#PE=3) – FOIL succeeds in inducing the correct expression for the concept. The following experiment tries again a reduction in the number of negative, maintaining the reduced number of positive as the previous experiments and FOIL ends without inducing any expression.

Table 10. Learning *during/4* based on Figure 3(g) where X: 1,2,3,4,5,6,7 (for FOIL)

LE	PE(during(X,X,X,X))			NE			IC
#1	3,4,2,5 3,4,1,7 3,5,1,7 3,4,2,6 3,5,2,6 2,5,1,6 3,4,1,6 3,5,1,6 2,5,1,7 3,4,2,7 3,5,2,7 3,6,2,7 3,6,1,7			2,5,2,3 2,5,2,6 2,5,3,6 2,5,3,4 2,5,6,7			during(A,B,C,D):- lessthan(C,A).
#2	3,4,2,5 3,4,1,7 3,5,1,7 3,4,2,6 3,5,2,6 2,5,1,6 3,4,1,6 3,5,1,6 2,5,1,7 3,4,2,7 3,5,2,7 3,6,2,7 3,6,1,7			2,5,2,3 2,5,6,7 3,6,4,5 2,5,2,6 3,6,4,6 3,6,1,2 2,5,3,6 3,6,2,6 2,5,3,4 3,6,2,5			during(A,B,C,D):- lessthan(B,D), lessthan(C,A).
#3	3,4,2,5 3,4,1,7 3,5,1,7 3,4,2,6 3,5,2,6 2,5,1,6 3,4,1,6 3,5,1,6 2,5,1,7 3,4,2,7 3,5,2,7 3,6,2,7 3,6,1,7			3,6,4,6 3,6,2,5 3,6,1,2 3,6,2,6 3,6,4,5			during(A,B,C,D):- lessthan(B,D).
#4	3,4,2,5 3,4,2,6 3,4,1,6			2,5,2,3 2,5,6,7 3,6,4,5 2,5,2,6 3,6,4,6 3,6,1,2 2,5,3,6 3,6,2,6 2,5,3,4 3,6,2,5			during(A,B,C,D):- lessthan(B,D), lessthan(C,A).
#5	3,4,2,5 3,4,2,6 3,4,1,6			2,5,2,3 3,6,2,5 2,5,2,6 3,6,4,5 2,5,3,6 3,6,1,2			***

5   Conclusions and Further Work

Allen's temporal interval logic goes far beyond the basic issues discussed in this paper since it is the basis for representing events and actions. As briefly mentioned in Section 3, Allen's temporal theory is based on a primitive object, the time period, and one primitive binary relation, the *meets* relation. Next, the theory introduces an axiomatization of the *meets* relation, by establishing 5 axioms based on the following intuitive notions: (1) every period has a period that meets it and another that it meets;

(2) time periods can be composed producing a larger time period; (3) periods uniquely define an equivalence class of periods that meet them (4) these equivalence classes also uniquely define the periods and finally (5) periods can be ordered. Based on both primitives i.e., time period and the *meets/2* relation, and considering the five axioms, several intuitive relationships that could hold between time periods could be defined, such as those already seen in tables 1, 2 and 3.

The work described in this paper will continue by (i) investigating the original time period representation proposed by Allen [14][30] i.e., as a primitive concept and not as a concept represented by time points as adopted in this paper; (ii) running automatic learning experiments with FOIL to evaluate the viability of having time period as primitive; (iii) comparatively evaluate results obtained with both temporal period representations taking into account the necessary examples and background knowledge given to the system for promoting the induction of a consistent expression of the target relation to be learnt.

As it is well established in the literature and very obvious from all the experiments described in this paper, the examples given to the learning system play a crucial role and are determinant for inducing a 'good' representation of the concept. Particularly when using ILP systems, the relevance of the examples and BK seems even more crucial. As can be seen in many of the experiments described in this paper, the use of the closed world assumption can be misleading and consequently, the 'right' choice of negative examples plays a fundamental role in inducing a sound and representative expression of the concept. Choosing a suitable set of negative examples, however, can be a particularly 'tricky' task which, most certainly, will not be feasible to be automatically conducted in a real time environment.

Acknowledgements

The authors thank the IFSC/USP (São Carlos) and CNPq for their financial support.

References

1. Bellini, P., Mattolini, R., Nesi, P.: Temporal logics for real-time system specification. ACM Computing Surveys 32(1), 12–42 (2000)
2. Schockaert, S., De Cock, M., Kerre, E.E.: Fuzzifying Allen's temporal interval relations. IEEE Trans. on Fuzzy Systems 16(2), 517–533 (2008)
3. Furia, C., Mandrioli, D., Morzenti, A., Rossi, M.: Modeling time in computing: a taxonomy and a comparative survey. ACM Computing Surveys 42(2), Article 6 (2010)
4. Knight, B., Ma, J.: Time representation: a taxonomy of temporal models. Artificial Inteligence Review (7), 401–419 (1994)
5. Long, D.: A review of temporal logics. The Knowledge Engineering Review 4(2), 141–162 (1989)
6. Chitaro, L., Montanari, A.: Temporal representation and reasoning in artificial intelligence: issues and approaches. Annals of Mathematics and Artificial Intelligence 28, 47–106 (2000)
7. Bettini, C.: Time dependent concepts: representation and reasoning using temporal description logics. Data & Knowledge Engineering 22(1), 1–38 (1997)

8. Ma, J., Knight, B.: A general temporal theory. The Computer Journal 37(2), 114–123 (1996)
9. Ma, J., Knight, B.: Reified temporal logics: an overview. Artificial Intelligence Review 15, 189–217 (2001)
10. Ladkin, P.: Time representation: a taxonomy of interval relations. In: Proc. of the National Conference on Artificial Intelligence, Philadelphia, Pennsylvania, pp. 360–366 (1986)
11. Bouzid, M., Combi, C., Fisher, M., Ligozat, G.: Guest editorial: temporal representation and reasoning. Ann. Math. Artif. Intelligence 46, 231–234 (2006)
12. Vila, L.: A survey on temporal reasoning in artificial intelligence. AI Communications 7, 4–28 (1994)
13. Mani, I., Pustejovsky, J., Sundheim, B.: Introduction to the special issue on temporal information processing. ACM Trans. on Asian Language Information Processing 3(1), 1–10 (2004)
14. Allen, J.F.: An interval-based representation of temporal knowledge. In: Proc. of the 7th Int. Joint Conference on Artificial Intelligence (IJCAI-81), Vancouver, Canada, pp. 221–226 (1981)
15. Allen, J.F.: Maintaining knowledge about temporal intervals. Communications of the ACM 2(11), 832–843 (1983)
16. Allen, J.F.: Towards a general theory of action and time. Artificial Intelligence 23(2), 123–154 (1984)
17. Allen, J.F., Hayes, P.J.: A common-sense theory of time. In: Proc. of the 9th Int. Joint Conference on Artificial Intelligence (IJCAI 1985), pp. 528–531 (1985)
18. Hayes, P.J., Allen, J.F.: Short time periods. In: Proc. of the 10th Int. Joint Conference on Artificial Intelligence (IJCAI 1987), Milan, Italy, pp. 981–983 (1987)
19. Allen, J.F., Hayes, P.J.: Moments and points in an interval-based temporal logic. Computational Intelligence 5(4), 225–228 (1989)
20. Allen, J.F.: Time and time again: the many ways to represent time. International Journal of Intelligent Systems 4(5), 341–355 (1991)
21. Allen, J.F., Ferguson, G.: Actions and events in interval temporal logic. Journal of Logic and Computation, Special issue on actions and processes 4(5) (1994)
22. Trudel, A.: Representing Allen's properties, events, and processes. Applied Intelligence 6, 59–65 (1996)
23. Freksa, C.: Temporal reasoning based on semi-intervals. Artificial Intelligence 5(1-2), 199–227 (1992)
24. Quinlan, J.R.: Learning logical definitions from relations. Machine Learning 5, 239–266 (1990)
25. Cameron-Jones, R.M., Quinlan, J.R.: Efficient top-down induction of logic programs. SIGART 5, 33–42 (1994)
26. Muggleton, S.: Inductive logic programming: issues, results and the challenge of learning language in logic. Artificial Intelligence 114, 283–296 (1999)
27. Quinlan, J.R., Cameron-Jones, R.M.: FOIL: A midterm report. In: Proc. of the European Conference on Machine Learning, pp. 3–20 (1993)
28. Galton, A.: A critical examination of Allen's theory of action and time. Artificial Intelligence 42, 159–188 (1990)
29. Nebel, B., Bürckert, H.-J.: Reasoning about temporal relations: a maximal tractable subclass of Allen's interval algebra. Journal of the ACM 42(1), 43–66 (1995)
30. Lee, Y.J., Lee, J.W., Chai, D.J., Hwang, B.H., Ryu, K.H.: Mining temporal interval relational rules from temporal data. Journal of Systems and Software 82(1), 155–167 (2009)

Power Spectral Density Technique for Fault Diagnosis of an Electromotor

Hojjat Ahmadi[*] and Zeinab Khaksar

University of Tehran
Iran
hjahmadi@ut.ac.ir

Abstract. Developing a special method for maintenance of electrical equipments of industrial company is necessary for improving maintenance quality and reducing operating costs. The combination of corrective preventative and condition based maintenance will require applying for critical equipments of industrial company. This type of maintenance policy and strategy will improve performance of this equipment through availability of industrial equipment. Many vibration environments are not related to a specific driving frequency and may have input from multiple sources which may not be harmonically related. Examples may be excitation from turbulent flow as in air flow over a wing or past a car body, or acoustic input from jet engine exhaust, wheels running over a road, etc. With these types of vibration, it may be more accurate, or of more interest to analyze and test using random vibration. In this research we were calculated RMS and PSD (Power Spectral Density) of an electromotor in different faults situation. We were calculated Grms and PSD for different faults. The results showed that different faults were showed different PSD vs. frequency. The results showed that with calculating PSD we could find some fault and diagnosis of electromotor as soon as possible.

1 Introduction

It has been known for many years that the mechanical integrity of a machine can be evaluated by detailed analysis of the vibratory motion [1]. Vibration signals carry information about exciting forces and the structural path through which they propagate to vibration transducers. A machine generates vibrations of specific 'color' when in a healthy state and the degradation of a component within it my result in a change in the character of the vibration signals [2]. Machine condition monitoring has long been accepted as one of the most effective and cost-efficient approaches to avoid catastrophic failures of machines. It has been known for many years that the mechanical integrity of a machine can be evaluated by detailed analysis of the vibratory motion [3]. In this research, density data produced by vibration analysis was compared with previous data. Numerical data produced by power spectral density were compared with power spectral density in healthy electromotor, in order to quantify the effectiveness of the power spectral density technique [4, 5, and 6].

We were calculated Grms and PSD (Power Spectral Density) of an electromotor in different situation and different faults. The results showed that different faults were

---

* Corresponding author.

E.R. Hruschka Junior et al. (Eds.): INTECH 2011, CCIS 165, pp. 105–112, 2011.
© Springer-Verlag Berlin Heidelberg 2011

showed different power spectral density carves vs. frequency [7-6]. The results showed that with calculating power spectral density, we could diagnosis electromotor fault very fast. It was shown that power spectral density provides a good and rapid method to show faults of electromotor. The results of this paper were given more understanding on the dependent roles of vibration analysis and power spectral density carve in predicting and diagnosing of an electromotor faults. The objective of this research was to investigate the correlation between vibration analysis, power spectral density (PSD) and fault diagnosis.

2 Power Spectral Density (PSD)

Vibration analysis in particular has for some time been used as a predictive maintenance procedure and as a support for machinery maintenance decisions [8-18]. Condition monitoring is a valuable preventative maintenance tool to extend the operating life of an electromotor. Between of the techniques available, vibration monitoring is the most widely used technique in industry today.

Many vibration environments are not related to a specific frequency and may have input from multiple sources which may not be harmonically related. Examples may be excitation from turbulent flow as in air flow over a wing or past a car body, or acoustic input from jet engine exhaust, wheels running over a road, etc. With these types of vibration, it may be more accurate, or of more interest to analyze and test using random vibration [5, 6].

Unlike sinusoidal vibration, acceleration, velocity and displacement are not directly related by any specific frequency. Of primary concern in random testing is the complete spectral content of the vibration being measured or generated. Most random vibration testing is conducted using Gaussian random suppositions for both measurement and specification purposes. With Gaussian assumptions, there is no definable maximum amplitude, and the amplitude levels are measured in RMS (root-mean-squared) values [5, 6].

Random vibration can be thought of as containing excitation at all frequencies within the specified frequency band but no excitation at any specific single frequency [5, 6]. An acceleration spectrum is normally specified in terms of its' acceleration density using the units of g^2 per Hz. Acceleration density is defined as [5, 6]:

$$g_d = \lim{}^{a^2} / \Delta f \qquad\qquad \Delta f \geq 0$$

Where:
g_d=acceleration density
a = rms acceleration
Δf =bandwidth

A plot of the acceleration density for each component frequency verses frequency gives a curve of g^2/Hz over the frequency spectrum of interest. This curve is known as the PSD or Power Spectral Density curve. The PSD curve is the normal method used to describe random vibration specifications. Since the PSD curve is a plot of acceleration density, the overall rms acceleration can be found by summation of the density over frequency [5, 6].

$$g_{rms}^{2} = \sum_{f_1}^{f_2} g_d \Delta f \Rightarrow$$

$$g_{rms} = [\int_{f_1}^{f_2} g(f)df]^{\frac{1}{2}}$$

Where
g_{rms}=overall acceleration
f_1 and f_2=band frequencies

If a random specification calls for a flat PSD curve, the overall acceleration level is easily calculated from the following equation [5, 6].

$$g_{rms} = [(f_2 - f_1)g_d]^{\frac{1}{2}}$$

Bands of spectra with non-flat, but straight line (log-log), acceleration density characteristics can substitute the following equation for overall acceleration [5, 6].

$$g_{rms} = [(\frac{g_1}{f_1^{s}}) \frac{f_2^{s+1} - f_1^{s+1}}{s+1}]^{\frac{1}{2}}$$

Where g_1 and g_2= band limit levels

$$s = \log(g_2 / g_1) / \log(f_2 / f_1)$$

Bands of different acceleration density can be added as the areas under the PSD curve as follows [5, 6]:

$$g_{rms} = [(f_{21} - f_{11})g_{d1} + (f_{22} - f_{12})g_{d2} + ...]^{\frac{1}{2}}$$

3 Experimentation and Testing

The test rig used for the experimentation was an electromotor. The rig design incorporated an unbalance, a coupling disk system to impose shaft misalignment, and looseness. Electromotor was running under different faults. The coupling discs system was used to create an angular misalignment. The power of electromotor was 30 KW, three phase, variable speed.

Vibration data were collected on a regular basis after the run in period. The experimental procedure for the vibration analysis consisted of taking vibration readings at two select locations over the electromotor. There were taken on the drive end (DE) and non-drive end (NDE) of electromotor. Vibration measurements were taken on the DE and NDE of electromotor using an Easy -Viber (VMI was the manufacturer).

A coupling disc system was designed to impose shaft misalignment. The coupling system consisted of two discs: one attached to a short driven shaft and the other one attached to a longer shaft. This system was enabling us to considerable angular misalignment on the support bearing by moving the discs apart. The disks were moved relative to each other by tightening or loosening a grub screw, which pushes onto a key. The base screws of electromotor were loosed for losing the electromotor and we made unbalance our electromotor for unbalancing test.

It is very easy to describe the Grms (root-mean-square acceleration) value as just the square root of the area under the PSD vs. frequency curve, which it is. But to physically interpret this value we need to look at Grms a different way. The easiest way to think of the Grms is to first look at the mean square acceleration. Mean-square acceleration is the average of the square of the acceleration over time. Using the mean square value keeps everything positive. We were calculated the root-mean-square acceleration (Grms) response from a random vibration PSD curve. We were fixed our electromotor on different faults and measured the overall vibration of electromotor on that situation and calculated Grms and PSD (Power Spectral Density) of an electromotor in different situation and different faults. The results showed that different faults were showed different power spectral density carves vs. frequency [7-6].

4 Results and Discussion

Figures 1 until 4 showed frequency spectrum result of DE of electromotor in healthy, misalign, unbalance, and looseness, respectively.

The frequency spectrum of each fault was different and overall vibration values also were different at the same frequency.

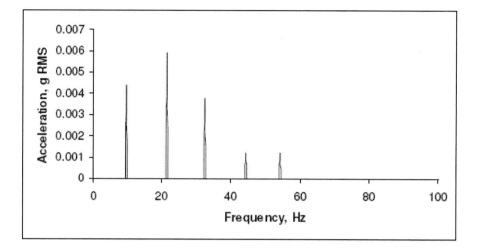

Fig. 1. Frequency spectrum result of DE of electromotor on healthy situation

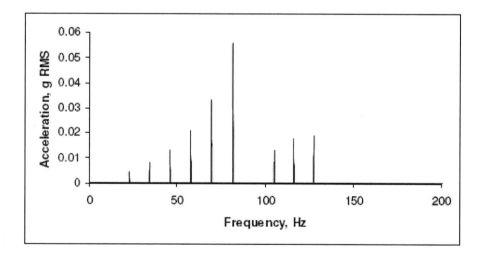

Fig. 2. Frequency spectrum result of DE of electromotor on misalign situation

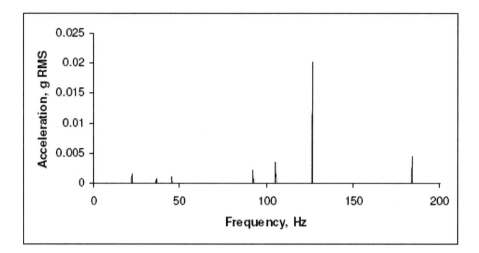

Fig. 3. Frequency spectrum result of DE of electromotor on unbalance situation

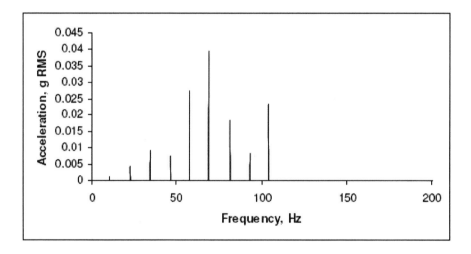

Fig. 4. Frequency spectrum result of DE of electromotor on looseness situation

The results showed that area under Power Spectral Density carves were indicated a problem. The more area below Power Spectral Density curve showed the faults were deeper. Figure 5 showed the power spectral density of DE of electromotor in different situation. There was big different between PSD of looseness fault and other faults.

The results showed that different faults were showed different PSD vs. frequency. The results showed that with calculating PSD we could find some fault and diagnosis of electromotor as soon as possible. Results showed that when we had deeper faults such as looseness the area under PSD carves was grown.

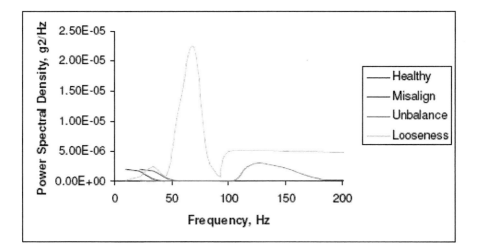

Fig. 5. Power Spectral Density result of electromotor on healthy, misalign, unbalance and looseness situations

5 Conclusions

Results showed that vibration condition monitoring and Power Spectral Density technique could detect fault diagnosis of electromotor. Vibration analysis and Power Spectral Density could provide quick and reliable information on the condition of the electromotor on different faults. Integration of vibration condition monitoring technique with Power Spectral Density analyze could indicate more understanding about diagnosis of electromotor.

Acknowledgment

Author has especially tanks for Sange Ahan Bafgh and Company University of Tehran about its concentration during this research.

References

1. Eisenmann, R.C.S.: Machinery Malfunction Diagnosis and Correction. Prentice-Hall, Englewood Cliffs (1998)
2. Williams, J.H., et al.: Condition-Based Maintenance and Machine Diagnostics. Chapman and Hall, Boca Raton (1994)
3. Eisenmann, R.C.S.: Machinery malfunction diagnosis and correction. Prentice Hall, Englewood Cliffs (1998)
4. Wowk, V.: Machinery vibration: Measurement and analysis. McGraw-Hill Inc, New York (1991)
5. http://www.labworksinc.com/enginfo/random_vib_test.htm
6. http://analyst.gsfc.nasa.gov/FEMCI/random/randomgrms.html

7. Peng, Z., Kessissoglou, N.J.: An integrated approach to fault diagnosis of machinery using wear debris and vibration analysis. Wear 255, 1221–1232 (2003)
8. Eisenmann, R.C.S.: Machinery Malfunction Diagnosis and Correction. Prentice-Hall, Englewood Cliffs (1998)
9. Barron, T.: Engineering condition monitoring. Addison-Wesley Longman, Amsterdam (1996)
10. Want, W.J., McFadden, P.D.: Application of wavelets to gearbox vibration signals for fault detection. J. Sound Vib. 192, 927–939 (1996)
11. Luo, G.Y., Osypiw, D., Irle, M.: Real-time condition monitoring by significant and natural frequencies analysis of vibration signal with wavelet filter and autocorrelation enhancement. J. Sound Vib. 236, 413–430 (2000)
12. Smith, J.D.: Vibration measurement and analysis. Butterworth & Co. Ltd (1989)
13. Barron, T.: Engineering Condition Monitoring. Addison-Wesley Longman, Amsterdam (1996)
14. Want, W.J., McFadden, P.D.: Application of wavelets to gearbox vibration signals for fault detection. J. Sound Vib. 192, 927–939 (1996)
15. Luo, G.Y., Osypiw, D., Irle, M.: Real-time condition monitoring by significant and natural frequencies analysis of vibration signal with wavelet filter and autocorrelation enhancement. J. Sound Vib. 236, 413–430 (2000)
16. Smith, J.D.: Vibration Measurement and Analysis. Butterworth & Co. Ltd (1989)
17. Wowk, V.: Machinery Vibration: Measurement and Analysis. McGraw-Hill Inc, New York (1991)
18. Peng, Z., Kessissoglou, N.J.: An integrated approach to fault diagnosis of machinery using wear debris and vibration analysis. Wear 255, 1221–1232 (2003)

Efficient ID-Based Multi-proxy Signature Scheme from Bilinear Pairing Based on *k-plus* Problem

Shivendu Mishra[1], Rajeev Anand Sahu[2],
Sahadeo Padhye[2], and Rama Shankar Yadav[1]

[1] Department of Computer Science and Engineering
[2] Department of Mathematics
Motilal Nehru National Institute of Technology
Allahabad-211004, India
2009is17@gmail.com, rajeevs1729@gmail.com,
sahadeomathrsu@gmail.com, rsy@mnnit.ac.in

Abstract. Proxy signatures are efficient alternatives to delegate the signing rights. In a proxy signature scheme, the original signer can delegate its signing rights to any other party, to make signature on its behalf. In a multi-proxy signature scheme, the original signer delegates its signing rights to a group of persons called proxy groups. With the exploit of bilinear pairing over elliptic curves, several ID-based multi-proxy signature schemes have been developed till now [5,9,17]. In this paper, we have proposed an ID-based multi-proxy signature, based on '*k-plus* problem'. The proposed scheme is secure under the INV-CDHP assumption. Moreover, our scheme is computationally more efficient than the schemes [5,9] and assure all the security requirements of a proxy signature, given in [11].

Keywords: ID-based signature, multi-proxy signature, bilinear pairing, *k-plus* problem, INV-CDHP.

1 Introduction

In traditional public key cryptography, when users want to communicate a message, they first obtain the authenticated public key from certificate authority. In that system, the problem is to maintain certificates of users, storage space and large overhead to transfer certificates that leads to increase the assosiated cost significantly. In 1984, Shamir [16] introduced the ID-based cryptography, that removes the need of certificate for public key and thus reduces the cost assosiated to the certificates. In ID-based cryptography, the users public and private keys are generated from their identities such as email address, IP-address etc.

Bilinear pairings are very efficient tools to make the computation easy and to reduce the assosiated costs. Boneh and Franklin [1] put forward the first secure and practical ID-based encryption scheme, using bilinear pairing. Since then many ID-based encryption and signature schemes from bilinear pairing

E.R. Hruschka Junior et al. (Eds.): INTECH 2011, CCIS 165, pp. 113–122, 2011.

have been proposed [2,4,6]. In 1996, Mambo *et al.* [12] proposed the first proxy signature scheme. In a proxy signature scheme, an original signer is authorized to delegate the signing rigths to any other user, called proxy signer. The concept of proxy signature is very much applicable when the original signer is absent to sign any document. The proxy signature scheme introduces, other additions also, such as multi-proxy signature, proxy multi-signature, multi-proxy multi-signature, threshold proxy signature etc. In 2005, Lee *et al.* [11] proposed the security requirements of a proxy signature.

In 2000, the first scheme of multi-proxy signature was introduced by S. Hwang and C. Chen. [7]. In a multi-proxy signature, the final signature is made by the group of proxy signers on behalf of the original signer, who delegates his signing rights to the proxy group. Their scheme [7] leads to many multi-proxy signature schemes [5,9,10].

1.1   Our Contribution

In 2005, Takeshi *et al* [13] suggested the '*k-plus*' and 'extended '*k-plus*' problems using bilinear pairing. In [13], they proposed a short signature scheme based on '*k*-plus problem' and a proxy signature scheme based on 'extended *k*-plus problem'. Security of their schemes depends on '*k-plus* problem' under the INV-CDHP assumption. In this paper, we have proposed an ID-based multi-proxy signature scheme, based on '*k-plus* problem' using the idea of Takeshi *et al* [13]. Our scheme is computationally more efficient than [5,9] and satisfies all security requirements of a proxy signature.

1.2   Roadmap

The rest of this paper is structured as follows. In Section 2, we describe some preliminaries. Security requirements of a proxy signature is described in Section 3. Our proposed scheme is depict in Section 4. Section 5 investigates the security and efficiency analysis of our scheme and finally Section 6 concludes the paper.

2   Preliminaries

In this section, we briefly describe the bilinear pairing and some related mathematical problems.

2.1   Bilinear Pairing

Let G_1 and G_2 be two groups of prime order q. Then a map $e : G_1 \times G_1 \to G_2$ satisfying the following properties, is called bilinear pairing:

(a)Bilinear: $e(aP, bQ) = e(P, Q)^{ab}$, for all a,b $\in Z_q$ and $P, Q \in G_1$.
(b)Non-Degeneracy: Existence of $P, Q \in G_1$ such that $e(P, Q) \neq 1$.
(c)Computability: There must exist an efficient algorithm to compute $e(P, Q)$ for any $P, Q \in G_1$.

2.2   Discrete Logarithm Problem (DLP)

For given two elements $P, Q \in G_1$, to compute an integer $n \in Z_q$, such that $P = nQ$.

2.3   Computational Diffie-Hellman Problem(CDHP)

For given $P, aP, bP \in G_1$, to compute $abP \in G_1$, where $a, b \in Z_q$.

2.4   Inverse Computational Diffie-Hellman Problem (INV-CDHP)

Given $P, aP \in G_1$, to compute $a^{-1}p \in G_1$, where $a \in Z_q$.

2.5   Bilinear Inversion Problem (BIP)

Given $P \in G_1$, and $e(P, Q) \in G_2$, to find $Q \in G_1$.

2.6   k-Plus Problem

For given $P, Pub = sP \in G_1, V = g^e \in G_2, e_1, e_2....e_k \in Z_q$, $\{\frac{e+e_1}{s}P, \frac{e+e_2}{s}P, ...\frac{e+e_k}{s}P\} \in G_1$, To find a pair $\{e', \frac{e+e'}{s}P\}$, where $e', e, s \in Z_q$, $e' \notin \{e_1, e_2....e_k\}$ and k is a constant number.

3   Security Requirements for Proxy Signature

A safe and sound proxy signature should satisfy the following security requirements [11]:

3.1   Strong Unforgeability

Only the legal proxy signer can generate a valid proxy signature on behalf of original signer. Even the original signer cannot make proxy signature.

3.2   Verifiability

Signature can be verified by anyone, and delegation warrant should be confirmed by the signed message.

3.3   Strong Identifiability

Identity of corresponding proxy signer can be determined by anyone.

3.4   Strong Undeniability

The proxy signer cannot deny his signature, which he generates ever.

3.5   Prevention of Misuse

The proxy signer should be unable to sign any unauthorized message.

4   Proposed Scheme

In this section, we describe our proposed ID-based multi-proxy signature scheme. In our scheme, the delegation security depends on the 'k-plus problem' and security of the partial signature generation depends on the combination of 'k-plus problem' and INV-CDHP. Our scheme is designed into five phases: System setup, Extraction, Proxy key generation, Multi-proxy signature and Verification.

4.1   System Setup

PKG generates the system's public parameters $prams = (K, G_1, G_2, q, e, H, H_1, P, g, Pub)$, where K is given security parameter, G_1 and G_2 are groups with prime order q, bilinear map $e : G_1 \times G_1 \to G_2$ is defined as above. $H : \{0,1\}^* \to Z_q$ and $H_1 : \{0,1\}^* \times G_2 \to Z_q$ are two hash functions for the security purpose. P is a generator of G_1, $g = e(p, p)$ is generator of G_2. System's public key is $Pub = sP \in G_1$, and $s \in Z_q$ is system's master key. PKG publishes the $params$ and keeps the master-key s secret.

4.2   Extraction

For given identity ID, the PKG computes public key and private key as follows

Public key: $Q_{ID} = H(ID)$
Private Key: $S_{ID} = \frac{Q_{ID}}{s}P$, where $P \in G_1$ is generator of G_1.

Thus the original signer (say A), has his public key Q_{ID_A}, and consequent private key S_{ID_A}. Similarily, for the l proxy signers, the public key is $Q_{ID_{P_i}}$ and consequent private key is $S_{ID_{P_i}}$ (for $1 \le i \le l$).

4.3   Proxy Key Generation

Through the signing warrant w, the original signer A delegates the signing capability to the l proxy signers in proxy group. The warrant w includes the delegation time, identity of original and proxy signers etc. Following is the process of delegation of warrant and proxy key generation.

Warrant Delegation: The original signer A randomly choses $r_A \in Z_q$ and computes

$V_A = g^{r_A}$,
$h = H(w)$ and
$S_A = (r_A + h)S_{ID_A}$,

then sends (S_A, V_A, w) to each proxy signer as a delegation value.

Each proxy signer P_i for $1 \leq i \leq l$, accepts the delegation value S_A on warrant w, if the equality

$$e(Pub, S_A) = (V_A.g^h)^{Q_{IDA}} \text{ holds.}$$

Finally, each proxy signer generates their proxy key as

$$d_{P_i} = S_A + S_{ID_{P_i}}, \text{ (for } 1 \leq i \leq l).$$

4.4 Multi-proxy Signature

Each proxy signer in proxy group, generates his partial proxy signature on message m that verifies the warrant w. One proxy signer in the proxy group is assigned as a clerk, whose task is to combine all the partial proxy signatures to generate the final multi-proxy signature. For that, each proxy signer P_i for $1 \leq i \leq l$
chooses randomly $r_i \in Z_q$ and
computes $V_i = g^{r_i Q_{ID_{P_i}}}$
then broadcasts their V_i to the other $(l-1)$ proxy signers.

Each P_i then computes

$$V_P = \Pi_{i=1}^l V_i$$
$$h' = H_1(m, V_P), \text{ and}$$
$$S_{P_i} = h'd_{P_i} + r_i S_{ID_{P_i}}$$

where m is the intended message. The partial proxy signature on message m is: (S_{P_i}, V_P). Each proxy signer P_i sends their partial proxy signatures to the clerk in proxy group.

Receiving the partial proxy signatures (S_{P_i}, V_P), for $1 \leq i \leq l$, the clerk verifies them checking whether the equality $e(Pub, S_{P_i}) = V_A^{h'Q_{IDA}}.g^{h'[hQ_{IDA}+Q_{ID_{P_i}}]}.V_i$
holds or not.

Once if all the partial proxy signatures are verified correct by the clerk, he finally generates the multi-proxy signature on message m as $(\mathbf{S_P, V_P, V_A, w})$.
Where $S_P = \sum_{i=1}^l S_{P_i}$

4.5 Verification

Getting a multi-proxy signature (S_P, V_P, V_A, w) and message m, the verifier proceeds as follows

(1) Checks whether or not the message m validates to the warrant w. If not, stop, continue otherwise
(2) Checks the authorization of l proxy signers by original signer in the warrant w. Stop the verification, if all or any one is not authorized by the warrant. Continue otherwise.
(3) Agree to the multi-proxy signature on message m, if and only if the following equality holds

$e(\mathbf{Pub}, \mathbf{S_P}) = V_A{}^{lh'Q_{ID_A}} \cdot g^{h'[lhQ_{ID_A} + \sum_{i=1}^{l} Q_{ID_{P_i}}]} \cdot V_P.$

Where, $Q_{ID_A} = H(ID_A)$, $Q_{ID_{P_i}} = H(ID_{P_i})$, $h' = H_1(m, V_P)$ and $h = H(w)$.

5   Analysis of Proposed Scheme

In this section, we prove the correctness of verification and compare the efficiency of our scheme with those of [5,9]. We show that our scheme is computationally more efficient than [5,9]. We also prove that the proposed scheme gratify all the security requirements of a proxy signature given in [11]

5.1   Correctness

The property of correctness is satisfied as follows-

$$
\begin{aligned}
\mathbf{e(Pub, S_P)} &= \mathbf{e(Pub,} \sum_{i=1}^{l}(\mathbf{S_{P_i}}) \\
&= e(Pub, \sum_{i=1}^{l}[h'd_{P_i} + r_i S_{ID_{P_i}}]) \\
&= e(Pub, \sum_{i=1}^{l}[h'(S_A + S_{ID_{P_i}}) + r_i S_{ID_{P_i}}]) \\
&= e(Pub, \sum_{i=1}^{l}[h'S_A + h'S_{ID_{P_i}} + r_i S_{ID_{P_i}}]) \\
&= e(Pub, \sum_{i=1}^{l}[h'S_A + (h' + r_i)S_{ID_{P_i}}]) \\
&= e(Pub, \sum_{i=1}^{l} h'S_A)e(Pub, \sum_{i=1}^{l}(h' + r_i)S_{ID_{P_i}}) \\
&= e(Pub, S_A)^{\sum_{i=1}^{l} h'} e(Pub, \sum_{i=1}^{l}(h' + r_i)\frac{Q_{ID_{P_i}}}{s}P) \\
&= e(Pub, S_A)^{lh'} e(Pub, \frac{P}{s}\sum_{i=1}^{l}(h' + r_i)Q_{ID_{P_i}}) \\
&= e(sP, S_A)^{lh'} e(sP, \frac{P}{s}\sum_{i=1}^{l}(h' + r_i)Q_{ID_{P_i}}) \\
&= e(sP, (r_A + h)S_{ID_A})^{lh'} e(P, P\sum_{i=1}^{l}(h' + r_i)Q_{ID_{P_i}}) \\
&= e(sP, (r_A + h)\frac{Q_{ID_A}}{s}P)^{lh'} e(P, P\sum_{i=1}^{l}(h' + r_i)Q_{ID_{P_i}}) \\
&= e(sP, \frac{P}{s}(r_A + h)Q_{ID_A})^{lh'} e(P, P\sum_{i=1}^{l}(h' + r_i)Q_{ID_{P_i}}) \\
&= e(P, P)^{lh'(r_A + h)Q_{ID_A}} e(P, P)^{\sum_{i=1}^{l}(h' + r_i)Q_{ID_{P_i}}} \\
&= \{g^{r_A}g^h\}^{lh'Q_{ID_A}} g^{h'\sum_{i=1}^{l} Q_{ID_{P_i}}} \cdot g^{\sum_{i=1}^{l} r_i Q_{ID_{P_i}}} \\
&= \{V_A g^h\}^{lh'Q_{ID_A}} g^{h'\sum_{i=1}^{l} Q_{ID_{P_i}}} \cdot \Pi_{i=1}^{l} g^{r_i Q_{ID_{P_i}}} \\
&= V_A^{lh'Q_{ID_A}} \cdot g^{h'lhQ_{ID_A}} g^{h'\sum_{i=1}^{l} Q_{ID_{P_i}}} \cdot V_P \\
&= V_A^{lh'Q_{ID_A}} \cdot g^{h'[lhQ_{ID_A} + \sum_{i=1}^{l} Q_{ID_{P_i}}]} \cdot V_P
\end{aligned}
$$

5.2   Security Analysis

In this section, we examine the security properties of our scheme. We will show that all the security requirements of a proxy signature mentioned in section 2 [11] are satisfied by our scheme, as the security requirements given in [11] can be analyzed also for ID-based multi-proxy signature schemes [10].

(i) *Strong unforgeability:* **Theorem:** The proposed ID-based multi- proxy signature is unforgeable under the DLP and INV-CDHP assumptions, if the 'k-plus problem' is hard in G_1.

Proof: The attempt to forge the multiproxy signature, can be made by either of the three parties, (1) The original signer (2) Proxy signers, and (3) Any third party who never take part in the entire protocol.

1. The original signer: The original signer can not generate a valid multi-proxy signature, because to do this, he will need to get the private keys $S_{ID_{P_i}}$ of each proxy signer. But as $S_{ID_{P_i}} = \frac{Q_{ID_{P_i}}}{s}P$, the attacker will have to solve the INV-CDHP in G_1, which is assumed to be hard.

In other way if the original signer wants to generate a valid partial proxy signature S_{P_i}, he will have to compute $\frac{r_i+h'}{s}Q_{ID_{P_i}}P$ as

$$S_{P_i} = h'd_{P_i} + r_i S_{ID_{P_i}}$$
$$S_{P_i} = h'(S_A + S_{ID_{P_i}}) + r_i S_{ID_{P_i}}$$
$$S_{P_i} = h'S_A + (r_i + h')S_{ID_{P_i}}$$
$$S_{P_i} = h'S_A + [\frac{r_i+h'}{s}]Q_{ID_{P_i}}P.$$ But computing $[\frac{r_i+h'}{s}]Q_{ID_{P_i}}P$ is equivalent to soloving k-plus problem, which is assumed to be hard. Hence the original signer is unable to get any valid multi-proxy signature.

2. Proxy signers: Suppose, the clerk in proxy group wants to sign any unauthorized message, he can maximum change his V_i, that leads to change in V_P and finaly change in h'. Then he will try to compute $S_P \in G_1$, such that the equality $e(Pub, S_P) = V_A^{lh'Q_{IDA}} . g^{h'[lhQ_{IDA} + \sum_{i=1}^l Q_{IDP_i}]} . V_P$ holds. But this is equivalent to solve the BIP, which is is reducible to CDHP in G_2 and can be condensed to DLP in G_2. Now since DLP is intractable in G_2 according to assumptions, hence the clerk cannot generate a valid multi-proxy signature on any unauthorized message. In other way, if the clerk tries to get the partial proxy signatures on the false message, he will need to break the combination of 'k-plus problem' and INV-CDHP to find $d_{P_i} = S_A + S_{ID_{P_i}}$, because S_A is based on k-plus problem and $S_{ID_{P_i}}$ is based on INV-CDHP, which are hard to solve. So, the clerk in proxy group can not forge the proposed multi-proxy signature. Moreover, since all other proxy signers are less priviledged than the clerk in our scheme, hence no proxy signer can forge the signature.

3. Third party: Any third party can not forge the proposed multi proxy signature, even having signature of the original signer. Because to forge the signature, he will be required the private key of original signer, which is impossible to get due to the hardness of 'k-plus problem'.

Hence, it is proved that the proposed scheme is unforgeable.

(ii) Verifiability: The correctness of the verification is discussed above so any verifier can validate the signature and can check whether the signed message authenticate to the delegation warrant or not.

(iii) Identifiability: Through the attached warrant, any one can determine the identity of proxy signers and original signer.

(iv) Strong undeniability: No proxy signer in proxy group can refuse their signature, they made in earlier session because the clerk validates the entire partial proxy signature by checking $e(Pub, S_{P_i}) = V_A^{h'Q_{ID_A}} . g^{h'(hQ_{ID_A} + Q_{ID_{P_i}})} . V_i$.

(v) Prevention of misuse: Due to the warrant, the proxy signers cannot sign any message which does not validates to the warrant and has not been authorized by the original signer.

5.3   Efficiency Comparison

Here, we compare the efficiency of our scheme with those of multi-proxy signature scheme given in [5,9].

Proxy key generation:

Scheme	Pairing	Hashing	Exponentiation
Li and Chen's scheme (2005) [9]	3	2	1
Cao and Cao's scheme (2009) [5]	3	3	0
Our scheme	**1**	**2**	**3**

Multi-proxy signature generation:

Scheme	Pairing	Hashing	Exponentiation
Li and Chen's scheme (2005) [9]	3	1	1
Cao and Cao's scheme (2009) [5]	5	1	1
Our scheme	**1**	**1**	**3**

Verification:

Scheme	Pairing	Hashing	Exponentiation
Li and Chen's scheme (2005) [9]	3	4	1
Cao and Cao's scheme (2009) [5]	4	5	0
Our scheme	**1**	**4**	**2**

From the above comparison, it is clear that our scheme is computationally more efficient than those of schemes given in [5,9].

5.4   Advantage and Application

Previously some ID-based multi-proxy signature schemes have been proposed [5,9] whose security depends on CDHP. Here, our scheme generates a multi-proxy signature employing the *k-plus* problem which is supposed to be more strong than CDHP, as the hardness of *k-plus* problem depends on computation of two unknown integers whereas hardness of CDHP depends on computation of a single unknown integer. Hence, our scheme is supposed to be more secure and strong than others. The proposed signature scheme is also applicable in many real word scenarios as in distributed system, grid computing, mobile agent environments etc. In distributed system, where the delegation of right is common in practice, this scheme can be used to delegate the right of execution to the person sitting in a connected computer in a network. Also in commercial transitions, this scheme can be employed in grid computing by any agent who wish to transfer his rights to some other person. This scheme also enjoys application in global distributed networks and distributed shared object system. To implement the proposed scheme, one can employ the proposed signature algorithm in various open source tools like sage [15], PBC library (http://crypto.stanford.edu/pbc/) etc.

6   Conclusion

In this paper, we have proposed an ID-based multi-proxy signature scheme based on k-$plus$ problem. Security of our scheme is based on k-$plus$ problem under the INV-CDHP and DLP assumptions. Our scheme is computationally more efficient than other existing schemes [5,9]. More over our scheme also satisfies all the security requirements of a proxy signature mentioned in [11].

References

1. Boneh, D., Franklin, M.: Identity-based encryption from the weil pairing. In: Kilian, J. (ed.) CRYPTO 2001. LNCS, vol. 2139, pp. 213–229. Springer, Heidelberg (2001)
2. Barreto, P.S.L.M., Libert, B., McCullagh, N., Quisquater, J.-J.: Efficient and provably-secure identity-based signatures and signcryption from bilinear maps. In: Roy, B. (ed.) ASIACRYPT 2005. LNCS, vol. 3788, pp. 515–532. Springer, Heidelberg (2005)
3. Boneh, D., Lynn, B., Shacham, H.: Short signatures from the weil pairing. In: Boyd, C. (ed.) ASIACRYPT 2001. LNCS, vol. 2248, pp. 514–532. Springer, Heidelberg (2001)
4. Cha, J.C., Cheon, J.H.: An identity-based signature from gap diffie-hellman groups. In: Desmedt, Y.G. (ed.) PKC 2003. LNCS, vol. 2567, pp. 18–30. Springer, Heidelberg (2002)
5. Cao, F., Cao, Z.: A secure identity-based multi-proxy signature scheme. Computers and Electrical Engineering 35, 86–95 (2009)
6. Hesss, F.: Efficient identity based signature schemes based on pairings. In: Nyberg, K., Heys, H.M. (eds.) SAC 2002. LNCS, vol. 2595, pp. 310–324. Springer, Heidelberg (2003)
7. Hwang, S., Chen, C.: New multi-proxy multi-signature schemes. Appl. Math.Comput. 147, 57–67 (2004)
8. Hwang, S., Shi, C.: A simple multi-proxy signature scheme. In: Proceedings of the 10th national conference on information security, Hualien, Taiwan, ROC, pp. 134–138 (2000)
9. Li, X., Chen, K.: ID-based multi-proxy signature, proxy multi-signature and multi-proxy multi-signature schemes from bilinear pairings. Appl. Math. Comput (2005)

10. Li, X., Chen, K., Li, S.: Multi-proxy signature and proxy multi-signature schemes from bilinear pairings. In: Liew, K.-M., Shen, H., See, S., Cai, W. (eds.) PDCAT 2004. LNCS, vol. 3320, pp. 591–595. Springer, Heidelberg (2004)
11. Lee, B., Kim, H., Kim, K.: Strong proxy signature and its applications. In: Proceedings of SCIS, pp. 603–608 (2001)
12. Mambo, M., Usuda, K., Okmamoto, E.: Proxy signatures: delegation of the power to sign message. IEICE Transaction Functional E79-A (9), 1338–1354 (1996)
13. Okamoto, T., Inomata, A., Okamoto, E.: A Proposal of Short Proxy Signature using Pairing. In: International Conference on Information Technology: Coding and Computing (ITCC 2005), vol. I, pp. 631–635 (2005)
14. Paterson, K.G.: Id-based signatures from pairings on elliptic curves, Cryptology ePrint Archive, Report 2002/004 (2002)
15. Stein, W.: Sage: Open Source Mathematical Software (Version 3.2.3). The Sage Group (2009), http://www.sagemath.org
16. Shamir, A.: Identity-based cryptosystems and signature schemes. In: Blakely, G.R., Chaum, D. (eds.) CRYPTO 1984. LNCS, vol. 196, pp. 47–53. Springer, Heidelberg (1985)
17. Sahu, R.A., Padhye, S.: An ID-based multi-proxy signature scheme. In: Proc. of IEEE Intl. Conf. Comp. Cumm. Tech (ICCCT 2010), IEEE explore, pp. 60–63 (2010)
18. Yi, X.: An identity-based signature scheme from the Weil pairing. IEEE Communication Letters 7(2), 76–78 (2003)
19. Yi, L., Bai, G., Xiao, G.: Proxy multi-signature scheme: a new type of proxy signature scheme. Electronics Letters 36(6), 527–528 (2000)
20. Zhang, F., Kim, K.: Efficient ID-Based Blind Signature and Proxy Signature from Bilinear Pairing. In: Safavi-Naini, R., Seberry, J. (eds.) ACISP 2003. LNCS, vol. 2727, pp. 312–323. Springer, Heidelberg (2003)
21. Zhang, F., Safavi-Naini, R., Susilo, W.: An efficient signature scheme from bilinear pairings and its applications. In: Bao, F., Deng, R., Zhou, J. (eds.) PKC 2004. LNCS, vol. 2947, pp. 277–290. Springer, Heidelberg (2004)

Decision Tree Technique for Customer Retention in Retail Sector

Rose Tinabo

Dublin Institute of Technology, School of Computing,
Kevin Street, Dublin 6, Ireland
rose.tinabo@student.dit.ie
http://www.comp.dit.ie/website07/

Abstract. Currently, data mining techniques are used in different areas, and numerous commercial data systems are available. The retail industry is a major application area for data mining techniques, since it collects large amount of data on sales, customer shopping history, goods transportation, consumption, and service. The quantity of data collected continues to expand rapidly, especially due to the increased ease, availability, and popularity of business conducted on the Web, or e-commerce. Therefore, most effective data mining technique must be identified from large number of the available data mining techniques. This paper explores four potential data mining techniques to the problem of customer retention in the retail sector and propose decision tree to be the most effective technique. The decision is made by considering the use and features of the retail datasets, such as size which include number of instances and number of attributes.

Keywords: data mining, decision tree, retail sector, customer retention.

1 Introduction

Data mining applications can be used in a variety of sectors: finance, health, manufacturing, bank, consumer product sales, utilities and insurance [1]. Therefore, the benefits of data mining apply to any sector where there are large quantities of data about its customers, suppliers, products, or sales [2]. However, the retail sector is one of the sectors where the importance of data mining to improve their processes has been widely recognised with a large amount of evidence of the application of data mining techniques to a variety of problems [3].

The retail sector is any sector that sells goods and services directly to consumers, either in small quantities or to individual consumer who will not resell them, but who buy those for their own uses [2,4]. Data mining is important in any business not only in attracting new customers but most important is in keeping existing customers from moving to their competitors. In the retail sector, data mining can be used to understand interactions and relationships among the customers and organisations or to improve marketing campaigns by using the outcomes to provide customers with more focused support and attention [5]. In

E.R. Hruschka Junior et al. (Eds.): INTECH 2011, CCIS 165, pp. 123–131, 2011.

the retail business context, knowledge obtained by data mining can be valuable in three ways; it can increase profit by lowering cost or raising revenue, or it can increase the stock price by holding out the promise of future increased profit [6].

The cost of acquiring new customers is much higher than the cost of retaining existing customers; therefore companies are mostly focusing on customer retention [7,4]. Businesses have had to become more competitive due to slow down of market growth and saturation of various markets as a result of different developments such as globalization and internet widening market. If a business is facing a competitive market fails to retain its customers then their market share will begin to decline, as a result profit will quickly disappear and the company will not be able to maintain itself [8]. Therefore, data mining can be used effectively to increase market share by knowing who your most valuable customers are, defining their features and then using that profile to either retain them or target new, similar customers [9].

2   Customer Retention

Customer retention can be defined as the customer taste, identification, commitment, trust, and willingness to recommend and purchase intentions [11]. Customer retention is essential to any organisation as a slight improvement, as little as 5%, in the customer retention can lead to profit improvements ranging between 25 and 80 %, depending on the cost of achievement [12,13]. This is an indicator of the importance of the customer retention. The loss of one or two of these customers could potentially reduce the business and revenue dramatically [2].

Customer retention needs to be determined in terms of defection as well as in terms of retention [14]. There are various reasons for the customer to move from one business to another. Customer defection can be mainly due to the High price reasons; poor product and service reasons especially when there is elsewhere where they can get quality service or product, and lastly changing of technology may cause customer to shift from one business to another [15]. In general, firms or industries need to modify their definitions depending on what they offer or what type of customer base they have.

Customers are the reason for businesses to exist. Customers spend their money that make business profitable, if they are not treated well they will go elsewhere, as long as there are other options available, even if the product they are buying is of good quality [5]. However, customers can only be retained if they are loyal and motivated to resist competition. Therefore holding on to valuable customers is essential for a businesss survival [14]. Companies with high customer retention grow faster as customers purchase increase, guaranteed base profit from existing customers, and lower operating and achievement cost as the customers are already exist [14,16].

It is not only companies who benefit with customer retention but customers themselves benefit. With customer retention, risk and stress to customers is rescued, customers receive higher quality products and services as the company knows what the existing customers want, and customers will avoid switching costs [16]. Therefore, it makes sense for all businesses in the retail sector to invest in improved customer retention.

3   Benefits of Data Mining Techniques in Retail Sector

Data is constantly being generated and corrected as proven by Ahmed [1]: in 1989 the total number of databases was estimated to be at 5 millions and that figure was almost reaching 10 millions by 2004. Thus, data mining tools are used to perform data analysis to uncover important data patterns from these stored data, that contributing greatly to support in making business strategies, and knowledge-driven decision [17]. Retail sectors have different sources for generating and correcting data such as Credit card transactions, loyalty cards, discount coupons, and customer complaint calls as well as increase of interest for customers to purchase online. As such many web sites are generating billions of transaction data that can be easily used for data mining purposes.

Different techniques to maintain and improve customer satisfaction and relationship with customers (customer retention) must be considered as important to any organisation. Data mining is one of the effective tools that can be used to explore through large volume of data to find certain patterns or events which can support organisation to identify characteristics of the customers, and managers can use the information to predict the needs of customers to the future [6,1].

Data mining are used in different areas of retail sector for different purpose for example; products are arranged in a supermarket based on the buying trends and information about associations between products. Credits bureau uses observations of people with similar income, credit and buying patterns to make decision if someone should be granted loan or not. Business companies use data mining to analyse prescriptions to send different promotions to targeted customers only [18].

Data mining can also be used to improve relationship between the customers and the organisation. The closer the retailer can get to the customer the better they can provide the service that the customer seeks. As there are different customers with different needs, classifying customers in retail sectors is very important. Customers can be classified by using one or combination of the following: behaviour, demographics, benefits, and psychographics [5].

Retail sectors are mainly using classification techniques to discover characteristics of customers who are likely to leave and provide a model that can be used to predict who they are. It can also help to determine which kinds of promotions have been effective in keeping which types of customers, so that an organisation could spend only as much money as necessary to retain a customer [1].

Therefore, through the use of data mining, organisations can learn critical information about their customers, and organisations are able to identify market segments containing customers or prospects with high potential, since organisations can do what customers want before the customers knew themselves, this increase customer satisfaction and trusting which will results to customer retention.

4   Features of the Retail Data

To come-up with the proposed data mining technique for customer retention in retail sector a good understanding of the objectives and the features of the retail data was required. Through the literature review conducted as part of this research, the objectives, aims of doing data mining, and features of the retail data, especially size were identified.

The first considered factor is the objective of performing data mining activity. It is important to understand the reasons for retail sectors to perform data mining, so that any data mining technique proposed will be able to meet their objectives. Even though, retail sectors used data mining for prediction, discovery of data patterns, associations, and structure also for recognition of data similarities and differences organisations in the retail sector are mainly using data mining for classifying different behaviours of the customers in order to retain those customers [2].

Another factor considered is the features of the data available in retail sectors in terms of size that includes number of instances and number of attributes. Retail data consists of large number of instances of pairs of individuals and events. An example is a set of retail items purchased by a customer and grouped into a market basket. Thus, most of retail data are transactional data with the following mainly characteristics [18]:

- *Massive numbers of records.* Millions of transactions are generated and corrected by large retail businesses per day.
- *Sparseness.* A usual basket contains only a small fraction of the total possible number of items; individual customers may have few baskets, perhaps only one.
- *Heterogeneity.* Purchasing behavior varies considerably, depending on individual tastes and means, along with individual purchasing patterns over time.

Therefore, these factors, especially massive numbers of records, together with the characteristics of the data mining techniques was used to come-up with the proposed data mining technique for customer retention in retail sector as discussed in the following section.

5   Characteristics of the Existing Data Mining Techniques

Before recommending more appropriate data mining technique for customer retention in retail sector depending on the literature review, this sub-section assess what each technique can and cannot do and then recommend the data mining technique that might be more appropriate for customer retention in retail sector and lastly provide the reason for the recommended technique.

5.1   Neural Networks

Neural networks are networks of simple computational units operating in a parallel and highly interconnected way [19]. Safavian and Landgrebe defines neural network as simply an acyclic directed graph that consist of several layers of simple processing elements known as neurons [20]. Therefore in general neural networks are the systems composed of many simple processing elements operating in parallel whose function is determined by network structure, connection strengths, and the processing performed at computing elements or nodes.

Neural networks techniques are good in providing general overview of the data, they can handle problems with very many parameters, and they are able to classify objects well even when the distribution of objects in the N-dimensional parameter space is very complex.

Neural networks can produce very good predictions, but they are neither easy to use nor easy to understand. To be able to get good results from neural networks an extensive data preparation is required, but also, the results are difficult to understand because a neural network is a complex nonlinear model that does not produce rules.

Neural networks also, can not provide quicker results as they are extremely slow, not only in the training phase but also in the application phase. Another significant disadvantage of neural networks is that it is very difficult to determine how the net is making its decision (black box). Consequently, it is hard to determine which of the features being used are important and useful for description and which are worthless, as the choice of the best features is an important part for knowing behaviours of the customers, and neural nets do not give much help in this process.

5.2   K-Nearest Neighbour

The k-nearest neighbour (k-NN) technique is the simplest form of case based reasoning and it has been selected for this research as it has been effectively applied to a variety of real world classification problems [21]. It can be represented by the following rule: to classify an unknown pattern, choose the class of nearest example in the training set as measured by a distance metric. A common extension is to choose the most common class in the k-nearest neighbors (k-NN).

k-NN techniques has the advantage that, they are easy to understand. They can also give quite good results if the features are chosen carefully (and if they are weighted carefully in the computation of the distance.)

There are several serious problems of the nearest-neighbour techniques. First, like the neural networks, they do not simplify the distribution of objects in parameter space to a clear set of parameters. Instead, the training set is retained in its entirety as a description of the object distribution. The method is also rather slow if the training set has many examples, as retail data. The most serious shortcoming of nearest neighbour techniques is that they are very sensitive to the presence of irrelevant parameters. Adding a single parameter that has a random value for all objects can cause these techniques to fail miserably.

5.3   Nave Bayes

Nave Bayes is one of the simplest and effective techniques for classification problem and is based on the so called Bayesian theorem. In this theorem, the final classification is produced by combining both sources of information, that is, prior probabilities for class membership and the likelihood (chances), to form a posterior probability using so called Bayes rule (named after Rev. Thomas Bayes 1702-1761) [22].

Nave Bayes is a simple technique which results in high accuracy, especially when combined with other methods. They are mostly suited in high dimensionality of the inputs, as data available in retail sector. The Naive Bayes techniques afford fast, highly scalable model building and scoring. It scales linearly with the number of predictors and rows. Naive Bayes can be used for both binary and multi-class classification problems.

The main problem of Nave Bayes is its strongly unrealistic assumption that all attributes are independent of each other given the background of the class and all other variables are directly dependent on the classification variable assumes that attributes are independent given the class which is almost always wrong in most of the real-world tasks.

5.4   Decision Tree

A decision tree is a repeated and special form of tree structure for expressing classification rules. In these tree structures, a leaf is associated with one class or the tree may consist of a test that has a set of mutually exclusive possible outcome together with a subsidiary decision tree for each such outcome [23]. Decision tree can be complex depending on the features that an organisation wants to analyse. To reduce the problem of complexity, smaller trees are more preferred because they are easier to understand and may also have higher predictive accuracy [22].

Main advantage of decision tree technique is their ability to provide enough description of the data; mostly it is possible to pick the most important variables for predicting particular outcome because these variables are chosen for splitting high in the tree. Decision tree are usually much faster in the construction (training) phase than neural network techniques, and they also tend to be faster during the application phase.

Their disadvantage is that they are not as flexible at modelling parameter space distributions having complex distributions as either neural networks or nearest neighbour techniques. In fact, even simple shapes can cause these techniques difficulties. Also, since every split in decision tree is a test on a single variable, decision tree can never discover rules that involve a relationship between variables. This adds responsibility on the miner to add derived variables to express relationships that are likely to be important.

6   Experiment Design and Results

The experiments start by downloading datasets from UCI datasets repository and then loading them from a file to the RapidMiner analysis software tool.The experiments were done by assessing the four data mining techniques: decision tree, neural network, nearest neighbour and nave Bayes. The techniques were applied independently to six different size datasets (as summarised in Table 1). As retail data have massive number of instances, the results of the datasets with large number of instances, the first three, were most considered.

Performance was measured using four evaluation metrics including predictive accuracy, precision, recall and area under the ROC curve, or simply AUC. Figure 1 shows the results for predictive accuracy of the four techniques on the six different datasets. All four evaluation metrics has the output as shown in figure 1 but due to space limit cannot be presented all in this paper.

Results for decision tree technique were high in almost all four evaluation metrics, therefore the author propose it to be the most appropriate technique for customer retention. The decision tree technique can support the organisation to gain insights into customer identification such as customers purchasing behaviours, which will support managers in decision making for customer retention. Therefore, effective application of the decision tree technique for customer retention actions can be the key to eventual retain customers.

Table 1. Features of the Used Datasets

Dataset	Number of Instances:	Number of attributes:	Dataset Characteristics	Attributes characteristics
Mushroom	8124	22	Multivariate	Categorical, Integer
Chess	3196	36	Multivariate	Categorical
Germany Credit	1000	20	Multivariate	Categorical, Integer
Breast Cancer	569	32	Multivariate	Real
Congressional voting record	435	16	Multivariate	Categorical
Japanese	125	16	Multivariate, Domain-Theory	Categorical, Real, Integer

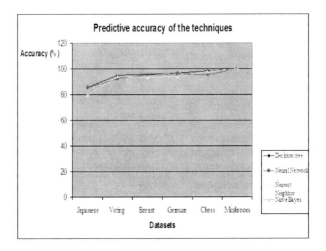

Fig. 1. Predictive accuracy of the four data mining techniques on the six different datasets

7   Conclusion

This paper explores four potential data mining techniques to the problem of customer retention in the retail sector and propose decision tree to be the most effective technique.The decision tree technique proposed to be used in retail sectors for customer retention based on the general characteristics of the retail dataset such as size, and objective of doing data mining in retail sectors. These characteristics are mainly for describing customers behaviours so that organisation can be able to use the descriptions obtained to make decision on how they can retain the customers.

To some extent generalisations may not be made for all other datasets as performance of the techniques depends also to other characteristics not only size. Also, in order to get a more accurate proposed data mining technique, the experiments could be done on the exactly retail dataset, but this was not possible as it is difficult to get free retail datasets that consists of behavioural information at the level of the individual customer. But organisations with specific retail dataset could use that specific datasets to prove the more appropriate data mining technique for customer retention.

References

1. Ahmed, S.R.: Applications of data mining in retail business. In: Proceedings Information Technology: Coding and Computing, ITCC 2004, pp. 455–459. IEEE press, Los Alamitos (2004)
2. Berry, M., Linoff, G.: Mastering data mining: The art and science of customer relationship management. John Wiley & Sons, Inc, New York (1999)

3. Chen, Y., Hu, L.: Study on data mining application in CRM system based on insurance trade. In: Proceedings of the 7th International Conference on Electronic Commerce, pp. 839–841. ACM, New York (2005)
4. Rud, O.C.: Data Mining, Cookbook: Modeling Data for Marketing, Risk and Customer Relationship Management. John Wiley & Sons, Inc, New York (2001)
5. Buckinx, W., Van den Poel, D.: Customer base analysis: partial defection of behaviourally loyal clients in a non-contractual FMCG retail setting. European Journal of Operational Research 164, 252–268 (2005)
6. Berry, M., Linoff, G.: Data mining techniques: for marketing, sales, and customer support. John Wiley & Sons, Inc, New York (1997)
7. Reinartz, W.J., Kumar, V.: On the profitability of long-life customers in a noncontractual setting: An empirical investigation and implications for marketing. The Journal of Marketing 64, 17–35 (2000)
8. Lambert, D., Pinheiro, J.C.: Mining a stream of transactions for customer patterns. In: Proceedings of the Seventh ACM SIGKDD International Conference on Knowledge Discovery and Data Mining, p. 310. ACM, New York (2001)
9. Dhond, A., Gupta, A., Vadhavkar, S.: Data mining techniques for optimizing inventories for electronic commerce. In: Proceedings of the Sixth ACM SIGKDD International Conference on Knowledge Discovery and Data Mining, pp. 480–486. ACM, New York (2000)
10. Perlich, C., Provost, F., Simonoff, J.S.: Tree induction vs. logistic regression: a learning-curve analysis. The Journal of Machine Learning Research 4, 211–255 (2003)
11. Stauss, B., Chojnacki, K., Decker, A., Hoffmann, F.: Retention effects of a customer club. International Journal of Service Industry Management 12, 7–19 (2001)
12. Reichheld, F.F.: Learning from customer defections. Harvard Business Review 74, 56–70 (1996)
13. Zhang, G.: Customer Retention Based on BP ANN and Survival Analysis. In: International Conference on Wireless Communications, Networking and Mobile Computing, WiCom2007, pp. 3406–3411. IEEE, Los Alamitos (2007)
14. Ahmad, R., Buttle, F.: Customer retention: a potentially potent marketing management strategy. Journal of Strategic Marketing 9, 29–45 (2001)
15. DeSouza, G.: Designing a customer retention plan. Journal of Business Strategy 13, 24–28 (1993)
16. Jobber, D.: Principles and practice of marketing. McGraw-Hill, Maidenhead (1995)
17. Fayyad, U., Piatetsky-Shapiro, G., Smyth, P.: From data mining to knowledge discovery in databases. AI magazine 17, 37 (1996)
18. Apte, C., Liu, B., Pednault, E.P.D., Smyth, P.: Business applications of data mining. Communications of the ACM 45, 49–53 (2002)
19. Lippmann, R.P.: An introduction to computing with neural nets. ARIEL 2009, 115–245 (1987)
20. Safavian, S.R., Landgrebe, D.: A survey of decision tree classifier methodology. IEEE Transactions on Systems, Man and Cybernetics 21, 660–674 (2002)
21. Van Der Merwe, N., Hoffman, A.J.: Developing an efficient cross validation strategy to determine classifier performance (CVCP). In: Proceedings International Joint Conference on Neural Networks, IJCNN 2001, vol. 3, pp. 1663–1668 (2002)
22. Amor, N.B., Benferhat, S., Elouedi, Z.: Naive bayes vs decision trees in intrusion detection systems. In: Proceedings of the 2004 ACM symposium on Applied computing, pp. 420–424. ACM, New York (2004)
23. Quinlan, J.R.: Simplifying decision trees. International Journal of Man-Machine Studies 27, 221–234 (1987)

Separation between Arabic and Latin Scripts from Bilingual Text Using Structural Features

Sofiene Haboubi, Samia Snoussi Maddouri, and Hamid Amiri

System and Signal Processing Laboratory,
National Engineering School of Tunis,
BP 37 Belvedere, 1002, Tunis, Tunisia
sofiene.haboubi@istmt.rnu.tn,
samia.maddouri@enit.rnu.tn,
hamid.amiri@enit.rnu.tn

Abstract. The identification of scripts is an important step in the characters recognition. In this work, we are interested in Arabic and Latin scripts. The identification is based on an approach to character recognition. The approach is structural feature. Selected characteristics of scripts are based on the geometric shape of the characters. Evaluations are conducted on a printed document Arabic and Latin, and with the neural networks functions. The results are interesting in the case of bilingual documents.

Keywords: Script identification, Structural features, Arabic script, Latin script.

1 Introduction

Discriminating between the languages a document image is a complex and challenging task. It has kept the scientists, working in this field, puzzled for quite some time now. Researchers have been emphasizing a lot of effort for pattern recognition since decades. Amongst the pattern recognition field Optical Character Recognition is the oldest sub field and has almost achieved a lot of success in the case of recognition of Monolingual Scripts.

One of the important tasks in machine learning is the electronic reading of documents. All documents can be converted to electronic form using a high performance Optical Character Recognizer (OCR) [1]. Recognition of bilingual documents can be approached by the recognition via script identification.

The digital processing of documents is a very varied field of research. Their goal is to make the machine able automatically to read the contents of a document, even of high complexity. Among the obtained results, we find the OCR (Optical characters recognition). This system makes to read the scripts form images, to convert them in numerical form. This system must know the language of script before the launching of process, to obtain good results. Also, the currently system does not treat two different languages in the same document. Like several researchers, our work is to introduce the Multi-language to our OCR, and we took the differentiation between the

E.R. Hruschka Junior et al. (Eds.): INTECH 2011, CCIS 165, pp. 132–143, 2011.
© Springer-Verlag Berlin Heidelberg 2011

Arab and Latin scripts our field of contribution. Existing methods for differentiation between scripts are presented by [2, 3] in four principal classes according to analyzed levels of information: methods based on an analysis of text block, methods based on the analysis of text line, methods based on the analysis of related objects and methods based on mixed analyses.

The identification of the language of script began in 1990 with Spitz [4]. According to the literature in journals and international conferences, Fig. 1 shows the evolution of the number of papers since 1990. According to the figure, the number of papers that focus on identifying of the scripts shows the importance of this problem in the field of automatic analysis of documents.

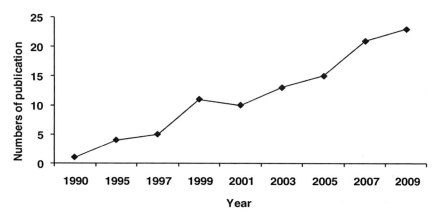

Fig. 1. The number of papers by years

2 Background

The identification of the language of script based on the fact that each script has a unique spatial distribution and unique visuals that can distinguish it from other scripts. So the basic task involved in the identification is to develop a technique to discover these features from a given document, then classes the documents. Based on the nature of the approach and features used, these methods can be divided into two main categories:

− methods based on the structure of scripts
− methods based on the visual appearance of scripts

Techniques for identifying the script in each of these two categories can be classified on the basis of the level to which they are applied in the document image: page-level, paragraph-level, line-level and word-level. The mode of application of a method depends on the minimum size of the text; from which the proposed features can be extracted.

The preliminary study, shown that the majority of differentiation methods treat only the printed text documents. Among the latter, the method suggested by [5], develops a strategy of discrimination between Arabic and Latin scripts. This approach is based on Template-Matching, which makes it possible to decide between the identified languages. In [6], the authors uses a supervised Multi-Classes for classification and the Gabor filter to identify the Latin script. The type of document used is printed with Latin scripts and mixed. Two methods are proposed by [7], with two approaches: Statistical and spectral by Gabor filter. This work is interested on Kannada and Latin scripts. The system of identification, proposed by [8], relates to Latin and not-Latin languages in printed documents. This method is based on the application of Gabor filter, the author classifiers for the identification of languages other than Latin. With statistical methods and on printed documents, [9] has interested by identification of Arabic, Chinese, Latin, Devanagari, and Bangla languages. The identification of the type of scripts (printed or handwritten) is treated by [10], on Korean language. This approach is based on an analysis of related components and contours. A spectral method is presented in [11]. This method is to classes the script to Chinese, Japanese, Korean or Latin language by Gabor filter. The Arabic script is cursive and present various diacritic.

In general, the methods used to differentiate between two or more scripts are: first that a statistical geometric aspect of dividing words into three parts (a central part, top part and bottom part) and then a calculation of pixel density or others that are based on edge detection, connected components, ... The second method is based on texture to characterize the scripts, such Gabor filters or other. In the same area and other than the script recognition, [12] interest on the recognition of numeric characters and [13] on finding the best algorithm for identification of the script language. [14] shows a method for extracting Chinese words from a document in English using neural networks.

Comparative studies between the various script identification techniques are presented by [2, 15, 16].

An Arab word is a sequence of letters entirely disjoined and related entities. Contrary to the Latin script, the Arab characters are script from the right to left, and do not comprise capital letters. The characters form varies according to their position in the word: initial, median, final and insulated. In the case of handwritten, the characters, Arabic or Latin, can vary in their static and dynamic properties. The static variations relate to the size and the form, while the dynamic variations relate to the number of diacritic segments and their order. Theirs increases the complexity of distinction between the languages.

3   Separation between Languages

The propose method consists of several stages (Fig 2). From a printed document, we must pass a filter to remove the diacritics dots. Then, extraction lines by horizontal projection. In the next step, we extract the words from lines; where each word will be treated separately.

We extracted the structural features for each word, and then passed to a stage of training or classification. In the training phase, we store all the results into a database, and in the classification phase, we use a classifier to determine the nature of language (Arabic or Latin).

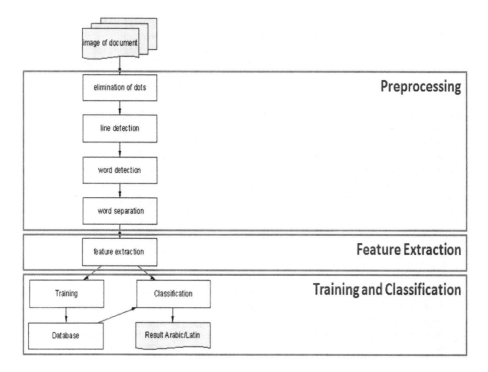

Fig. 2. System architecture

The extraction of structural features is based on three steps: pre-treatment, the determination of the baseline, and the detection of primitives.

The words to be recognized are extracted from their contexts check or postal letters. A stage analysis, segmentation and filtering of documents is required. This task is not part of our work. The words are supposed to be taken out of context without noise. Since our method of feature extraction is based mainly on the outline, the preprocessing step we have introduced in our system is the expansion in order to obtain a closed contour with the least points of intersections. Since the elimination of the slope may introduce additional distortions we have tried to avoid this step. It is for this reason that techniques of preprocessing, avoiding the inclination correction has emerged [17, 18].

3.1 Elimination of Dots

The challenge is the presence of eight different types of diacritical marks, used to represent Arabic or Latin letters. In written text they are considered as special letters where each one is assigned a single code, as with normal letters. In fully diacriticized text a diacritical mark is added after each consonant of the Arabic word. These diacritical marks play a very important role in fixing the meaning of words.

But these diacritics can cause problems in the detection and extraction lines. Because in some writing styles, the diacritics may leave the upper limit of the line or the lower limit. This can cause poor detection of lines. Their diacritics will be removed by morphological erosion followed by a morphological dilation.

3.2 Line Detection

To separate words from text document, we must first start with the detection of lines. There are several methods proposed by authors such as [19, 20]. But since we work with the Arabic and Latin, and our basic document that consists of text (without images and background), we chose to use the horizontal projection method. This method is still reliable in the absence of the inclination of lines. Fig 3 shows the application of the horizontal projection.

The judge Al-Moaafi bin Zakariyya narrated from Ibrahim bin Faz'l, from Faz'l bin Yousuf, from Hasam bin Saber, from Wakee', from Hisham bin Urwah, from his father, from Ayesha, who said: |

The Messenger of Allah ﷺ said, "Mentioning Ali bin Abi Taleb is worshipping Allah.

حدثنا ابو القاسم جعفر بن مسرور اللحام رحمه الله قال حدثني الحسين بن محمد عن ابراهيم بن محمد عن بلال عن ابراهيم بن صالح الأنماطي عن عبد الصمد عن جعفر بن محمد عن ابيه عن علي بن الحسين عن ابيه قال:

سئل النبي صلى الله عليه وآله عن قوله تعالى طوبى لهُمْ وَ حُسْنُ مآبٍ قال نزلت في أمير المؤمنين علي و طوبى شجرة في داره و هي في الفردوس ليس من أثمار دور الجنة شيء إلا و غصنٌ منها فيها.

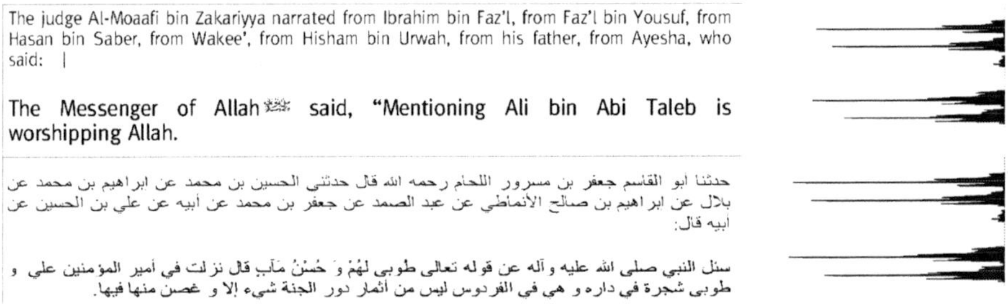

Fig. 3. Line detection from Arabic/Latin Text

3.3 Word Detection and Separation

The detection and separation of words from a text document, is a conventional step in the automatic document processing. This step makes it difficult in the case of multilingual documents. This difficulty because of the large difference between the Arabic printed script and Latin printed script.

The Arabic handwriting is cursive. It is writing where the letters are linked to each other. This is not only in the case of handwriting; it is also the case of printed letters. The Latin alphabet is not cursive writing in the case of printed letters. In Arabic, the writing is always attached, even with print. This break is a problem in the step of separation between words; since both languages are present in the same text together.

Fig 4 shows the difference in dispersal areas in the case of Arabic (AR) and Latin (LA) scripts. To see this difference we used a Latin text and its similarity in Arabic, they have almost the same amount of information. We measured the distance (in pixels) between characters, and we calculated the number of occurrences of each distance found. In the case of the Arabic script, there are not much of separators between the characters, because of its nature cursive. In contrary, in the case of the Latin script, the distance is the dominant separators between the characters of the same word. But these two types of scripts have a common point at the threshold between the distances "between words" with the distances "between characters" (e.g. 6 pixels).

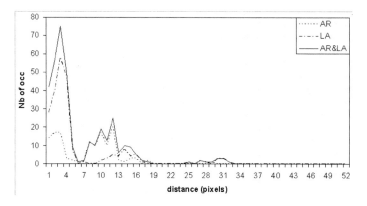

Fig. 4. Dispersal spaces between characters and words

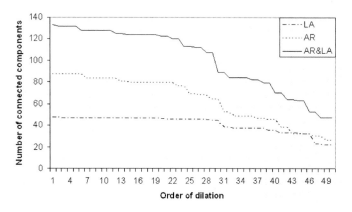

Fig. 5. The impact of dialtion on the number of connected components

Our idea of separation of words is to use the Morphological image analysis to know the limits of the word (lower, upper, right and left). The structuring element for morphological dilation is a horizontal line form. The size of this line is the threshold that separates the distances between words and the distances between characters. In Fig 5 we show the impact of the order of dilation (size of the structuring element) on the number of connected components. The search for the ideal size of dilation is difficult with Fig 5.

In our case (Arabic and Latin text printed), the sequential dilation causes a decrease in numbers of connected components thereof (the characters of same word stick), then there is a stabilization, then there is a second decrease (the words stick). The difference between the two phases of reductions is stabilization, which is shown in Fig 6. Stability is the first value where the standard deviation of the variation in the number of related components vanishes.

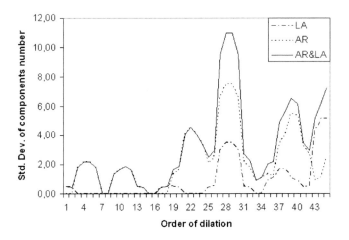

Fig. 6. The standard deviation of the impact of dilation on the number of connected components

After choosing the size of the structuring element, and after dilation of the original image, we determine the boundaries of each word in the Arabic and Latin text. The Fig 7 shows an example of results found.

4   Feature Extraction

4.1   Determination of Baselines

From the word we can extract two baselines. A upper and lower baseline. These two baselines divide the word into three regions. The poles "H" and diacritical dots high "P" which are regions above the upper baseline. The jambs "J" and diacritical dots lower "Q" correspond to regions below the lower baseline. The body of the word is the region between the two baselines. In general, the loops are in the middle.

The judge Al-Moaafi bin Zakariyya narrated from Ibrahim bin Faz'l, from Faz'l bin Yousuf, from Hasan bin Saber, from Wakee', from Hisham bin Urwah, from his father, from Ayesha, who said:
The Messenger of Allah said, "Mentioning Ali bin Abi Taleb is worshipping Allah.
حدثنا أبو القاسم جعفر بن مسرور اللحام رحمه الله قال حدثني الحسين بن محمد عن ابراهيم بن محمد عن بلال عن ابراهيم بن صالح الأنماطي عن عبد الصمد عن جعفر بن محمد عن أبيه عن علي بن الحسين عن أبيه قال:
سئل النبي صلى الله عليه وآله عن قوله تعالى طوبى لهُمْ وَ حُسْنُ مَآبٍ قال نزلت في أمير المؤمنين علي و طوبى شجرة في داره و هي في الفردوس ليس من أثمار دور الجنة شيء إلا و غصن منها فيها.

Fig. 7. Distinction of words from bilingual text

4.2 Extraction of the Poles and Jambs

A pole is all forms with a maximum above the upper baseline. Similarly, jambs and all maxima below the lower baseline. The distance between these extrema and the baseline is determined empirically. It corresponds to:

MargeH = 2(lower baseline – upper baseline) for the poles
MargeJ = (lower baseline – upper baseline) for the jambs.

4.3 Detection of Diacritical Dots

The diacritical points are extracted from the contour. Browsing through it, we can detect those that are closed. From these closed contours, we choose those with a number of contour points below a certain threshold. This threshold is derived from a statistical study to recognize the words taken from their context (checks, letters, mailing ...). It is estimated in our case the recognition of literal amounts to 60 pixels.

4.4 Determination of Loops from the Contour

A closed contour length below 60 pixels corresponds to a loop if some contour points are between the two baselines. The problems encountered during the extraction of loops are:

- Some diacritical dots can be confused with the loops if they are intersecting with the baselines.
- Some loops may be longer than 60 pixels and cannot be taken into account.

After a first selection step loops, a second step of verifying their inclusion in another closed loop is completed. This method involves:

– Looking for word parts that can include the loop.
– Stain the relevant section blank, if the contour points disappear when the latter is included in the word color and is part of the list of loops.

4.5   Detection of Pieces

Given the variability of the shape of characters according to their position, an Arabic word can be composed by more than one party called for Pieces. Detection of Pieces is useful information both in the recognition step in the step of determining the position of structural features in the word.

4.6   Position Detection Primitives

The shape of an Arabic character depends on its position in the word. A character can have four different positions which depend on its position in the word. We can have single characters at the beginning, middle or end of a word. This position is detected during the primary feature extraction. Indeed, the extracted areas are defined by local minima. These minimums are from the vertical projection and contour. The number of black pixels is calculated in the vicinity of boundaries demarcated areas and between the two baselines above and below. If this number is greater than 0 at the left boundary and equal to 0 on the right, the position is the top "D", etc ... Fig 8 and 9 shows the various positions found in the Arabic and Latin scripts.

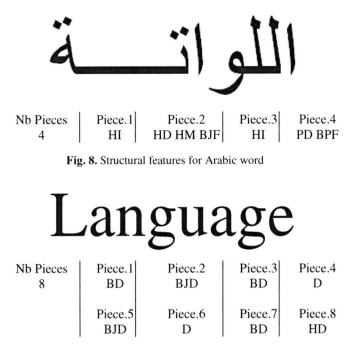

Nb Pieces	Piece.1	Piece.2	Piece.3	Piece.4
4	HI	HD HM BJF	HI	PD BPF

Fig. 8. Structural features for Arabic word

Nb Pieces	Piece.1	Piece.2	Piece.3	Piece.4
8	BD	BJD	BD	D
	Piece.5	Piece.6	Piece.7	Piece.8
	BJD	D	BD	HD

Fig. 9. Structural features for Arabic and Latin Printed word

5 Training and Classification

The recognition of the language of the document is regarded as a preprocessing step; this step has become difficult in the case of bilingual document. We begin by discriminating between an Arabic text and a Latin text printed by the structural method. Considering the visual difference between writing Arabic and Latin script, we have chosen to discriminate between them based on the general structure of each, and the number of occurrences of the structural characteristics mentioned above. Indeed, in analyzing a text in Arabic and Latin text we can distinguish a difference in the cursivity, the number of presence of diacritical dots and leg in the Arabic script. To printed Latin script, it is composed mainly of isolated letters.

The first step in the process regardless of the Arabic script from a text document is extracted lines and words. The extraction of lines is done by determining the upper and lower limit using the horizontal projection. For each line, there are the words using the method of dilation. Each word will be awarded by a system for extracting structural features.

From image of the word, we extract the feature vector that can discriminate between writing languages. This vector represents the number of occurrences of each feature in the word. It is to count the number of each feature: Hampe (H), Jamb (J), Upper (P) and Lower (Q) diacritic dots, Loop (B), Start (D), Middle (M), End (F) and Isolated (I). Our vector is composed of selected features

− the number of Pieces and the number of characters :

   {NbPieces, NBL}

− the number of occurrences of each feature :

   {H, J, B, P, Q, R, D, M, F , I}

− the number of occurrence of each feature taking into account their position :

   {HD, HM, HF, HI, JF, JI, PD, PM, PF, PI, QD, QM, QF, QI, BD, BM, BF, BI}.

To evaluate our method, we used 57 documents Arabic and Latin text. After the step of separation into words, we found 4229 words. From each word, we generate its feature vector. For learning and testing, we used the Multilayer Perceptron function (MLP). The learning database contains 80% of all words, and the test database contains the rest. In practice, we used the WEKA [21, 22] software to evaluate our method.

6 Results

In the test phase, we used 846 words (440 Arab and 406 Latin). After evaluating the test split, we found 798 words correctly classified and 48 words incorrectly classified. Who gave a classification rate equal to 94.32% and an error rate equal to 5.68%. From the confusion matrix, we found 37 Arabic words incorrectly classified and 11 Latin words incorrectly classified.

7 Conclusion

According to the method of discrimination presented, we showed that discrimination between Arabic and Latin is possible. The text documents used are in Arabic and Latin at the same time. The techniques used for discrimination are: mathematical morphology for separation into words, and structural characteristics for identification, and neural networks for classification. The levels found are too motivating to treat the case of handwritten documents.

References

1. Guyon, I., Schomaker, L., Plamondon, R., Liberman, M., Janet, S.: UNIPEN project of on-line data exchange and recognizer benchmarks. In: Proceedings of the 12th IAPR International Conference on Computer Vision & Image Processing Pattern Recognition, vol. 22, pp. 29–33 (1994)
2. Ghosh, D., Dube, T., Shivaprasad, A.P.: Script Recognition-A Review. IEEE T. Pattern Anal. 32, 2142–2161 (2010)
3. Kanoun, S., Ennaji, A., LeCourtier, Y., Alimi, A.M.: Script and Nature Differentiation for Arabic and Latin Text Images. In: Proceedings of the Eighth International Workshop on Frontiers in Handwriting Recognition (IWFHR 2002), vol. 309, IEEE Computer Society, Los Alamitos (2002)
4. Spitz, A.L.: Multilingual Document Recognition. Electronic Publishing Document Manipulation and Typography 193–206 (1990)
5. Elbaati, A., Charfi, M., Alimi, A.M.: Discrimination de Documents Imprimés Arabes et Latins Utilisant une Approche de Reconnaissance. Journées GEI (2004)
6. Ma, H.F., Doermann, D.: Font identification using the grating cell texture operator. Document Recognition and Retrieval XII 5676, 148–156 (2005)
7. Dhanya, D., Ramakrishnan, A.G., Pati, P.B.: Script identification in printed bilingual documents. Sadhana-Acad. P. Eng. S 27, 73–82 (2002)
8. Jaeger, S., Ma, H., Doermann, D.: Identifying Script onWord-Level with Informational Confidenc. In: ICDAR 2005: Proceedings of the Eighth International Conference on Document Analysis and Recognition, pp. 416–420 (2005)
9. Pal, U., Chaudhuri, B.B.: Script line separation from Indian multi-script documents. IETE J. Res. 49, 3–11 (2003)
10. Jang, S.I., Jeong, S.H., Nam, Y.-S.: Classification of Machine-Printed and Handwritten Addresses on Korean Mail Piece Images Using Geometric Features. In: ICPR 2004: Proceedings of the Pattern Recognition, 17th International Conference on (ICPR 2004), vol. 2, pp. 383–386 (2004)
11. Pan, W.M., Suen, C.Y., Bui, T.D.: Script Identification Using Steerable Gabor Filters. In: ICDAR 2005: Proceedings of the Eighth International Conference on Document Analysis and Recognition, pp. 883–887 (2005)
12. Lehal, G.S., Bhatt, N.: A recognition system for devnagri and english handwritten numerals. In: Tan, T., Shi, Y., Gao, W. (eds.) ICMI 2000. LNCS, vol. 1948, pp. 442–449. Springer, Heidelberg (2000)
13. Kastner, C.M., Covington, G.A., Levine, A.A., Lockwood, J.W.: HAIL: a hardware-accelerated algorithm for language identification. In: International Conference on Field Programmable Logic and Applications, 2005, pp. 499–504 (2005)

14. Yang, H.-C., Lee, C.-H.: Automatic category structure generation and categorization of chinese text documents. In: Zighed, D.A., Komorowski, J., Żytkow, J.M. (eds.) PKDD 2000. LNCS (LNAI), vol. 1910, pp. 673–678. Springer, Heidelberg (2000)
15. Abirami, S., Manjula, D.: A Survey of Script Identification techniques for Multi-Script Document Images. International Journal of Recent Trends in Engineering (IJRTE) 1(2), 246–249 (2009)
16. Artemenko, O., Mandl, T., Shramko, M., Womser-Hacker, C.: Evaluation of a language identification system for mono- and multilingual text documents. In: Proceedings of the 2006 ACM symposium on Applied Computing, pp. 859–860. ACM, Dijon (2006)
17. Coté, M., Cheriet, M., Lecolinet, E., Suen, C.Y.: Automatic Reading of Cursive Scripts Using Human Knowledge. In: Proceedings of the International Conference on Document Analysis and Recognition, pp. 107–111. IEEE Computer Society, Los Alamitos (1997)
18. Madhvanath, S., Govindaraju, V.: Contour-based Image Preprocessing for Holistic Handwritten Word Recognition. In: ICDAR 1997: Proceedings of the 4th International Conference on Document Analysis and Recognition, pp. 536–539 (1997)
19. Bouriel, K., Samoud, F.B., Abed, H.E., Maddouri, S.S.: Stratégies d'évaluation et de comparaison de méthodes d'extraction de la ligne de base de mots manuscrits arabes. In: Actes du dixième Colloque International Francophone sur l'Écrit et le Document, CIFED (2008)
20. Pechwitz, M., Maddouri, S.S., Margner, V., Ellouze, N., Amiri, H.: IFN/ENITdatabase of handwritten arabic words. In: Actes du Colloque International Francophone sur l'Écrit et le Document (CIFED), pp. 127–136 (2002)
21. Ian, H.W., Eibe, F.: Data Mining: Practical Machine Learning Tools and Techniques, 2nd edn. (2005) ISBN 0-12-088407-0
22. Hall, M., Frank, E., Holmes, G., Pfahringer, B., Reutemann, P., Witten, I.H.: The WEKA Data Mining Software: An Update. SIGKDD Explorations 11(1) (2009)

Introducing a New Agile Development for Web Applications Using a Groupware as Example

Vinicius Pereira and Antonio Francisco do Prado

Federal University of Sao Carlos – UFSCar, Department of Computing,
Via Washington Luis, km 234, CEP: 13565-905, Sao Carlos – SP, Brazil
{vinicius_pereira,prado}@dc.ufscar.br

Abstract. The purpose of this paper is introduce a new agile methodology for Web development based on User Stories and that use some concepts of Scrum like Product Backlog and Sprint. The methodology is divided in three disciplines: Communication, Modeling and Construction; each one refining the User Stories, from requirements specification with the User and the use of the Navigation Model and Story Cards until the execution of these User Stories to guide the coding. Thus, the development team can use these User Stories as acceptance tests, which represent the User behavior when using the system. The code written to pass in those tests can generate, through reverse engineering, design for the team to evaluate how the Web application is being developed and evolved. In the end, the team has more guarantees that the Web application developed represents what the User wanted in the beginning.

Keywords: Agile Process, User Story, Navigation Model, Web Development.

1 Introduction

In the early versions of the Web there was little room for its users to publish information and interaction was very restrictive. At that time, the Web consisted specially of static HTML pages and/or some very few Java applets. With the Web 2.0 [1] new technologies began to gain the moment, opening the Web for social collaboration. Good examples of this are the social networks [2], with the growing focus on groupware (or collaborative software) [3] [4]. Collaborative software is designed to facilitate interactions between groups of individuals that share a common objective. This is just to show how the Web (with the Internet) changes the way that people interact with the computer and others devices with Web interfaces.

Considering the growth tendency of collaborative software in many areas, like education, trading, healthcare and others, a more participative and agile approach becomes necessary for corporations and institutions. These ideas, together with the new technologies available today are promising to accelerate the development process. A good example to illustrate that tendency is Twitter, a social network focused on the concept of micro blogging that allows its users to publish personal updates and see updates from the others in a computer or in a smartphone, for example.

E.R. Hruschka Junior et al. (Eds.): INTECH 2011, CCIS 165, pp. 144–160, 2011.

This article presents an agile process for the development of Web applications using the concept of User Stories and making sketches of the Navigation Model to guide the construction and details these Stories in conversations with the User. Modern techniques and concepts are the basis for the development of this agile methodology.

2 Concepts and Techniques

This section presents the main concepts and techniques behind the proposed methodology. The main concept is the User Stories [5]. There are also brief descriptions regarding Test Driven Development (TDD) [6], Web Engineering (WebE) [7] and Scrum [8]. WebE was the starting point that led the studies to other techniques and concepts. The use of TDD is heavily encouraged in the proposed methodology. Concepts of the Scrum are reused in some points in this process.

2.1 User Stories

User Stories describes functionally what it is requested and valuable for the User. In a User Story there are 3 C's which are: Card, Conversation and Confirmation, and follows the principle of INVEST: Independent, Negotiable, Valuable for the user, Estimable, Small and Testable. One of the C's cited previously, the Story Card is the User Story written and formalized. From this card can be seen the other two C's.

The idea of the User Story be written in a card instead of another media have the purpose to maintain the principle of Small (so the story gets short). If a User Story exceeds the card limit maybe it is time to break it. The important is that there is no limit to write User Stories since they are in the pattern [5]. An informal example is: "Students can purchase parking passes". In his book Mike Cohn suggests a more formal approach to writing User Stories [5]. He suggests the format: As a *"role"* I want *"something"* so that *"benefit"*. This approach helps to think about why a certain feature is built and for whom, and as a result is the approach that is typically taken. The same example in this approach is: "As a student I want to purchase a parking pass so that can drive to school". As can be seen, the formality brings a greater understanding of the problem.

Agile methodologies favor face-to-face communication over comprehensive documentation and quick adaptation to change instead of fixation on the problem. User Stories achieve this by: (1) they represent small chunks of business value that can be implemented in a period of days to weeks; (2) needing very little maintenance; (3) allowing developer and the client representative to discuss requirements throughout the project lifetime; (4) allowing projects to be broken into small increments; (5) being suited to projects where the requirements are volatile or poorly understood; (6) require close customer contact throughout the project so that the most valued parts of the software gets implemented. Some of the limitations of user stories in agile methodologies: (1) they can be difficult to scale to large projects; (2) they are regarded as conversation starters and nothing more.

2.2 Web Engineering (WebE)

The World Wide Web has become a crucial platform for the delivery of a variety complex and diversified corporative applications in many business domains. Besides its distributed aspect, these Web applications require constant improvements in usability, performance, security and scalability. However, the vast majority of the aforementioned applications are still being developed with an ad hoc approach, contributing for usability problems, maintenance, quality and reliability [9][10]. Even considering that the Web development can benefit from methodologies inherited from other areas, it has very specific characteristics that require a special approach. Among these characteristics there are the network traffic, parallelism, unpredictable load, performance, availability, focus on data, context sensitivity, continuous evolution, urgency, security, and aesthetics [7].

Web Engineering allows a systematic, disciplined and quantifiable approach for high quality development focused on Web applications [11]. Focusing on methodologies, processes, techniques and tools applied in different abstraction levels, from the conception to development, evaluation and maintainability.

The principles of WebE include: (1) a different and unique process of Web development [12]; (2) multidiscipline. It is very unlikely that a single discipline can offer a complete theoretical basis, with knowledge and practice to guide the Web development [13]; (3) the continuous evolution and the management of the life's cycle of a software (cycles as short as possible) when compared to the traditional development methods; and (4) the applications can be pervasive and non-trivial. The Web perspective as a platform will continue to grow and should be addressed as one.

2.3 Test Driven Development (TDD)

Created by Kent Beck, *Test Driven Development* is an approach to deal with analysis and specifying behavior based on automated tests. TDD introduces the concept of Red-Green-Refactor: (1) write a test and watch it fail; (2) write the minimum code necessary to make the test passes; and (3) apply refactoring with design patterns [14] to eliminate redundancies or duplicated codes.

Kent Beck considers that TDD encourages simple code design and increases confidence in the final product [6]. With TDD, according Feathers, programmers can improve legacy code without the fear of changing the existing behavior [15]. In TDD, a test is a piece of software that has two main goals: (1) specification: establishing a rule that the software has to follow and (2) validation: verify that the rule is properly implemented by the software. With this, it is possible to generate clean code, which according to Robert Martin [16], is the code that reflects exactly what it had been designed to do, without trickery or obscurity.

The main advantages of using TDD are: (1) the code has less coupling and greater cohesion; (2) the code has greater quality because it is fully tested; (3) refactoring can be executed without fear of breaking behavior; (4) it is possible to know clearly when a task is done – when the corresponding test is passing; (5) the test suite serves as a basis for automated regression tests without need further development; (6) the vast majority of the bugs are found earlier, which make the effort to fix them cheaper.

2.4 Scrum

Scrum is a framework for agile software development that is iterative and incremental. Initially it was conceived as a project management style for the automobilist and consumables industries. They noticed that on projects using small multidisciplinary (cross functional) teams where the result were considerably better. In 1995, Ken Schwaber formalized the definition of Scrum [8] and helped to introduce it to the software development worldwide.

The primary function of Scrum is to be used for management of software development projects, it can be used to run software maintenance teams, or as a general project/program management approach. It can be too, theoretically, applied to any context in which a group of people needs to work together to achieve a common goal.

Scrum has three main roles: (1) the *Scrum Master*, who maintains the processes; (2) the *Product Owner*, who represents the stakeholders and the business; (3) the *Team*, a cross-functional group of about 7 people who do the actual analysis, design, implementation, testing, among another tasks.

During each *Sprint*, typically a two to four week period, the Team creates a potentially shippable product increment. The set of features that go into a sprint come from the *Product Backlog*, which is a prioritized set of high level requirements of work to be done. Which backlog items go into the Sprint is determined during the *Sprint Planning Meeting*. During this meeting, the Product Owner informs the Team of the items in the Product Backlog that he or she wants completed. The Team then determines how much of this they can commit to complete during the next Sprint. During a Sprint, no one is allowed to change the *Sprint Backlog*, which means that the requirements are frozen for that sprint. Development is time boxed such that the Sprint must end on time; if requirements are not completed for any reason they are left out and returned to the Product Backlog. After a Sprint is completed, the Team demonstrates how to use the software to the User.

3 Introducing a New Agile Development for Web Applications with a Groupware as Example

With the knowledge about these key concepts and techniques, and focused on improving the process of Web development, this article presents the results of a research project to Web development that focus on agile process. This methodology has as a goal to offer a greater margin of cover for developing a Web application. Another goal is explicitly join the process disciplines, showing for the development team that an artifact really helps in obtain other artifact, leaving visible that the requirement was actually implemented. Thus, the methodology wants that people of the development team valorizes the artifacts and get a bigger (and better) understanding of what must be done to create the Web application requested by the User.

This process is called RAMBUS (*Rambus Agile Methodology Based on User Stories*) and is defined with three disciplines: *Communication, Modeling* and *Construction*. The process follows the concept of using User Stories to get the requirements with Story Cards, and using Navigation Model to define them. Like in Behavior Driven Development (BDD) [17] these Stories are used as an acceptance tests when the development team is coding the application. Moreover, the process makes uses of ideas and concepts of the Scrum, among them *Product Backlog* and *Sprint*, as well suggest the use of some practices of the eXtreme Programming (XP) [18], like *Pair Programming* and *Continuous Integration*. Lastly, it also makes use, in a lower degree, of the concept of Evolutionary Design proposed by Fowler [19]. The Figure 1 shows a brief version of the proposed process.

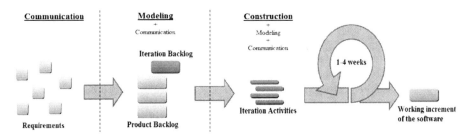

Fig. 1. Brief version of the proposed process

The name of the discipline in bold and in underline is where the main focus of the development team at the moment. So when it is done the requirements specification, the team's focus is on Communication. When is created the product backlog and is selected what will be done in the iteration, the team is focused on Modeling. And finally, when the team starts the iteration, the team's focus is in Construction. However, nothing prevents the previous disciplines occur with less intensity in the present moment of the team. To complement the understanding of this process the Figure 2 shows, in a diagram SADT (Structured Analysis and Design Technique) [20] [21], a more detailed version of the process with the artifacts that are generated in each discipline. The process is executed in cycles to create the Web application which is requested by User.

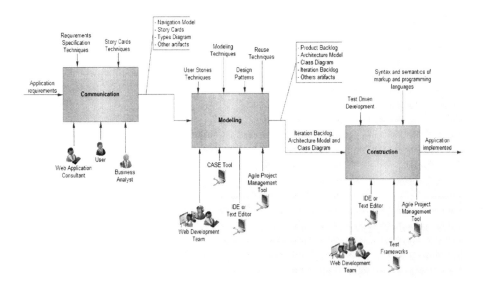

Fig. 2. The New Agile Development for Web Applications

It is suggested to the consultant that he gets as much information as possible on the requested Web application in early conversations with the User. This amount of information will be vital for the development team to analyze and project the time and effort to accomplish the implementation of the system. People involved in the project should realize that having "as much information as possible" does not imply implement everything at once. The requirements specified in this information will be broken into shorter (and functional) cycles of iterations. More details about this will be discussed throughout the article.

Another fact can be that some of the features will be only requested when the User interact with the application. The team should have in mind that a Web application will be always evolving. Test the ideas and collect the feedback for these tests before going ahead. The earlier the mistakes were discovered, the fewer resources and time will be spent to fix them.

In general, this type of development involves a large quantity of changes along the project. The process is based in iterations according to the User Stories originated in the conversations with the User. The prototypes developed in each iteration constitute mini-projects that slowly include all the functionality of the software, based in the functionalities and/or characteristics that these Stories request.

In general, this type of development involves a large quantity of changes along the project. The process is based in iterations according to the User Stories originated in the conversations with the User. The prototypes developed in each iteration constitute mini-projects that slowly include all the functionality of the software, based in the functionalities and/or characteristics that these User Stories request.

For better understanding, a clarification is needed. The term "Story Card" is used in Communications to express a User Story in card format, like Mike Cohn proposes in his book [5]. And the term "User Story" in Modeling and Construction disciplines, is used to express the format proposed by Dan North [17], with some key words that will be useful in these disciplines.

To assist in the presentation of the disciplines is used as an example of a Web application a kind of social software, the groupware (specifically a wiki). Therefore, all figures show a part of the specification of a wiki to help illustrate the description of artifacts.

3.1 Communication

In this discipline, the main focus is to extract information in conversations with the User. The concern is to raise as much information as possible about how the system should behave. To assist in requirements gathering, the proposed approach makes use of Story Cards and the Navigation Model.

There is no rule saying which of the two types of artifacts should be generated first, because the process assumes that one complements the other. At the end of the conversation with the User, the Story Cards and the Navigation Model should be made (remember, with as much information as possible at the moment) and use them together should show the overall picture of the problem.

To present the methodology, the first type of artifact to have explained their preparation and use is the *Story Card*. Based on the example of a groupware Figure 3 shows the front of a Story Card requesting the management of pages in a wiki.

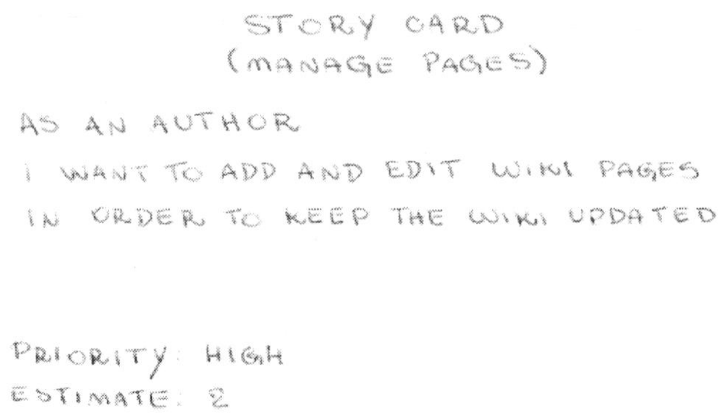

STORY CARD
(MANAGE PAGES)
AS AN AUTHOR
I WANT TO ADD AND EDIT WIKI PAGES
IN ORDER TO KEEP THE WIKI UPDATED
PRIORITY: HIGH
ESTIMATE: 2

Fig. 3. Example of a Story Card to a wiki

As can be seen in the figure, the Story Card is as simple and objective as possible. The user can have a greater sense of being understood and can come to collaborate more with the identification of requirements. But such information is of a very high level of abstraction, even if we consider what is written on the back of the Card, which will be shown later. The User said "what" expects that the application does, but not "how" expects that the application works.

This is where it is necessary to use the *Navigation Model*, to extract the User information about how the application will be used. One of the best ways to achieve this result is to draw the model with pen and paper, as show Figure 4, or on a whiteboard. This informality is a good way to encourage the User to interact.

LOGIN
name
password
MENU
PAGE
MAINT
ORPHAN
PAGES
title
CREATE
title
CREATE
CREATE
title
content
date
user
SHOW
title
content
EDIT
date
user

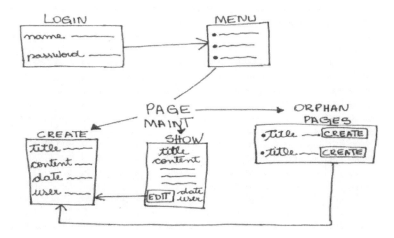

Fig. 4. Part of the Navigation Model of a wiki

During these conversations, using both the Navigation Model and the Story Cards, the requirements are more detailed. This is the gain about using these two artifacts together. Rules that are not explicit in the Navigation Model, or even to make them clearer, may be written on the back of the corresponding Story Card, as can be seen in Figure 5. Other way to see these "requirements more detailed" in the back of the Story Card is like confirmations. Confirmations are "questions" that may appear in a talk with the User, an iteration plan or in the implementation time.

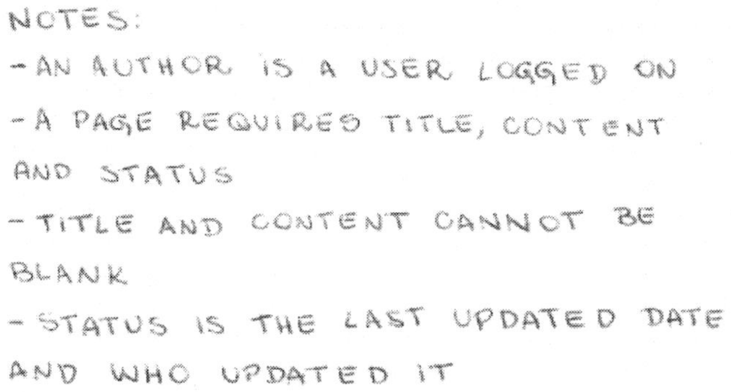

NOTES:

− AN AUTHOR IS A USER LOGGED ON

− A PAGE REQUIRES TITLE, CONTENT AND STATUS

− TITLE AND CONTENT CANNOT BE BLANK

− STATUS IS THE LAST UPDATED DATE AND WHO UPDATED IT

Fig. 5. Back of the Story Card of Figure 3

Importantly, the ideal to have as much information as possible in these conversations is to send the most experienced Web Application Consultant with the skills necessary to interact with the User. If possible, the same consultant must have some knowledge in the user's business. Otherwise, send a Business Analyst with the consultant. These skills, besides assist in the extraction of requirements, are used to estimate the difficulty of accomplishing what is explicit in the union of the Story Cards and the Navigation Model. This estimate must be noted on the corresponding Story Card.

Another necessary note and extremely useful is "what" the User considers most urgent to be delivered in early iterations of the project, if possible. Therefore, each Story Card should have a priority and an estimate of difficulty.

Nothing prevents other artifacts from be created in the search for more requirements. The more practical, but with content, the artifact is greater is the likelihood of having a User interaction. An example is the Types Diagram [22], which is extremely simple, showing only the entities (with attributes) and their relationships. The User does not need to know what an entity is necessarily, for example, just understand what the drawing represents and interact with it. The diagram types can also be used to specify information in a legacy database that will be used by Web application, for example.

Technical issues such as infrastructure are not discussed in the Story Cards but they should be noted for later analysis by the development team. If these issues have a direct relationship with a Story is important to note it in the back of the corresponding Story Card.

At the end of the Communication, at least two types of artifacts (as shows in the Figure 1) should have been made: the Story Cards and the Navigation Model. Both serve to guide the next discipline.

3.2 Modeling

The development team, in this discipline, uses the Story Cards, the Navigation Model and any other artifacts that were created in *Communication* to create or redefine (in case of fixing) the application specifications. They should be transcribed to an electronic format which means using any graphical tool or CASE tool.

The team should draw a *Class Diagram* or refine the Types Diagram previously created. This should be doing because this type of diagram helps the development team see what they will implement. The Figure 6 shows a more refined version of the Class Diagram for the wiki example.

This Class Diagram, initially much simple, is refined in each iteration, according to the concept of Evolutionary Design [19]. It is noteworthy that this diagram should represent how the requirements of the artifacts of the *Communication* will be treated. Like, for example, the necessity of create an abstract class or an interface. It is the discretion of the team using the Class Diagram to create the database (if it is not a legacy database) or create a Database Model. Thus, the team can create a database as complete as possible to deal with the application that will be created in cycles. If the opposite occurs (create the database gradually, according to application needs at the moment), that will increase the chance of having to remodel the database and spend more resources fixing the problem.

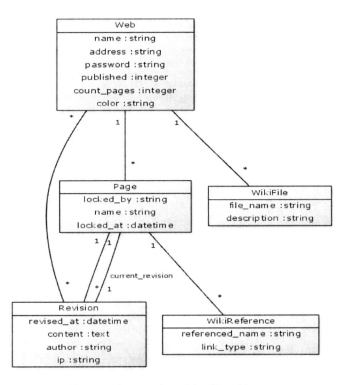

Fig. 6. Refined version of the Class Diagram

The next step is write the *User Stories* based on the artifacts that were elaborate until now. These User Stories are written in a language proposed by Dan North [17] which enables a simpler way to communicate with the User and obtain their understanding. The User can check the User Stories and approves them or not, for example. Or the team may assume that these Stories represent as faithfully as possible was expressed by the User in the Story Cards and the Model of Navigation. The Figure 7 shows a transcript of a User Story from the Story Card of Figure 3, its back in Figure 5 and the Navigation Model in Figure 4.

A User Story transcribed in this language represents an executable description without losing the sense that was specified in the identification of requirements (in the previous discipline). This description provides an element that was implicit in the cards: the Scenario. The Scenario is a using perspective in the User Story that contains one or more criteria for acceptance. A User Story will be finished when all the acceptance criteria for each Scenario are attended.

```
 1 Feature: Manage pages in the wiki
 2     In order to keep the wiki updated
 3     As an author
 4     I want to add and edit pages
 5
 6     Scenario: Create a page
 7         Given I am on the wiki creation page
 8         When I fill in "Title" with "Test - create page"
 9         And I fill in "Content" with "Checking the content..."
10         And I press "Save"
11         Then I should see the new page
12         And I should see the revision date
13         And I should see the author`s name
14
15     Scenario: Update a page
16         Given that I have created a page "First wiki page"
17         When I press "Edit"
18         And I fill in "Content" with "Updating the content..."
19         And I press "Update"
20         Then I should see the updated page
21         And I should see the new revision date
22         And I should see the authors name
```

Fig. 7. User Story transcribed

Despite the example shown above, it is important to realize that one way to improve the use of User Stories is create it only for business rules. The CRUD (Create, Read, Update and Delete) [23], once well defined in a Class Diagram, can be generated automatically from various CASE tools. This helps in saving development time, not only in the coding of this part but also in the maintenance of this automatic code. The development team may raise questions about the information obtained in the communication to better understand the issue if necessary. It is important that the User is willing to be asked to solve the doubts of the team.

Analyzing the User Stories and the others artifacts, the team should look for what can be reused from previous applications or which may give rise to an artifact reusable in future applications of this domain. Also, it is valid identify where a pattern can be included to facilitate understanding and further maneuver of the application.

Another team's function is to verify that non-functional requirements (which are the technical issues, which as mentioned in the end of *Communication*) are also necessary for a User Story to be considered complete. At last, the team must verify the behavior with the recycling of some component or framework with patterns adopted and between the User Stories and technical issues. In such cases, it is necessary to create "techniques stories" called *Tasks*. These Tasks have the same treatment of the User Stories. However, as the name suggests, they may not have as an origin a Story told by the User.

A person responsible for managing User Stories, to accept them or not, should create a *Product Backlog* (like the Product Owner on Scrum). This Backlog consists of the User Stories and the Tasks.

To control the Product Backlog, a good idea is to use an agile project management tool. Thus, the items in this Backlog can be divided into: the current iteration, waiting for future iteration and those that have not yet been confirmed by the User (he is not sure about the need for such functionality). Figure 8 shows a part of the Product Backlog for the wiki example, created in an agile project management tool.

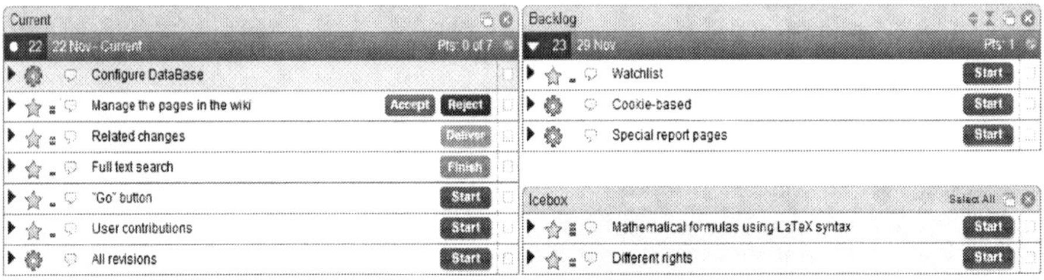

Fig. 8. A part of the Product Backlog for the wiki

It is suggested that the User Stories and Tasks to be printed. It is valid put them together in a board visibility for the whole team like the style of KanBan [24] [25]. It is also necessary to analyze which framework for acceptance tests will be used to perform the User Stories. Some of these frameworks are: Cucumber, JBehave, NBehave, easyb and Jasmine, among others. The choice should consider what the most appropriate for the programming language that will be adopted and how much work will be to integrate this framework in the process.

Another recommendation is to use patterns like the MVC (Model-View-Controller) [26] [27], to better separate the layers between the data and interface (view). Another advantage of the MVC pattern is that the frameworks which should be used in the next discipline can generate error messages more comprehensible for each layer based on the User Stories.

To determine what will be developed in each iteration must be taken into account the priorities established with the User (in *Communication*) and what is really possible to be done so that the iteration has the shortest duration possible. This will be the *Iteration Backlog* (similar to the *Sprint Backlog* on Scrum).

According to Pressman [7], it is recommended that one iteration of Web applications do not take more than a few weeks. This period of "few weeks", considering the guidelines of the Scrum Sprint, usually lasts one to four weeks. All

User Stories, and the relative Tasks, chosen to participate in the iteration must be completed within the cycle. This is a commitment from the development team.

Other decisions in the Modeling are related to hardware and software platforms adopted for the project. For example, is defined the programming language will be Ruby with the Rails framework. So, in this case, is necessary creating an *Architecture Model* that shows how the MVC works with Ruby and Rails (as can be seen in Figure 9). Another decision is about which DBMS (DataBase Management System) will be used in the case of creating a database.

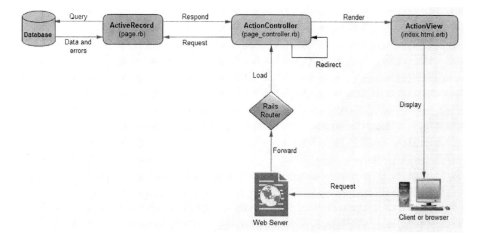

Fig. 9. Architecture Model using Rails framework

Thus, in the end of the Modeling discipline, as show in the process figure (Figure 1), the new artifacts are the User Stories transcribed, the Product Backlog, the Iteration Backlog, the Class Diagram and the Architecture Model. Like in *Communication*, nothing prevents other artifacts from be created in this discipline to help the team comprehend the problem.

3.3   Construction

This discipline covers the coding and testing. By representing the implementation of Web application, this discipline can be considered as equivalent to the *Sprint* of the Scrum. However, this process goes into more detail on how the implementation should be made in search of an application closer to the ideal for the User. Practices such as *Daily Meeting* (Scrum), *Pair Programming*, *Continuous Integration* and *Standardized Code* (XP) are very welcome, like any other practices that help the team to develop the Web application.

It encouraged the use of tests before coding. Therefore, if possible, the tests (in addition to acceptance tests, which are the User Stories) must be created before any code to help plan what will be done. This concept is known as *Test Driven Development* (TDD). This is not mandatory in the process, but it is good practice and should be considered.

Based on these artifacts: Class Diagram, Architecture Model and the User Stories; the development team must create the necessary infrastructure to support the iteration. Probably the first iteration will need more activities, like to create the database with the information collected in *Communication* and analyzed in *Modeling*, for example. It is recommended to take this moment to generate all possible automatic codes and then write (and test) the code concerning about the business rules.

Making use of the Iteration Backlog, the development team must execute the User Stories under it and start coding based on the error messages that the test framework for User Stories returns. Figure 10 shows the first error in the execution of the User Story of Figure 7.

```
(::) failed steps (::)

Can't find mapping from "the wiki creation page" to a path.
Now, go and add a mapping in /home/vinicius/Projects/wiki/features/support/paths.rb (RuntimeError)
./features/support/paths.rb:27:in `rescue in path_to'
./features/support/paths.rb:21:in `path_to'
./features/step_definitions/web_steps.rb:20:in `/^(?:|I )am on (.+)$/'
features/manage_pages.feature:7:in `Given I am on the wiki creation page'

Failing Scenarios:
cucumber features/manage_pages.feature:6 # Scenario: Create a page

2 scenarios (1 failed, 1 undefined)
14 steps (1 failed, 6 skipped, 7 undefined)
0m0.895s
```

Fig. 10. First error when executing the User Story of Figure 7

At this point can be seen the need to have been adopted a framework for acceptance tests in *Modeling*. It is important to realize that by correcting the errors occurring in the implementation of User Stories, the development team can create features to the application based on a simulation of use by the User. And these are precisely the features most important to the application as it represents the business rules that the User must have the application.

As previously mentioned, the use of TDD may be necessary to test methods that are part of one or more features requested by the User Stories. Therefore, these testing methods are of a lower-level of abstraction, being indicated not enter these kinds of details in the User Stories. Such tests prevail, for example, if the calculation of any monetary value is correct or even the proper use of the MVC layers to ensure future maintenance. Based on a figure of The Book RSpec [28], the Figure 11 shows the relationship between high-level of abstraction of a User Story and low-level of abstraction achieved using unit tests, for example.

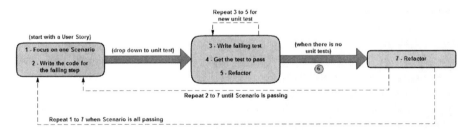

Fig. 11. Relationship between high-level of abstraction (User Story) and low-level of abstraction (unit tests)

The implementation process (preferably of business rules) starts with the tests being executed in a User Story. It is focused on one of the Scenarios, normally the first with errors (1). A step is written. This step refers to the acceptance criteria of the current Scenario (2). When the need arises for specialization, a unit test should be created. Any time a unit tests fails, for make it pass, it is necessary to go through TDD (3 to 5). As long as there are acceptance criteria unmet in the current scenario (6 and 7), the steps 2 to 7 should be re-run. When the Scenario is attended, the process restarts (1) for the next Scenario (as it is on the same User Story or on the next one). When there is no specialization (unit test), the cycle constitutes of only the User Story, with the activities 1, 2 (coding to pass this step) and 7.

This process repeats itself iteratively, by creating tests for each acceptance criteria, of each Scenario, of each User Story. The code necessary is implemented, until the functional requirement for the User Story is fulfilled and all the tests (unit and acceptance) are passing. By the end of the iteration cycle, a fully functional prototype is ready.

At the end of Construction, the prototype should be presented to the User analyze. Because it was created from simulations of use, the chance that the User accepts the product is great. Nothing prevents the User wants to put this prototype into production. In this case, the prototype must be refined in relation to the design of interfaces because they are as simple as possible.

The User may or may not request changes. If he requests, the code leaner may be easier to be changed. Both changes as other features not seen before are treated in a new iteration, returning in the stage of *Communication*. If no change or no new functionality is required, the process returns to *Modeling*, where the team discusses what was done and seek improvements, besides selecting the next User Stories for the new iteration.

Nothing prevents the User requests to modify the priorities of the Story Cards (or even User stories) before iteration begins. If he requests during an iteration the team must negotiate the possibility of change it or not. User Stories, registered in the agile project management tool, may have changed his priorities, besides being marked as "delivered" or "not acceptable". Please note that the User shall, at all times, be aware of the Product Backlog and the current Iteration Backlog.

If the implementation involves changes in the *Modeling*, the artifacts must be updated to a new version, to make the documentation consistent. For example, the Navigation Model has navigation between pages different of what was previously specified. The updated artifacts (i.e., Class Diagram) can even be generated from code by reverse engineering, according to the ideas of Fowler [19].

4   Related Works

In addition to previously mentioned, other processes were analyzed. The process Agile Web Development with Web Framework (AWDWF) [29], according to the authors, consists in use frameworks to guide the Project discipline of traditional Software Engineering. The proposal is to use the frameworks for the part of the development that is not linked to business logic, thus increasing the stability and efficiency, and ensure quality in Web application. This way, the team focus stays in the business logic. Also, cites that the communication with the Customer must be continuous.

In comparison, the procedure proposed in this article, in addition to using frameworks, show how to interact with the Customer and how to use the artifacts of this interaction to guide the coding of Web application. It also shows the need to write tests before the code and the gain that it generates.

Another case considered was proposed by Altarawneh and El Shiekh [30]. Here is proposes improvements in the life cycle of XP and added an activity of project management. This addition, it is justified because the project management of XP to be considered limited. The process is separated into six steps: (1) start with small Web projects, (2) adopt the modified XP process, (3) apply XPMM (eXtreme Programming Maturity Model) [31], (4) education and training, (5) internal evaluation and lighter formal reviews and (6) external evaluation. All these steps should be implemented with the best practices in Web Engineering.

The proposed process is based not only on eXtreme Programming, but also in other methods such as Pressman's Web Engineering and Scrum. Another difference is that the process presented uses the concept of behavior driven development, to the tests be as close as possible to the User expects. Furthermore, the process is based on the concept of test driven development to generate the minimal code needed for the Web application be built without unnecessary functions.

In the Agile Software Engineering Environment proposed by Mikio Aoyama [32], is shown an integrated software engineering environment developed to manage what he labeled as the Agile Software Process [33]. Mikio presents a way of dealing (in a more high-level) with an agile development. It is an excellent and comprehensive way to manage an agile project. However, this proposal does not demonstrate the low-level part of the development (the coding) with more details, which is what the methodology proposed here aims to do. In the opinion of the authors to ensure that what was requested by User, in the specification of requirements, is well developed by the team has to have a direct relationship between requirements and code, that is, as the first directly implies the second.

5   Conclusion

The agile methodology for Web development proposed here is a way to connect the areas of Requirements (Communication), Analysis and Design (Modeling), and Implementation (Construction) through artifacts that are highly related. To write and test the application code in *Construction* is necessary to run a User Story, which was created in *Modeling*. The way that the User Story has been created it will be used. The same thinking applies to the creation of the User Story. It was created from the requirements of *Communication*, through the Story Cards and Navigation Model. The methodology thus shows an efficient way to prove that the condition requested by the User was in fact implemented.

There are limits to this approach. The larger the system, the greater will be the difficulty to deal with Story Cards and create the Model Navigator, and later the User Stories, besides the fact that it consuming more time in conversations with the User. Thus, the methodology is suitable for Web applications to small and medium businesses. Another limit is the fact that non-functional quality attributes are hard to be placed as User Stories.

Future works includes the refinement and a more formal approach, with the study of a form to deal with the guarantee of quality in non-functional attributes and maintenance of the whole project, besides the construction of tools and other resources to support the process. A case study will also be conducted to prove the viability of the process and collect data such as effort, time and level of maintenance compared to other agile methods.

Acknowledgments. The authors would like to thanks to the people from their laboratory for their support and cooperation. Thanks also to The National Council for Scientific and Technological Development (CNPq) for financial support. V.P. gives sincere thanks to his friends Mozair Alves do Carmo Junior and Luiz Fernando Amorim Ribeiro for valuable discussions and suggestions during this work. V.P wants also to thanks his girlfriend Maria Fernanda Pinto, always by his side.

References

1. O'Reilly, T.: Web 2.0 Compact Definition: Trying Again. O'Reilly Network (2006)
2. Recuero, R.C.: Redes sociais na Internet: Considerações iniciais. In: XXVII INTERCOM (2004)
3. Carstensen, P.H., Schmidt, K.: Computer supported cooperative work: new challenges to systems design (1999),
   http://citeseer.ist.psu.edu/cartensen99computer.html
4. Beyerlein, M., Freedman, S., McGee, G., Moran, L.: Beyond Teams – Building the Collaborative Organization. The Collaborative Work Systems series. Wiley, Chichester (2002)
5. Cohn, M.: User Stories Applied: For Agile Software Development. Addison-Wesley Professional, Reading (2004)
6. Beck, K.: Test-Driven Development by Example. Addison-Wesley, Reading (2003)
7. Pressman, R., Lowe, D.: Web Engineering: A Practitioner's Approach. The McGraw-Hill Companies, Inc., New York (2009)
8. Schwaber, K.: Agile Project Management with Scrum. Microsoft Press, Redmond (2004)
9. Pressman, R.: Can Internet Applications be Engineered? IEEE Software 15(5), 104–110 (1998)
10. Pressman, R.: What a Tangled Web we Weave. IEEE Software 18(1), 18–21 (2001)
11. Ginige, A., Murugesan, S.: Web Engineering: An Introduction. IEEE Multimedia 8(1), 14–18 (2001)
12. Kappel, G., Proll, B., Seiegfried, R.W.: An Introduction to Web Engineering. In: Kappel, G., et al. (eds.) Web Engineering, John Wiley and Sons, Heidelberg (2003)
13. Deshpande, Y., Hansen, S.: Web Engineering: Creating Discipline among Disciplines. IEEE Multimedia 8(1), 81–86 (2001)
14. Fowler, M.: Refactoring: Improving the design of existing code. Addison-Wesley, Reading (1999)
15. Feathres, M.: Working Effectively with Legacy Code. Prentice-Hall, Englewood Cliffs (2004)
16. Martin, R.: Clean Code: A Handbook of Agile Software Craftsmanship. Prentice Hall PTR, Upper Saddle River (2008)

17. North, D.: Introducing Behavior Driven Development. Better Software (2006)
18. Beck, K.: Extreme Programming Explained: Embrace Change. Addison-Wesley, Reading (1999)
19. Fowler, M.: Is Design Dead? In: The XP Conference (2000)
20. Ross, D.T.: Structured Analysis: A Language for Communicating Ideas. IEEE Transactions on Software Engineering, Special Issue on Requirements Analysis 3(1), 16–34 (1977)
21. Marca, D.A., McGowan, C.L.: SADT – Structured Analysis and Design Technique. McGraw-Hill, New York (1988)
22. D'Souza, D.F., Wills, A.C.: Objects, Components, and Frameworks with UML: The Catalysis(SM) Approach. Addison-Wesley Professional, Reading (1998)
23. Kilov, H.: Business Specifications: The Key to Successful Software Engineering. Prentice-Hall, Englewood Cliffs (1998)
24. Ohno, T.: Toyota Production System - beyond large-scale production. pp. 25–29, Productivity Press (1988)
25. Anderson, D.: Kanban. Blue Hole Press (2010)
26. Reenskaug, T.: MVC. XEROX PARC 1978-1979 (1979)
27. Loyd, D., Rimov, M.: Expresso Developer's Guide. J. Corporate Ltd (2004)
28. Chelimsky, D., Astels, D., Dennis, Z., Hellesøy, A., Helmkamp, B., North, D.: The RSpec Book: Behaviour-Driven Development with RSpec, Cucumber, and Friends. Pragmatic Bookshelf (2010)
29. Ran, H., Zhuo, W., Jun, H., Jiafeng, X., Jun, X.: Agile Web Development with Web Framework. In: 4th WiCOM (2008)
30. Altarawneh, H., El Shiekh, A.: A Theoretical Agile Process Framework for WebApplications Development in Small Software Firms. In: 6th SERA (2008)
31. Nawrocki, J.R., Walter, B.: Toward Maturity Model for eXtreme Programming. In: 27th Euromicro Conference: A Net Odyssey, pp. 0233 (2001)
32. Aoyama, M.: Web-Based Agile Software Development. IEEE Software 15(6), 56–65 (1998)
33. Aoyama, M.: Agile Software Process and Its Experience. In: 20th ICSE, pp. 3–12. IEEE Computer Soc. Press, Los Alamitos (1998)

Hardware/Software Co-design for Image Cross-Correlation

Mauricio A. Dias* and Fernando S. Osorio

University of Sao Paulo - USP
Institute of Mathematics and Computer Science - ICMC
Mobile Robotics Lab - LRM
Sao Carlos, Sao Paulo, Brazil
{macdias,fosorio}@icmc.usp.br
http://www.lrm.icmc.usp.br

Abstract. Cross-correlation is an important image processing algorithm for template matching widely used on computer vision based systems. This work follows a profile-based hardware/software co-design method to develop an architecture for normalized cross-correlation coefficient calculus using Nios II soft-processor. Results present comparisons between general purpose processor implementation and different customized soft-processor implementation considering execution time and the influence of image and sub-image size. Nios II soft-processors configured with floating-point hardware acceleration achieved a 8.31 speedup.

Keywords: Cross-Correlation, Hardware/Software Co-Design, Profile-Based Method.

1 Introduction

Cross-correlation is a widely used algorithm for image processing, computer vision [10] [25] [24] and visual robotic navigation fields [20]. The main goal of this algorithm is to find the portion of an image that is most similar to a sub-image. This process can be extremely time-consuming depending on the size of the image and sub-image because the method calculates the coefficient for each pixel of the image using a sliding window that sweeps across the whole image searching for a match. Coefficient values indicate the degree of similarity between the sub-image and the current portion of an image.

Normalized cross-correlation (NCC) is a modification of the original algorithm that normalizes the coefficient values between -1 and 1. In this case, coefficient normalization makes the algorithm invariable to image and sub-image changes on brightness and scale. Visual navigation for mobile robotics is an example of

---

* The authors acknowledge the support granted by CNPq and FAPESP to the INCT-SEC (National Institute of Science and Technology of Critical Embedded Systems Brazil), processes 573963/2008-8 and 08/57870-9. Also acknowledge CNPq for financial support of this research.

E.R. Hruschka Junior et al. (Eds.): INTECH 2011, CCIS 165, pp. 161–175, 2011.
© Springer-Verlag Berlin Heidelberg 2011

current researching area that uses cross-correlation algorithms for visual-based navigation methods[15]. Researchers[24] suggested that the speedup of execution can be obtained using a specific hardware for this purpose.

In these work we have particular interest in the usage of the NCC algorithm applied to visual navigation for mobile robotic. Some facts should be considered in this type of application, once mobile robots are embedded systems which have some particularities and constraints. In most cases embedded systems have limited capacity of processing and memory. Embedded systems development for robotics is a complex task because these systems share computational resources with sensors data acquisition and processing, decision and actuators control. The combination of these facts justifies the adoption of more robust techniques considering performance, costs, energy consumption, processing and execution time.

The first and most intuitive solution for embedded systems design is to implement algorithms directly in hardware. Entire hardware designs solutions nowadays have been replaced by hardware/software co-designs [16]. Hardware/ software co-design is a design method that proposes a hardware and software concurrent development. This method is used to decide which part of the system will be implemented in hardware and which will be implemented in software. This classic problem is called hardware/software partitioning.

Choice for adopting hardware/software co-design is based on increasing complexity of embedded systems and reduction of time-to-market for embedded systems design. Also the increasing availability of complex hardware with lower costs is creating a phenomenon known as the SoC (System on a Chip) design gap [1]. Complexity of available hardware and embedded systems projects is the cause of this gap that can be softened by new approaches as hardware/software co-design [1]. Co-design methods usually require flexible development tools that allow rapid prototyping. One way to achieve desired flexibility level is to develop hardware with reconfigurable computing[3] using devices such as FPGA's[3].

FPGA's are flexible devices because, among various features, allow hardware to be described using Hardware Description Languages (HDL's) and several hardware reconfigurations (custom hardware design). In this work specifically, there is a free soft-processor [31] provided by FPGA's manufacturer that can be used for co-design development.

A soft-processor is an Intellectual Property (IP) core which is 100% implemented using the logic primitives of the FPGA. Other definition is: a programmable instruction processor implemented in the reconfigurable logic of the FPGA [31]. Soft-processors have several advantages and one of the most relevant for actual designs is the possibility to implement multi-core solutions defining the exact number of soft-processors required by the application. Since it is implemented in configurable logic (FPGA), a soft-processor can be tuned by customizing its implementation and complexity, by changing its internal configuration, processor functional blocks or even adding new instructions to the processor, in order to match the exact requirements of an application [31].

The remainder of the paper is organized as follows: section 2 presents some recent hardware development using NCC. In section 3, concepts of hardware/software co-design and profiling-based methods are presented. Section 4 contains proposed method description followed by the results section (5). At last section 6 presents authors' conclusions based on achieved results, followed by selected references.

2   Related Works

This work is related to hardware/software co-design, profile-based methods, image processing, reconfigurable computing and vision navigation for mobile robotics areas. In these areas there are important recent works and some of them are presented in this section.

Birla & Vikram [2] presents an architecture that uses partial reconfiguration for computer vision algorithms. Hardware is developed for people detection and the reconfiguration is used to choose between using the whole image or select some specific features extracted from the image. In [17] Kalomiros & Lygouras developed a reconfigurable architecture used to select important features for robot navigation. These features are points selected on images by an image consistency verification system. Visual vocabularies were used online in [22] to detect already visited regions. These vocabularies associate images that have similar characteristics.

Lee et. Al. [18] analyzes the future of hardware and software technologies related to visual computing. Main areas of their analysis are video coding, video processing, computer vision and computer graphics. Authors' conclusions indicate that algorithms and architectures optimization should consider concurrent operations, demonstrating the importance of parallel processing in this type of application. Lu et. Al. [19] also presents the use of GPU solutions for real-time image-based rendering. This kind of hardware is usually placed on general purpose computers but can also be used when a huge amount of processing is needed.

Other works present different cross-correlation coefficient calculus [8][28][5]. These works have poor comparisons between the proposed method and the common NCC coefficient. The proposed algorithm, FNCC (Fast normalized cross-correlation), is an implementation that uses a table of values that consumes additional significant amount of memory, usually not available on embedded systems.

Recent works, [32] and [27], present dedicated hardware architecture solutions (not programmable) for NCC algorithm, that achieved acceptable execution time. In this case some parts of proposed architectures are not detailed. Recent results of other applications for NCC algorithm can be found in [9][12][23]. Next sections presents some important concepts related to this work's development.

3   Hardware/Software Co-design

Electronic systems nowadays have become more complex because of the rising number of functionalities that are requested on projects. As electronic circuits become more complex, technical challenges in co-design will also increase [29]. These circuit systems can be classified as a joint operation component group developed for some task resolution [13] and, this components, can be implemented in hardware or in software depending on what are the system's constraints.

Hardware/Software co-design means the union of all system goals exploring interaction between hardware and software components during development [26]. This method tries to increase the predictability of embedded system design by providing analysis methods that tell designers if a system meets its performance, power, size and synthesis methods that let researchers and designers rapidly evaluate many potential design methodologies [29].

Hardware/Software co-design is a hard task and computational tools appeared to make this work faster, and also increase the system's degree of optimization. The introduction of programmable devices like FPGA's (Field Programmable Gate Arrays) on circuit co-design enabled flexibility and made prototyping easier. This fact is really important because the circuit can be developed and tested before be manufactured, reducing costs and design time. This flexibility opens new digital circuit applications and the rise of new Hardware/Software co-design problems [21].

Hardware/software partitioning problem has a first level impact on system's performance because a wrong choice can result in an increased development time and a final product out of specification. A good partitioning that fit all implementation requirements optimizes operation and minimizes costs usually resulting on an efficient project.

Firstly, partitioning problem was solved by developers with their experience and previously released works. In case of complex systems, this work became arduous and this fact inducted this research field interest on automating the process using techniques like evolutionary computing and artificial neural networks [7]. This automation can be achieved with EDA (electronic design automation) tools or methods that allow a fast search for good solutions on search space. Among existing methods, the profiling-based methods are being widely used nowadays.

3.1   Profiling-Based Methods

There are many methods for hardware/software co-design and the most commonly used nowadays are the profiling-based methods [14].

The increasing complexity of codes raised the need for profiling tools. Profiling tools make code analysis and indicate several system features like functions execution time and memory usage. Each tool gives a specific group of information and most of them are based on clock cycle information. Table 1 presents some other relevant information about profiling tools [14].

Table 1. Profiling Tool's Comparison

	Memory	Power	Per Funct	Per Line	Call Grph
Gprof	-	-	x	x	x
HDL Profiling	x	x	-	-	-
ATOMIUM	x	-	x	-	x
MEMTRACE	x	x	x	x	-

After obtaining profiling information, system can be modified to achieve expected performance. Usually the critical parts of the system (intensive processing and time consuming routines) start been optimized with by modifications and improvements, then followed by hardware development on extreme cases. This is a cyclic refinement process and usually stops when co-design performance constraints or maximum time-to-market are achieved.

One of the most important features of this kind of method is that the critical part of the co-design, hardware/software partitioning, is performed during a practical refinement process. Due to this fact there is a high probability that the final system has one of the best system partitioning of the search space. Nowadays hardware/software co-design is using soft-processors because they allow software execution, and also designed hardware to be included as custom instructions for validation.

4 Method

Previous sections presented this work's development context. Considering this, the main goal is to implement normalized cross-correlation coefficient calculus in an embedded platform and achieve acceptable execution time using a profile-based hardware/software co-design development method.

4.1 NCC Coefficient Calculus

The computational cost of the cross-correlation coefficient calculus without normalization is lower then normalized, but the results are sensible to image and sub-image brightness and scale changes [10]. So the normalization of this coefficient solves these two important image processing problems. As presented in Section 2 there are other ways to calculate cross-correlation coefficient but they have disadvantages for hardware implementation. Presented facts justified the choice for NCC algorithm implementation.

$$\gamma(s,t) = \frac{\sum\sum[f(x,y) - \bar{f}]\sum\sum[w(x-s,y-t) - \bar{w}]}{\{\sum\sum[f(x,y) - \bar{f}]^2 \sum\sum[w(x-s,y-t) - \bar{w}]^2\}^{\frac{1}{2}}} \qquad (1)$$

Equation 1 presents the normalized cross-correlation coefficient. f represents an image of $M \ x \ N$ size, w represents a sub-image of $m \ x \ n$ where $m \leq M$ and $n \leq N$. Values s and t represents the position of the sub-image center. In this

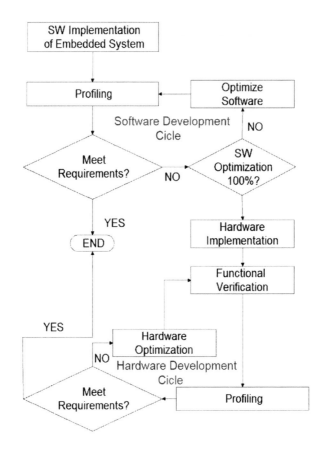

Fig. 1. Modified Profile-Based Method

equation, $\bar{w}$ and $\bar{f}$ are respectively the mean value of the sub-image (that is calculated only once) and the mean value of the image region where the sub-image is placed. In this case of template matching $\bar{w}$ refers to what region has to be discovered on in image $\bar{f}$.

4.2   Method Implementation

NCC algorithm was implemented and testes on a general purpose processor (Intel Core i3). After that the proposed hardware/software co-design method (figure 1) was applied. This previous implementation allowed the evaluation of image and sub-image size changes impacts on coefficient calculus. Considering that Nios II soft-processor can be programmed in C language, this procedure will generate a program that can be used on proposed method's first step without increasing development time.

It's important to know the effects of larger images and sub-images in the total computational cost, so general purpose processors were used to evaluate the execution times before porting the program to the soft-processor. This analysis will show what sizes of images run considerably fast on a general purpose processor and these sizes will be the references for soft-processor's algorithm evaluation. General purpose processor implementation allow also software optimization evaluation before being used on the soft-processor.

After this initial step, the proposed co-design method will be applied in order to select the configuration of the soft-processor, aiming to fit system constraints as area consumption, execution time and development time. Selected soft-processor will receive modifications on the software and hardware components according to profile results aiming better execution time. This method is interesting because partitioning, that is considered one of the most important parts of hardware/software co-design, is done implicitly during method execution.

Figure 1 illustrates the flowchart of proposed profile-based method. There are two main cycles were the first one refers to software development and the second one to hardware development. Sometimes system requirements can be satisfied only doing software optimizations. When software optimizations reach the limit without satisfying requirements, hardware development starts. On embedded systems design hardware development is a costly task comparing to software development, so a large amount of time can be saved choosing this modified method. Together with this fact the final solution can be more interesting considering cost, performance and energy consumption because only the portion of the system that needs acceleration will be implemented in hardware.

Basically this method needs the definition of two important things: the profile tool and the soft-processor. In this project the profile tool used was GNU Profiler [11] and the soft-processor was Altera Nios II. The Altera's Nios II [6] soft-processor has a lot of interesting characteristics and the most importants are: (i) the processor can be programmed on C programming language, using tools like GCC compiler and Grpof; (ii) there are three different ways to include custom-designed hardware into the FPGA-based system [16]; (iii)we have two different development platforms available in our lab based on Altera FPGAs (Terasic DE2-70 and Arrow BeMicro).

Nios II has three basic soft-processor configurations: (i) economic (e); (ii) fast (f) and (iii) standard (s). Soft-processors for this work had the same basic configuration with the CPU, on-chip memory, two timers (system timer for clock and another one), JTAG interface for communication. The BeMicro needs extra RAM configured in the FPGA for data storage and a PLL 50 MHz clock and other small features. The main difference between these three processors is that Nios II /e doesn't have instruction pipeline and embedded multipliers, and Nios II /f has hardware improvements on execution time like dedicated hardware for functions and acceleration between pipeline stages. None of them have floating-point unit. It's important to know that these results, except for execution times, are valid for any other soft-processor.

Altera provides softwares for hardware configuration (Quartus II IDE) and for code development and interface with Nios II soft-processor (Nios II EDS). These two softwares have free versions that were used for this work. Developed software will be executed on all different soft-processors to compare their performance, to choose the best between them for this work, and continue the co-design development method with hardware improvements if necessary.

5   Results

Following proposed method, initial results are about the influence of image size and sub-image size changes on execution time for the algorithm. These results are presented graphically on Fig. 2 and Fig. 3. Sub-image sizes are represented by the number of pixels as 10x10, 20x20 and so on, and images are the common sizes of images that are 352x288, 256x192 to 1024x768. These execution image sizes were chosen based on characteristics presented in [4].

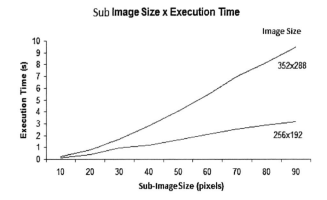

Fig. 2. Sub-Image Size Results for General Purpose Processor

Based on [30], chosen optimization techniques applied to softwares developed for embedded system are: use of unsigned variables, change functions for equivalent expressions (change pow(x,2) for x*x), use of common operators for simple attributions (change $x\ +=$ for $x = x\ +$), loop unrolling and use of vectors instead of matrices.

Results show that the only technique that is really efficient in this case is the loop unrolling. The reason is the fact that compilers apply the first three optimization techniques automatically and the last one is only effective when using operating systems that store matrix data away from each other. The problem of using loop unrolling technique is that the algorithm became more specific

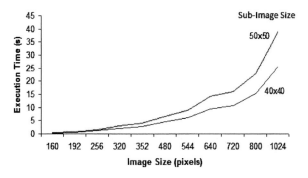

Fig. 3. Image Results for General Purpose Processor

Table 2. Software Optimization Results

	Mean Execution Time (s)	Size (KB)
Initial	0,047	25,6
Unsigned Variables	0,047	25,6
Function Changing	0,047	25,6
Operator Changing	0,047	25,6
Loop Unrolling	0,0235	26,6

as long as loop unrolling is applied. Other important things are that there is a maximum number of iterations to unroll after that point the execution time became higher again, and the code size also increases. In our tests the maximum number of unrolled iterations was 4.

To evaluate the influence of soft-processor features changing and achieve good results on co-design methodology, the experiments have been done with nine different Nios II hardware configuration in two different FPGAs platforms (Terasic DE2-70 and Arrow BeMicro). Both FPGAs executed the algorithm that implements normalized cross-correlation coefficient described in previous sections.

Starting with pipelined processor influence on execution time and area consumption, three basic processors were configured initially: Nios II /e, /s and /f. This work considers Nios II /e as the reference software implementation of the algorithm because it has no hardware accelerations or improvements as instruction pipelining, hardware multipliers or divisors. After profiling the code the parts that consumed the higher percentage of execution time were the floating point operations. So, the other six possible configurations for Nios II soft processor were implemented using floating point unit (FPU) and hardware division.

Table 3. Comparing Developed Hardware

	bET (s)	bLE	bMB	bP	Clock	tET (s)	tLE	tMB	tP
Nios II /e	5600	14%	53%	30%	50	-	3	72%	<1%
Nios II /s	1260	22%	60%	30%	50	-	4	75%	<1%
Nios II /f	980	26%	63%	30%	50	-	4	77%	<1%
Nios II /ef	4057	22%	53%	30%	50	-	4	72%	<1%
Nios II /sf	980	31%	60%	30%	50	-	6	75%	<1%
Nios II /ff	840	35%	63%	30%	50	-	7	77%	<1%
Nios II /efd	3888	53%	53%	30%	50	-	11	72%	<1%
Nios II /sfd	-	-	-	-	50	856,7	13	75%	<1%
Nios II /ffd	-	-	-	-	50	673,5	14	77%	<1%

FPGAs chosen for this work are Cyclone II and Cyclone III manufactured by Altera Corporation and part of DE2-70 and Arrow BeMicro development boards respectively. These boards are interesting because DE2-70 has a considerable number of I/O and BeMicro is similar to a pen-drive where power is provided from USB connection that consumes a slow amount of power. Only Cyclone II allowed floating point unit configuration with hardware division for Nios II /f and Nios II /s. Fitter of Quartus II wasn't able to fit the complete design (FPU + division) on Cyclone III FPGA so the software could be executed only on seven different soft-processors.

Table 3 shows the results for the execution on all configured soft-processors (Nios II /xf - represents FPU, Nios II /xfd - represents FPU+HW Divisor) and boards (indicating a b before - BeMicro board and a t before - DE2-70 board) for a 160x120 pixel image and a sub-image of 10x10 pixels (Execution Time (ET), Logic Elements (LE), Pins (P), Memory Bits (MB), Clock).

Execution time using was significantly reduced after including FPU unit without division hardware and on Nios II /e with division hardware. In the other hand, the execution time using DE2-70 was also significantly reduced after including FPU unit, but in this case including the division hardware in all configurations. Based on this results the soft processor Nios II /f with FPU (BeMicro) and Nios II /f with FPU + Division Hardware (DE2-70) were chosen to execute some different sizes of images and templates. Some higher image sizes that execute very fast on the general purpose computer achieve non-acceptable time on Nios II for this implementation as can be seen on table 3. To compare the influence of sizes on the soft-processor some smaller images and sub-images where chosen from 9x9 to 200x200 pixels images and from 3x3 to 11x11 pixels sub-images. These results can be seen in Fig. 5 and Fig. 4.

During hardware optimization step of the proposed methodology, the speedup of the resulting hardwares was calculated. Graphic of Fig.6 shows the speedup values for each development step.

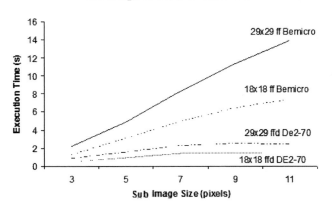

Fig. 4. Sub-Image Results for Nios II Processors

6   Conclusions

The results presented on previous section show that the proposed architecture achieves acceptable execution time only for small-size images. Initially chosen FPGA, Cyclone III wasn't huge enough to configure Nios II /f with floating point unit and hardware division. Despite of it, if small images can be used this system is very interesting for energy consumption constraints. Development time using chosen IDE's was also interesting because the configuration of the soft-processor became a less arduous task. On DE2-70 the results for the same images were better, representing almost half of the execution time on Bemicro. This improvement occurred because of the division hardware added into floating point unit on co-design hardware development phase. Presented results showed that chosen method is efficient and effective.

Extending this analysis, the speedup rate achieved after hardware development was 8,31. This number is related to all software execution time on Nios II /e processor, equivalent to 5600 seconds, divided by Nios II /f with FPU and hardware division 673,5 seconds. This speedup is due to FPU hardware together with pipeline of 6 stages from Nios II fast processor, and with hardware acceleration for integer multiplies and division. All these modifications can be considered hardware development and can be applied to any soft-processor.

Compilers already do automatically some software optimization operations and this fact justifies the fact that only with loop unrolling technique achieved significant code optimizations as presented on table 2. Using vectors instead of matrices are a good technique only when the operating system doesn't allows a better structured representation of the matrix.

The analysis of image sizes and sub-image sizes impacts on execution time showed that, on general purpose computers with high processing power, grayscale

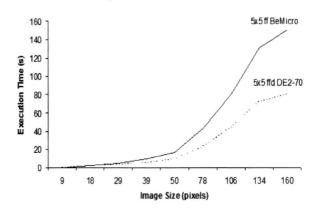

Fig. 5. Image Results for Nios II Processors

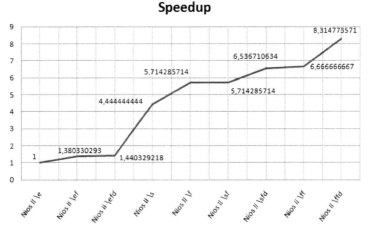

Fig. 6. Speedup during development

images of 320x240 can achieve acceptable execution time with small sub-images (Fig. 2). This analysis also indicates that the main relative problem is not the image size for the execution time but the sub-image size. There is a point that the sub-image gets so large that the number of calculus is small and execution time start to fall again, due to the reduced sliding window area.Software implementation on soft-processor showed to be more sensitive for both cases related to image sizes, but sub-image size still remains the main problem (Fig. 5).

The comparison between implemented soft-processors also confirms that the usage of the processor with higher computational power (Nios /f + FPU + Hardware Divison) is the right choice for this work and the area that is necessary to configure it on an FPGA compared to simpler processors is an acceptable counterpart. In order to implement this system in an actual autonomous robot navigation system, it will be possible only with improvements on algorithm's limitations related to image sizes that can be executed on acceptable time.

Future works directions include performing tests on larger FPGA's, so the Nios II soft-processor can be implemented with better hardware accelerations and the algorithm can probably achieve more interesting execution times. Other soft-processors can also be tested and compared. Code profile shows that the main problems of this algorithm are the floating point operations, so hardware structures should be included to parallelize code execution of sums and compensate part of the time wasted on divisions and square root operations.

References

1. Atasu, K.: Hadware/Sotware Partitioning for Custom Instruction Processors. Ph.D. thesis, Insitute for Graduate Studies in Science and Engineering (2007)
2. Birla, M., Vikram, K.N.: Partial run-time reconfiguration of fpga for computer vision applications. In: IPDPS, pp. 1–6 (2008)
3. Bobda, C.: Introduction to Reconfigurable Computing: Architectures, Algorithms, and Applications. Springer Publishing Company, Heidelberg (2007) Incorporated
4. Bourque, P.: Image dimensions (2010), http://local.wasp.uwa.edu.au/./imagedim/ (acesso: 25/10/2010)
5. Briechle, K., Hanebeck, U.D.: Template Matching Using Fast Normalized Cross Correlation. In: Proceedings of SPIE: Optical Pattern Recognition XII, vol. 4387, pp. 95–102 (2001), http://dx.doi.org/10.1117/12.421129
6. Corp., A.: Altera.com (2010), http://www.altera.com/literature (acesso: 22/05/2010)
7. Dias, M.A., Lacerda, W.S.: Hardware/software co-design using artificial neural network and evolutionaryy computing. In: 5th SPL., pp. 153–157 (April 2009)
8. Feng, Z., Qingming Huang, W.G.:Image matching by normalized cross-correlation. In: ICASSP 2006 Proceedings IEEE International Conference on Acoustics, Speech and Signal Processing, pp. II 729 – II 732 (2006)
9. Fernandes, C.W., Bellar, M.D., Werneck, M.M.: Cross-correlation-based optical flowmeter. IEEE T. Instrumentation and Measurement 59(4), 840–846 (2010)
10. Gonzalez, R.C., Woods, R.E.: Digital Image Processing, 3rd edn. Prentice-Hall, Inc., Upper Saddle River (2006)
11. Honeyford, M.: Speed your code with the gnu profiler (2010), http://www.ibm.com/developerworks/library/l-gnuprof.html (acesso: 17/07/2010)

12. Hongcheng, Y., Liu, W.: Design of time difference of arrival estimation system based on fast cross correlation. In: Proceedings of 2nd International Conference on Future Computer and Communication, vol. 2, pp. 464–466. IEEE Computer Society Press, Los Alamitos (2010)
13. Houssain, S.T.: An introduction to evolutionary computation (1998)
14. Hübert, H., Stabernack, B.: Profiling-based hardware/software co-exploration for the design of video coding architectures. IEEE Trans. Cir. and Sys. for Video Technol. 19(11), 1680–1691 (2009)
15. Jones, S., Andresen, C., Crowley, J.: Appearance based process for visual navigation. In: Proceedings of the 1997 IEEE/RSJ International Conference on Intelligent Robots and Systems IROS 1997, vol. 2, pp. 551–557 (September 1997)
16. Joost, R., Salomon, R.: Hardware-software co-design in practice: A case study. In: in Image Processing, In Proceedings of the 32 nd Annual Conference of the IEEE Industrial Electronics Society, IECON (2006)
17. Kalomiros, J., Lygouras, J.: A reconfigurable architecture for stereo-assisted detection of point-features for robot mapping (2009)
18. Lee, G.G., Chen, Y.K., Mattavelli, M., Jang, E.: Algorithm/architecture co-exploration of visual computing on emergent platforms: Overview and future prospects. IEEE Transactions on Circuits and Systems for Video Technology 19(11), 1576–1587 (2009)
19. Lu, S.J., Rogmans, Lafruit, G., Catthoor, F.: Stream-centric stereo matching and view synthesis: A high-speed approach on gpus. IEEE Transactions on Circuits and Systems for Video Technology 19, 1598–1611 (2009)
20. Matsumoto, Y., Inaba, M., Inoue, H.: Visual navigation using view-sequenced route representation. In: Proceedings IEEE International Conference on Robotics and Automation, 1996, vol. 1, pp. 83–88 (April 1996)
21. de Micheli, G., Gupta, R.K.: Hardware/software co-design. Proceedings of IEEE 85, 349–365 (1997)
22. Nicosevici, T., Garcia, R.: On-line visual vocabularies for robot navigation and mapping. In: IEEE/RSJ International Conference on Intelligent Robots and Systems, IROS 2009, pp. 205–212 (October 2009)
23. Pei, L., Xie, Z., Dai, J.: Fast normalized cross-correlation image matching based on multiscale edge information. In: Proceedings of International Conference on Computer Application and System Modeling, vol. 2, pp. 507–511. IEEE Computer Society Press, Los Alamitos (2010)
24. Russ, J.C.: Image Processing Handbook, 4th edn. CRC Press, Inc., Boca Raton (2002)
25. Sonka, M., Hlavac, V., Boyle, R.: Image Processing, Analysis, and Machine Vision. Thomson-Engineering (2007)
26. Straunstrup, J., Wolf, W.: Hardware Software Co-Design: Principles and Parctice, 1st edn. Springer, Heidelberg (1997)
27. Tao, Z., Feng-ping, Y., Hao-jun, Q.: An optimized high-speed high-accuracy image matching system based on fpga. In: Proceedings of the International Conference on Information and Automation, pp. 1107–1112. IEEE Computer Society Press, Los Alamitos (2010)
28. Tsai, D.-M., Lin, C.-T.: Fast normalized cross correlation for defect detection. Pattern Recogn. Lett. 24, 2625–2631 (2003), http://dx.doi.org/10.1016/S0167-86550300106-5

29. Wolf, W.: A decade of hardware/software codesign. Computer 36(4), 38–43 (2003)
30. Wolf, W.: High-Performance Embedded Computing: Architectures, Applications, and Methodologies. Morgan Kaufmann Publishers Inc., San Francisco (2006)
31. Yiannacouras, P., Rose, J., Steffan, J.G.: The microarchitecture of fpga-based soft processors. In: CASES 2005: Proceedings of the 2005 Int. Conf. on Compilers, Arch. and Synthesis for Emb. Sys., pp. 202–212. ACM, New York (2005)
32. Yonghong, Z.: An nprod algorithm ip design for real-time image matching application onto fpga. In: International Conference on Electrical and Control Engineering, pp. 404–409 (2010)

Author Index